CRAG CLIMBS
IN CHAMONIX

By the same authors:

"Climbs in Spain", Out of printing
"Mont Blanc. Easy ascents an glacier hike" 2009
"Mont Blanc off piste" 2008
"Thailand rock climbing" 1994

Cover:

François Burnier
Baptiste Lepoidevin in "Le Louis dort", 6c, La Flégère

Printed in Italy

www.topos-vamos.com

Imprimerie Marcoz s.n.c. - Place E. Chanoux, 1
11017 Morgex - Vallée d'Aoste (Italie) - Tel. +39 0165 809640

Drawings by Dominique Potard.
Pictures François Burnier.

I.S.B.N.: 2-910672-29-4 - 9th edition, revised.
I.S.B.N.: 2-910672-29-4 - 8th edition, revised.
I.S.B.N.: 2-910672-20-4 - 7th edition, revised.
I.S.B.N.: 2-910672-13-1 - 6th edition
I.S.B.N.: 2-910672-11-5 - 5th edition
I.S.B.N.: 2-910672-04-2 - 4th edition, revised.
I.S.B.N.: 2-910672-00-X - 3rd edition
I.S.B.N.: 2-9503673-5-6 - 2nd edition
I.S.B.N.: 2-9503673-0-5 - 1st edition

Copyright registered: April 2023

CRAG CLIMBS
IN CHAMONIX

François BURNIER
Dominique POTARD
Mountain Guides

Translation:
Nicole LEHMANN
Hillary SHARP
Claire TAILLARD
Philippa ZUCCHERO

vamos
280 rue Joseph Vallot - 74400 CHAMONIX MONT-BLANC - FRANCE

Thanks

We would like to thank the following for their kind assistance:

Michel ARIZZI
Luc AUBERTIN
Murray BALL
Julia and Leif BERKLINT
Mehdi BIDAULT
Lucien BOUCANSAUD
Lionel BRIAND
Gilles BRUNOT
Claude BUGNY
Luci BURNIER
Philippe COLLET
Jean-François and Laurent COLLIGNON
Elke COLLOC
Jonathan CHARLET
Christophe DAT
Jon DE MONTJOYE
Victor DECAMP
Romain DESGRANGES
Laurence DEVEAU
Vincent DOMINGUEZ
Jean-Claude GILLES
Fabrice JUDENNE
Ilan and Jean Sebastien KNÖERTZER
Marie Pierre LAFONTAINE
Nicole and Robert LEHMANN
Baptiste LEPOIDEVIN
Yves-Marie MAQUET
Dominique MARCHAL
Benoît MOUSSEUX
Alain PAYOT
Lionel PERNOLLET
Benoît PEYRONNARD
Benjamin, Nicolas and Nathalie POTARD-FEUTRY
Denis POUSSIN
Gaspard RAVANEL
Ludovic RAVANEL
Roland RAVANEL
Sylvain RAVANEL
Brian RAWCLIFFE
Thierry RENAULT
Dominic ROBERTS
Bernard ROLLAT
Nadège SECARDIN
Hilary SHARP
Jean-Marc TROUSSIER
Luc VERRIER
Laura and Victor

This book is dedicated to the memory of Hervé BIDAULT, mountain guide and leading light in the development of the Vallorcine crag. Hervé died on the 4th May 1994, descending the canyon at Les Marecottes.

Practical information

PERSONAL EQUIPMENT

Both experienced climbers and beginners use more or less the same equipment. For "equipped" areas:

- a main climbing rope, at least 60 m long;
- about a dozen quick-draws per rope;
- a belay device, (fig 8, stitch plate, grigri, camming device...);
- a "cow's tail" with screw gate carabiner (permanently attached to the harness).

For "semi equipped" areas, it is advisable to add:

- a few slings of different sizes;
- a few chocks, preferably mechanical stoppers ("Friends");
- a 2x50 m abseil rope.

A helmet is strongly recommended, (stone fall at certain over used locations). Sports shops in the valley hire out rock boots and harnesses.

LEARNING TO CLIMB

We strongly encourage beginners, both children and adults, to discover climbing under the guidance of a professional, (a guide or a climbing instructor). Individual or group courses, day or half day are offered by.

USEFUL ADDRESSES

- Compagnie des Guides de Chamonix: Maison de la Montagne, place de l'Eglise de Chamonix. chamonix-guide.com. Tel 04 50 53 00 88.
- Evo 2: maisondesguides-chamonix.com. Tel 04 50 55 90 22
- Centre U. C. P. A. d'Argentière, ucpa.com. Tel. 04 50 54 07 11.
- Bureau des Guides de Vallorcine, place de la Gare. Tel. 04 50 54 60 69.

SAFETY

Rescue: 04 50 53 16 89.

Simple, common sense precautions can often prevent dangerous situations:

- Check your tie-in knot (twice is better than once!).
- Ensure that the rope is long enough when lowering off, at least twice the length of the route (if in doubt, the belayer should tie on).
- Check the security of the belay anchors.
- When setting up an abseil or top rope, use only the anchors provided for that purpose, (chains, maillons, cemented-in rings).
- Belay yourself with a "cow's tail" and screw gate carabiner when untying from the rope.
- Don't set up a top rope, or lower off, directly through a sling or a rope loop; it will be burnt by the friction of the rope.
- Never set up two ropes in the same anchor, friction between them will cause damage.
- Generally keep an eye on any other people anywhere near your belay.

BUS AND TRAIN

It is easy to reach most of the climbing sites by bus or by train. Informations:

- chamonix.montblancbus.com
- chamonix.com

EQUIPMENT OF ROUTES

The quality of the equipment on routes varies from one location to another. The climbers has the responsibility to evaluate the strength of protection and belays points.

GRADING

Until the start of the 80s, the sites in the valley were training grounds for routes in the high mountains. The characteristic crack and slab climbing of the Mont-Blanc massif has plenty to challenge today's climbers who often begin climbing on indoor climbing walls. We have revised and increased the grading of routes for each re-edition to allow for wear. For example, the large slab in Vallorcine which was 6a is now a good 6b. Bear this in mind before heading off on classic high altitude routes which often retain their original grades.

Grading of pitches: 1-9 with a,b,c indications for each level, a + indicates increased difficulty within the grade.

Grading of boulder routes: as above but taking off half to a grade compared to the crag grading.

Multi pitch routes:

F = easy. PD = low difficulty; moves at grade 3. AD = moderate difficulty; moves from 4a - 4c. D = difficult; moves from 5a - 5c. TD = very difficult; moves from 5c - 6a+. ED = extremely difficult; moves from 6b - 6c. ABO = "Abominablement Difficile"; moves from 6c - 7b. Each grade can be given a + or - to show higher or lower difficulty within the grade.

Compulsory moves: when "compulsory" or "unavoidable" is indicated, this is an unavoidable move at the grade indicated.

Aid climbing: the term A0 is the first level of artificial climbing. It is used to refer to pulling on or standing on devices in place to progress on a climbing route. For ex. A route graded A0/5b means that the difficulty is 5b if the climber pulls on the quickdraw.

Introduction

This tenth edition presents the main climbing sites in the Chamonix Valley and Vallorcine (l'Eau Noire). It covers 4 bouldering sites, and 33 crags. Also included is a selection of several pitches situated in the mountains, easily accessible directly from the valley or by using lifts.

This guide doesn't include sectors which we consider less interesting, nor those which have a long term ban on access (because of private property or for reasons of security).

Thanks in particular to the enthusiastic new routers who give their time freely to do the often tortuous and difficult job of cleaning and equipping so as to provide the climbing community with these great routes.

⚠ **WARNING**

Rock climbing presents serious risks of injury or death. It requires a real knowledge of progression techniques and in the use of safety equipment. In natural surroundings it really comes down to the responsibility of the climber to assess the strength of the protection points and the rock.

Despite every effort in the care taken to write this guide, errors or omissions are possible.

The information given here is purely indicative and in no circumstances should replace the judgment of the climber at the site.

Symbols

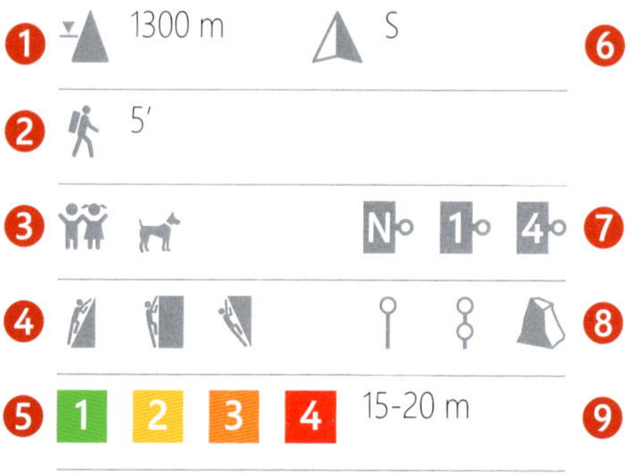

1 **Altitude:** of the site or the highest point of the cliff if the route is multi-pitch.

2 **Access:** approach time on foot from the start (parking, station, bus-stop)

3 **Children:** the cliff access and crag base are suitable for children.
Dogs: there is no restriction on the presence of dogs. The access and crag base are suitable for dogs.

4 **Type of climbing:** slab, vertical wall, overhang.

5 **Colour grades:**

Green: number of routes or boulder problems grade 3 and 4.

Yellow: number of routes or boulder problems grade 5.

Orange: number of routes or boulder problems grade 6.

Red: number of routes or boulder problems grade 7 and above.

6 **Orientation:** general aspect of the cliff.

7 **Equipment:** our opinion on the quality of the gear as well as the potential for a bad fall. Conditional on the climber being experienced in the standard techniques of clipping gear and using anchors safely.

4 - The protection points are basically considered safe for a fall. The protection points have been spaced and placed so as to minimize any risk of injury in the event of a fall.

3 - The protection points are basically considered safe for a fall. The hardest sections of the route are well protected for a fall; however, the spacing between points on the easier sections can be up to 4m and therefore a fall on these sections could be serious.

2 - Some protection points should be considered suspect. Some protection points are spaced far apart. A fall on certain parts of the route could be serious.

1 - The protection points will almost certainly not hold a fall and are very spaced.

N - No fixed gear.

8 Route: one pitch or multi-pitch, boulder.

9 Height: height of the climbing.

Mehdi Bidault in Korigan, 6c+

The locations

The locations

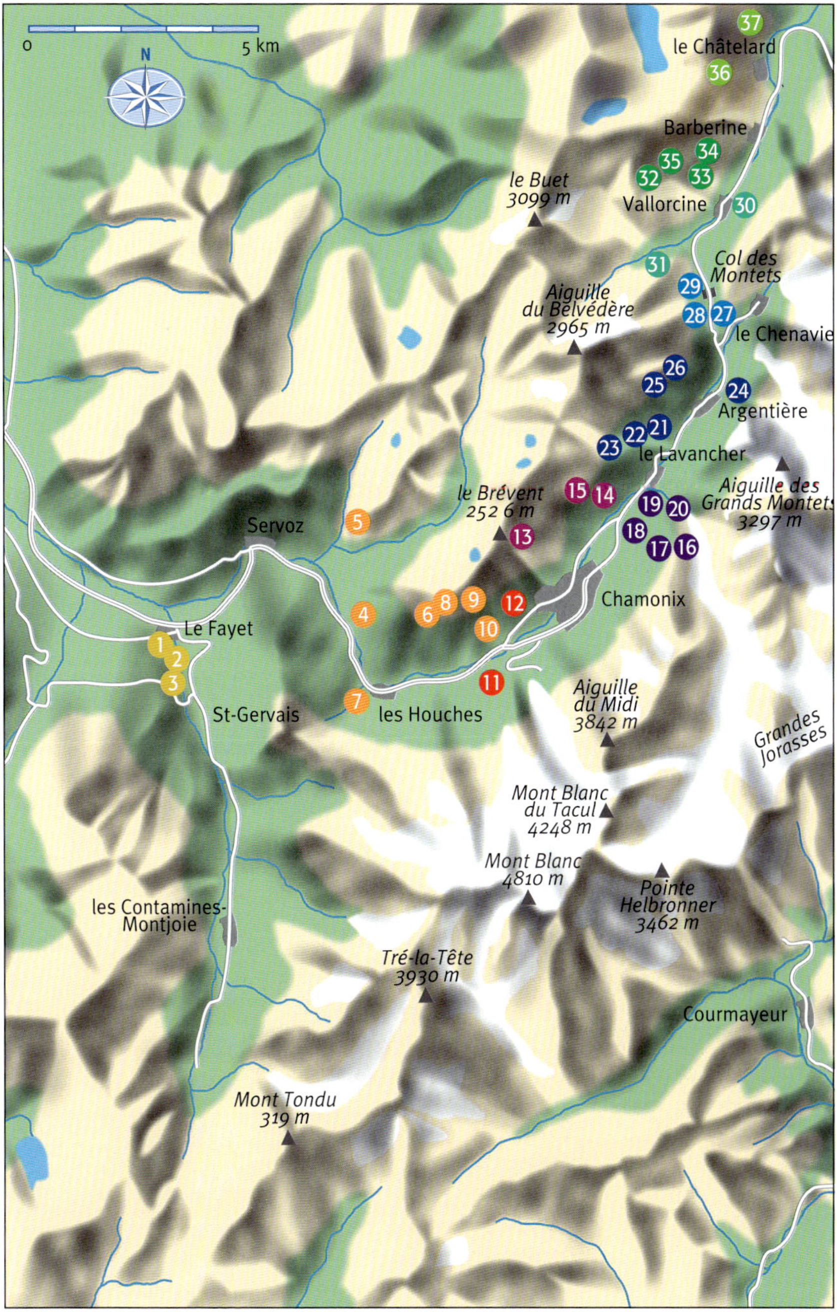
0
5 km
N
le Châtelard
Barberine
le Buet
3099 m
Vallorcine
Col des
Montets
Aiguille
du Belvédère
2965 m
le Chenavie
Argentière
le Lavancher
le Brévent
2526 m
Aiguille des
Grands Montets
3297 m
Servoz
Chamonix
Le Fayet
St-Gervais
les Houches
Aiguille
du Midi
3842 m
Grandes
Jorasses
Mont Blanc
du Tacul
4248 m
Mont Blanc
4810 m
Pointe
Helbronner
3462 m
les Contamines-
Montjoie
Tré-la-Tête
3930 m
Courmayeur
Mont Tondu
319 m
1
2
3
4
5
6
7
8
9
10
11
12
13
14
15
16
17
18
19
20
21
22
23
24
25
26
27
28
29
30
31
32
33
34
35
36
37

Area **01**

Le Fayet

Le Fayet

Three crags in the "Parc Thermal". "Fayet du bas" for beginners; the two others are more difficult.

Access : from Chamonix, follow the "Route Blanche" to Le Fayet.

By train: station in Saint-Gervais-le Fayet. Then 10 mins walk toward the "Parc Thermal" (follow the Mont Blanc railway in the main street) of "le Fayet".

By car: 16km from Chamonix. Follow N 205 toward Saint Gervais-le Fayet.

The entrance to the "Parc Thermal" is in the middle of the town. Follow the signposts to the car park at the foot of the crag.

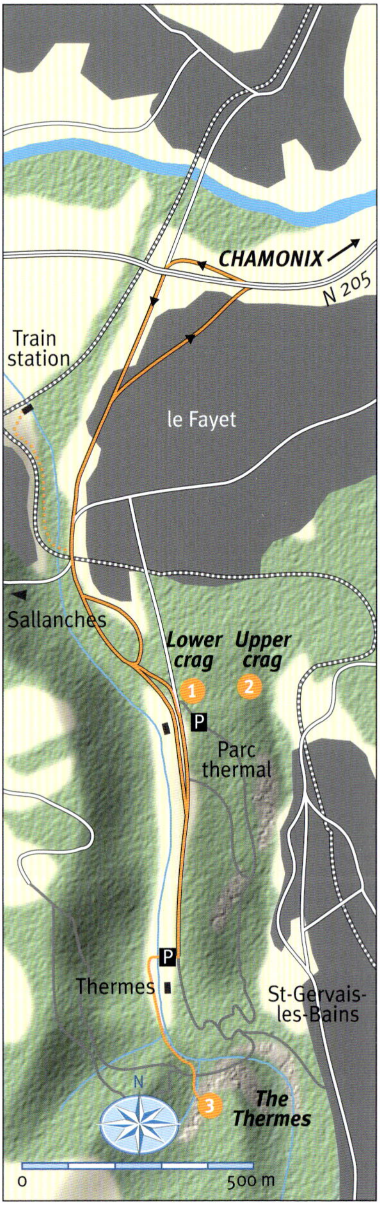

Le Fayet - Lower crag

650 m NW

1'

3

17	17	0	0	20-40 m

Situated in the middle of the "Parc Thermal" in Le Fayet, this small beginners' crag is very busy in summer. The rock is a granular gneiss, good for building confidence in footwork. The routes are equipped with cemented-in ring bolts.

The site : good for families. Carpark nearby. Close to a bar and restaurant (100m).

Access : follow the signposts to the car park at the foot of the crag.

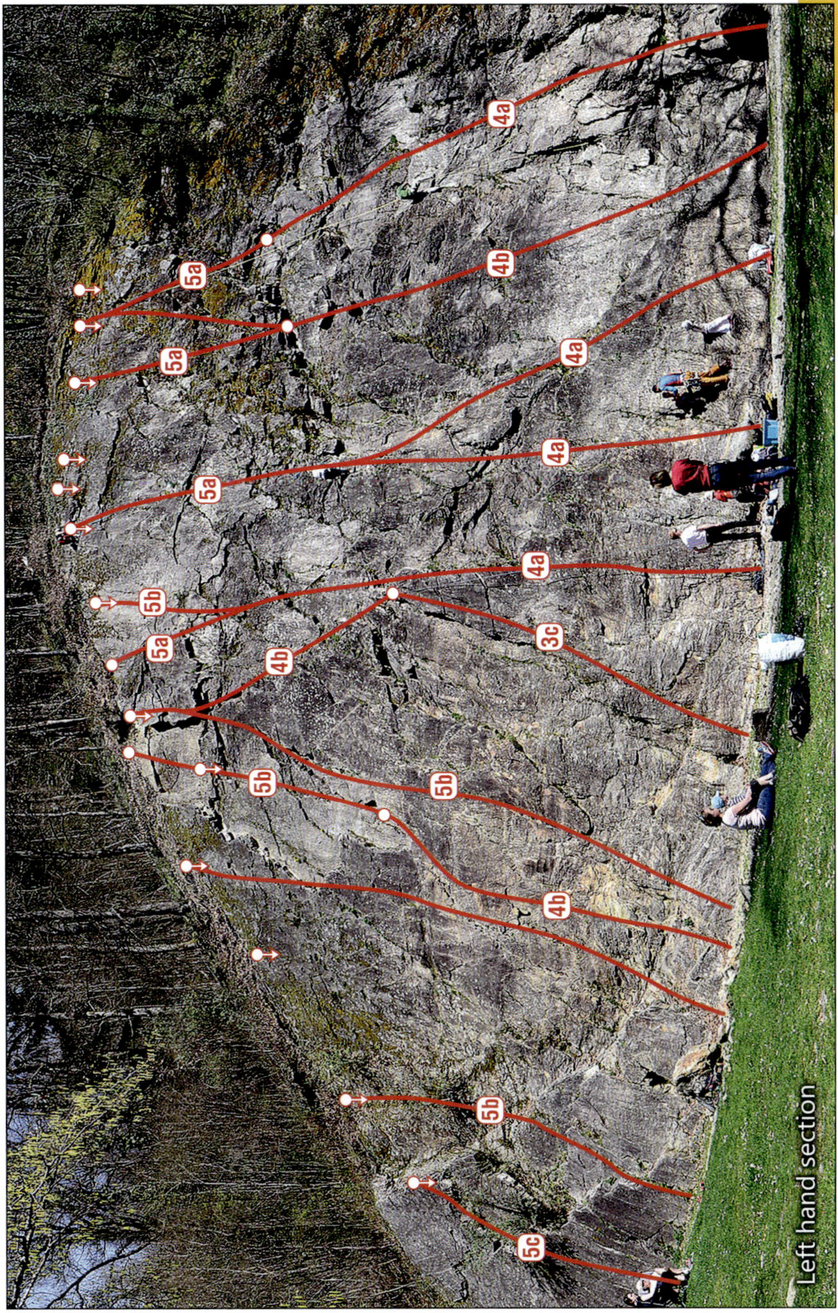
4a
5a
4b
5a
4a
4a
5a
4a
5b
5a
3c
4b
5b
5b
4b
5b
5c
Left hand section

AUX HOUCHES

Mont-Blanc Escalade

Un condensé de montagne à la portée de tous

La salle Mont-Blanc Escalade se place dans la continuité du fabuleux environnement qui nous entoure.

Notre leitmotiv : rester dans l'esprit de la haute altitude, omniprésent dans la vallée du Mont-Blanc. Mais aussi savoir redescendre sur le plancher des vaches : Mont-Blanc Escalade met la grimpe à la portée de tous.

Des voies de tous les niveaux, des encadrants diplômés et une ambiance décontractée.

La météo ne vous permet pas de partir vers les sommets ? Passez faire un tour, c'est ici que ça se passe : un nouveau mur fraîchement installé et 1 250 m² de surface grimpable, 15 m de hauteur, 45 couloirs de grimpe, cette salle possède environ 110 voies de tous niveaux.

Située au cœur de la vallée de Chamonix, dans le village des Houches, elle offre tous les ingrédients ludiques, techniques et de sécurité pour la pratique de l'escalade.

Un bar avec vue plongeante sur la salle, vous permettra de faire une petite pause.

Tous les premiers mercredis de chaque mois, à partir de 18h, Mont-Blanc Escalade **offre une entrée** pour toute entrée achetée**.** Consultez le site internet,la page Facebook ainsi que la page Twitter pour connaître les horaires.

Possibilité de privatiser la salle le matin (sur demande).

Ouvert 7 jours sur 7, pour tous les âges, du débutant au plus accro.
Cours sur réservation
Tél : 04 50 54 76 48 - www.montblancescalade.com

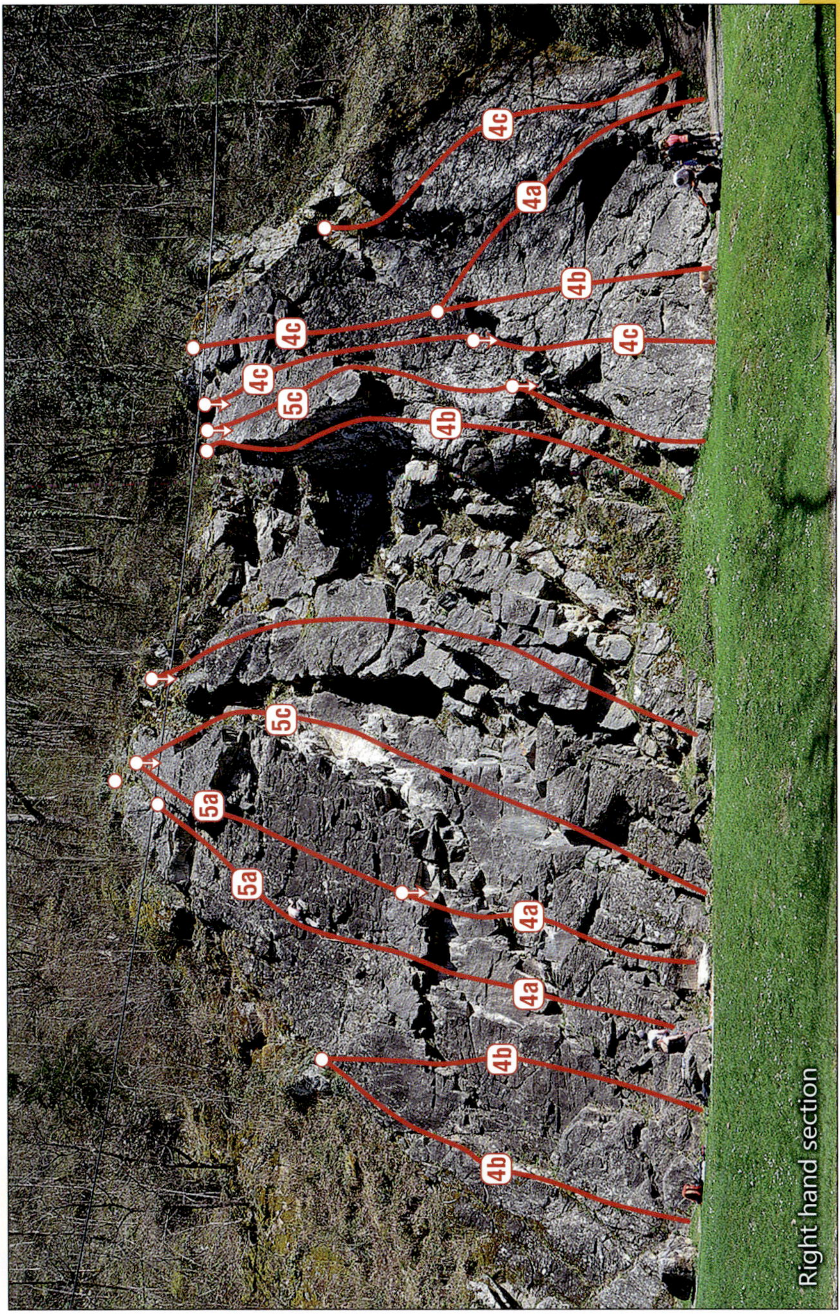
Right hand section
4c
4a
4b
4c
4c
4c
5c
4b
5c
5a
5a
4a
4a
4b
4b

Le Fayet - Upper crag

700 m | N

8'

3

0 | 0 | 27 | 7 | 8-60 m

It is possible to climb here, under the overhangs, even when it is raining. The climbing is on flat, often dusty, holds. 60m high, the crag offers several routes which go right to the top, plus some shorter routes at the bottom.

Equipment : cemented-in ring bolts at the bottom / bolts with hangers on the upper part.

Descent : descent from the long routes is either by a 50m abseil from the niche, or walking down, by a steep path on the left.

Access : follow the signposts to the lower crag. From here go up a path on the left, which bends sharply to end up above the lower crag.

The longer routes

1 - **Bras cassé**:
P1: 6b+; **P2**: 6c+. (**P1+P2**): 6c+; 40m. Athletic climb.

2 - **La mort du bûcheron**: **P1**: 6b+; **P2**: 6c. (**P1+P2**): 6c+, 40m.

3 - **Viol de nuit**: **P1**; 6b; **P2**: 6c+. (**P1+P2**) 7a. Friction!

4 - **Mitsou**: **P1**: 6a; **P2**: 6a+.

7 - **Jours de pluie**: **P1**; 6c; **P2**; 6c+, loose rock section.

8 - **Massacre**: **P1**: 6a; **P2**: 6b. (**P1+P2**): 40m. The most interested one.

9 - **Massacre directe**: 6c.

10 - **Popeye**: **P1** 6c; **P2**: 7a+, 40m.

11 - **Brutus**: 6b+.

12 - **L'ours**: **P1**: 6a; **P2**: 7a+. (**P1+P2**): 7a+. 40 m. What a journey!

12' - **Variante de L'ours**: 6a+.

13 - **Overdose**: **P1**: 6c; **P2**: 7a; **P3**: 7a+. (**P1+P2**): 7a; 35m.

Left hand section

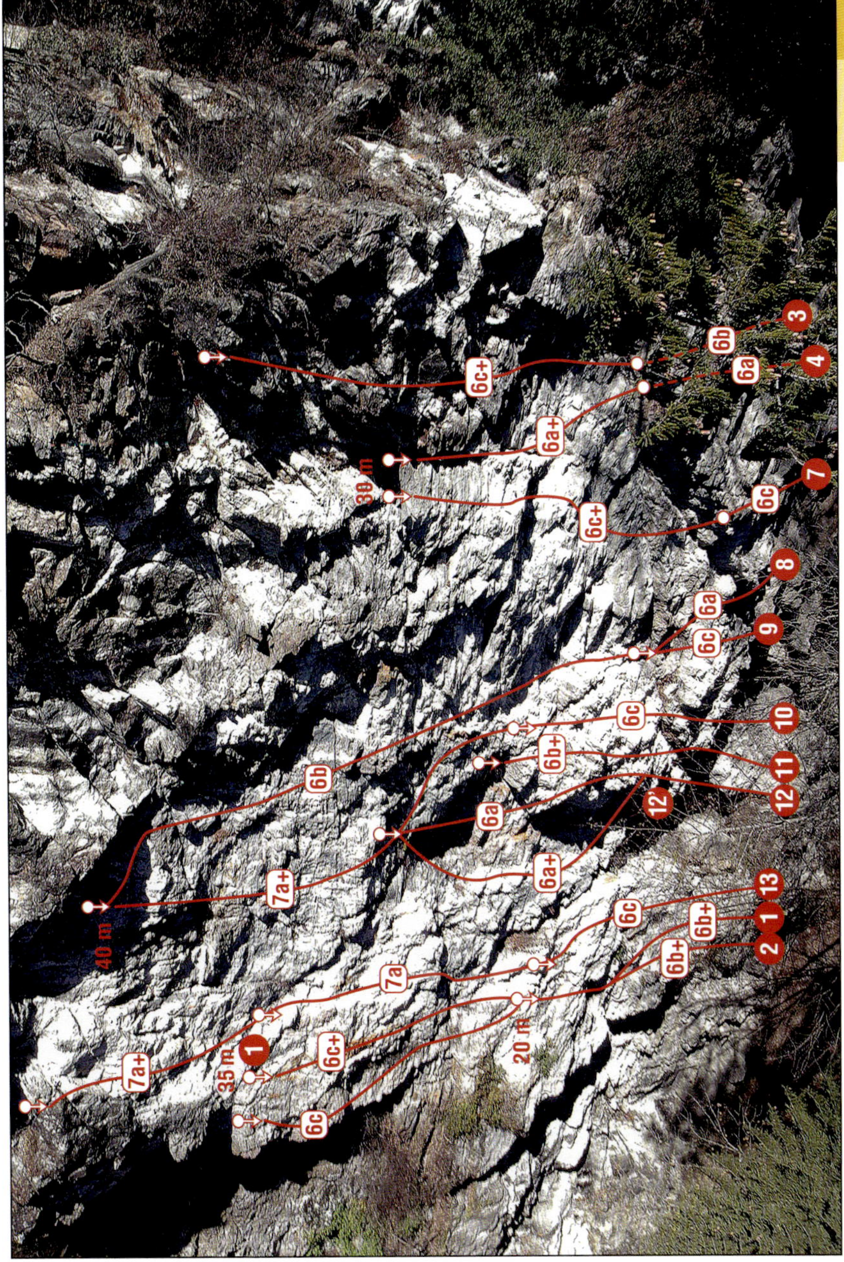

UPPER CRAG
Shorter climbs

All these routes are athletic, which sometimes makes the grades seem tough... The holds are often flat and must be used "in the right way"! Equipment is, on the whole, decent. The routes vary from 8 to 25 metres in length. Names of routes are generally written at the bottom.
10 quickdraws + belay.

Right hand side

1 - **Un toit pour elle**: athletic. A roof with tiles that are sometimes shaky... 7a.

2 - **Sans Toi ni Loi**: 6c.

3 - **Viol de nuit**: 6b. **P1+P2**: 32m, 7a.

4 - **Mitsou**: a good warm up pitch, 6a.

5 - **Petite Frappe**: 6b+.

6 - **Pétard**: demanding crack, 6b.

7 - **Jour de pluie**: 6c (quite committing).

8 - **Massacre**: slightly committing start, 6a. **P1+P2**: 35m, 6b.

9 - **Massacre direct**: heel hooks, 6c.

10 - **Popeye**: well named, don't forget the spinach! 6c+.

11 - **Brutus**: 6b+.

12 - **L'ours**: 5c+, athletic.

12' - **Variante de l'ours**: 6a+.

Left hand side

1 - **Bras cassé**: 6b+, 20m. Traverse left after the second point.

2 - **La mort du bûcheron**: 6b+, 20m. **P1+P2**, 6c, 40m.

3 - **Spartacus**: superb, 6c. Crux at the end.

4 - **Dièdre de droite**: 6b.

5 - **Rambo**: 6b+, athletic.

6 - **Résurgeance**: 7a.

7 - **Inifada**: 6c+, shaky key hold.

8 - **Dièdre de gauche**: 6b.

9 - **Jumbo**: 7a, delicate pull-up.

10 - **La plume**: 6c+.

11 - **Royal Bourin**: 7a+.

12 - **Guyon**: 6b+.

13 - **Ultime surprise**: 7a.

14 - **Les lierres**: 7a.

Right hand side
6c
6a+
5c+
6b+
6c+
6c
6a
6c
6b
6b+
6a
6b
6c
7a
1
2
3
4
5
6
7
8
9
10
11
12
12'
13

Left hand side
7a
7a
6b+
7a+
6c+
7a
6b
6c+
7a
6b+
6b
6c
6b+
6b+
1
2
3
4
5
6
7
8
9
10
11
12
13
14

Le Fayet - The Thermes

700 m E

10'

3

0 0 3 6 20 m

This is the most recently developed area, and is the only limestone crag in the upper Arve valley.

Rock : the pocketed limestone gives "Buoux-like" climbing.

Climbing : to this day 9 interesting routes have been equipped: 5 routes on a beautiful pocketed wall (15 to 20 metres high) and 4 on a steep overhang.

Equipment : cemented-in bolts and rings

The site : the crag is in a forest and doesn't get much sun. The base is steep and would be dangerous for children. There is seepage after rain.

Access : from Chamonix, follow the "Route Blanche" to Le Fayet. The entrance to the "Parc Thermal" is in the town centre. Park your car at the end of the road in the "Parking des Thermes".

Approach : 10 mins. Cross the bridge and take the path following the river. Climb some wooden steps to reach a point where you can clearly see the footbridge which crosses the gorge. From here you can just make out the crag through the vegetation. Reach it by a vague path which follows a small gorge to the right of the main path.

Names

(written at the bottom)

1 - **Gypaète interdit**: 7c.
2 - **La râpe démente**: 8b.
3 - **Les autres mondes**: 7b.
4 - **L'âge de cristal**: 7a, the crux is at the end.
5 - **Tostaky**: 6b, good warm up.
6 - **Absolom 2022**: 6c+.
7 - **Free State**: 7b.
8 - **Péril Jaune**: 7b.
9 - **Enjoy the silence**: 6c+, some typical "boulder" and spider moves.

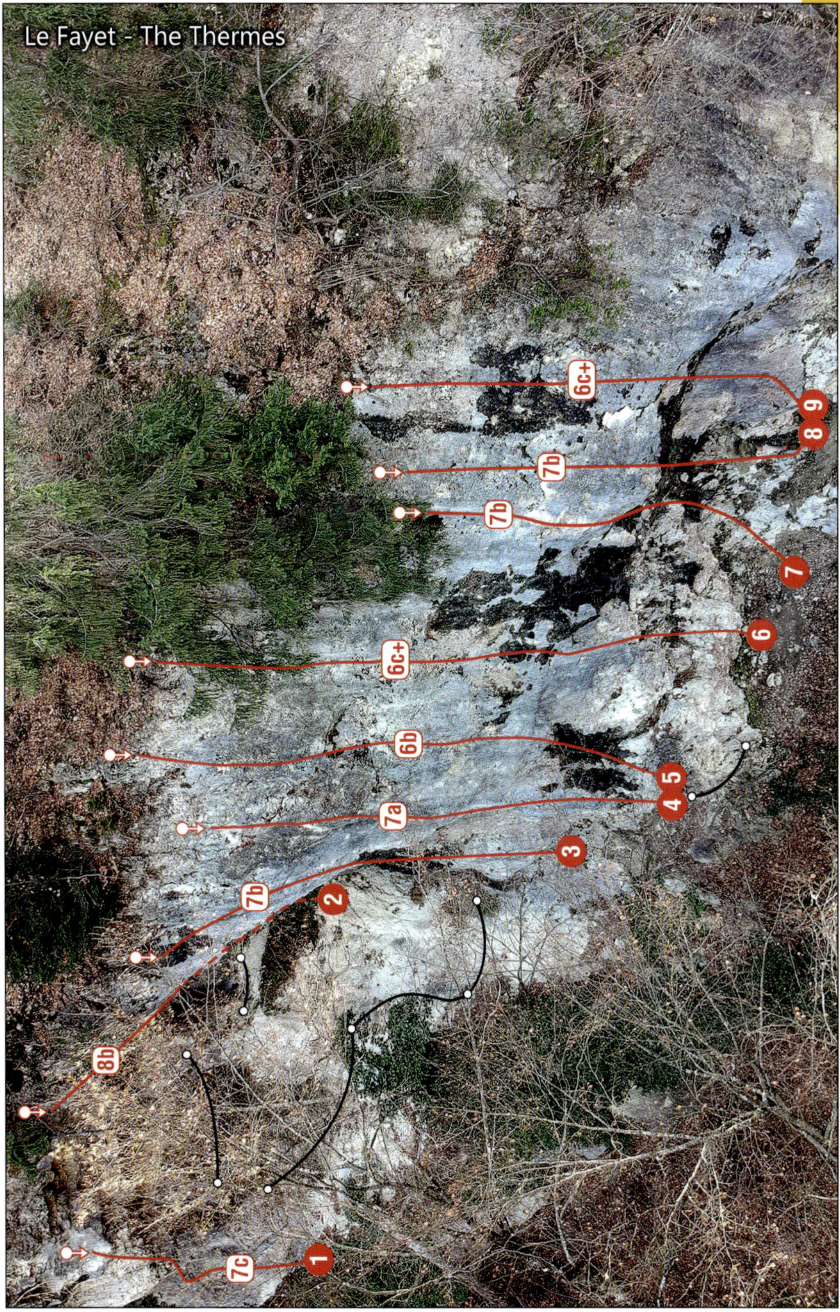
Le Fayet - The Thermes
1
7c
8b
2
7b
3
4
7a
5
6b
6
6c+
7
7b
8
7b
9
6c+

Area 02

Servoz
La Paré
Le Labo
Les Chavants
Coupeau
Roc Dément
Roc des Os

Servoz

800 m | W

0'

3

10 10 12 2 | 12-45 m

Servoz is the crag of good holds.

Rock : schist with very well-proportioned holds (ie. jugs!).

Climbing : part of the crag is sheltered from the rain under the big overhang. Most of the routes, especially on the lower part of the wall, are graded no harder than 5. The upper section offers several overhanging pitches for athletic climbers.

The site : cool in the mornings. Beginner's section. Run offs after rainfall. Next to a road, not too much traffic.

Access : **by bus**: line 3. **By train**: Servoz station 15 mins. Go through Servoz village center (Le Bouchet) then cross the Diosaz bridge and follow the road D13 for 500 m in the direction of Les Houches. **By car** from Chamonix: 14 km. Follow the N 205 (route Blanche) for 13km in the Geneva direction. Turn off to the right at the Servoz/Gorge de la Diosaz sign onto the D13. After a kilometer the crag is on the right by the roadside.

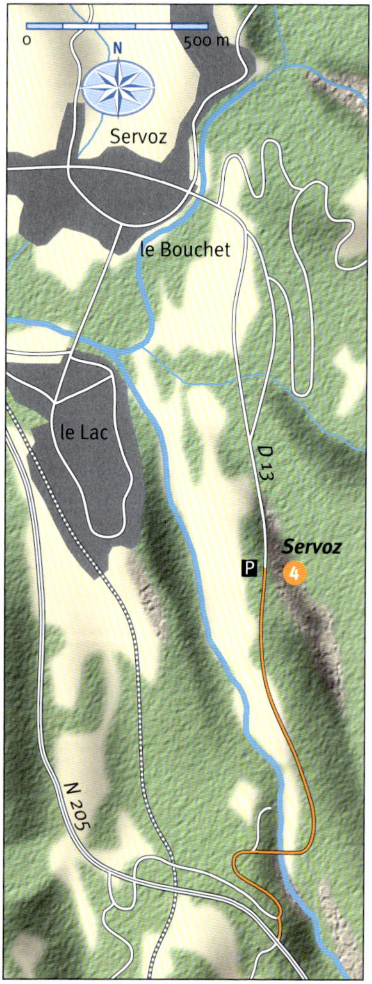

The routes

1 - **Voie de l'Arbre ou Bonzaï**: 4b, 25m, classic.

2 - **Le dièdre du facteur**: 5b, 15m.

3 - **?**: 4a, 25m.

4 - **?**: **P1**: 4b, 15m; **P2**: 5b, 15m. An athletic first move.

5 - **Le fil à plomb**: **P1**: 5b; **P2**: 5c. Nice climb.

6 - **Surbac à bras**: 6b, superb. Access through routes 4 or 5.

6' - **Le bombé à Jacquot:** 7b, 15m. Short boulder movements.

7 - **La Directe du Fil à plomb**: **P1**: 4c; **P2**: 5c, 30m.

8 - **Les bras m'en tombent: P1**: 5a; **P2**: 5c; **P3**: 6a+. 40m.

9 - **Les doigts m'en tombent**: 6b; 10m. An alternative exit to the route 8.

10 - **La Cheminée**: 45m, a nice classic ending with an airy chimney. **P1**: overhang 4a; **P2**: 4a; **P3**: 5b.

A - **La Traversée des Dieux**: 4c, 45m. A long, nearly horizontal traverse, which finishes in a very exposed positive flakes.

11 - **Perds pas les pédales**: **P1**: 5a, 15m; **P2**: 6c, fun.

12 - **?**: 5a, 10m. One tricky slab move, friction.

13 - **?**: 5a, 10m. One tricky slab move, friction.

14 - **?**: 5b, 10m. Athletic finish.

15 - **La Fernandise**: 6a.

16 - **Réta-mine**: 6b.

17 - **?**: 5b, 10m. Good holds.

18 - **?**: 6a, 10m. An aggressive move at the overhang.

19 - **?**: **P1**: 4c, 15m. Same start than 20.

20 - **Sur prise**: **P1**: 4b, 25m. **P2**: 6b (several uneasy holds).

21 - **Prends la cinquante**: **P1**: 4b; **P2**: 5c. Nice climbing. **P1+P2**: 45m, 18 quickdraws.

22 - **Attention au plafond**: **P1**: 4a, 25m; **P2**: 6b, 15m. A series of athletic moves.

23 - **Six sept à l'envers**: **P1**: 6a+, 15m; **P2**: 7a, 10m. Nice overhang. 10 moves with a surprise at the last hold. **P1+P2**: 15 quickdraws.

24 - **Ça béne**: **P1**: 3a, 25m; **P2**: 6c. Overhang with good but spaced holds.

25 - **La quartzite**: 6a+, 15m. Crack/corner, beautiful rock.

26 - **?**: 2c, 12m.

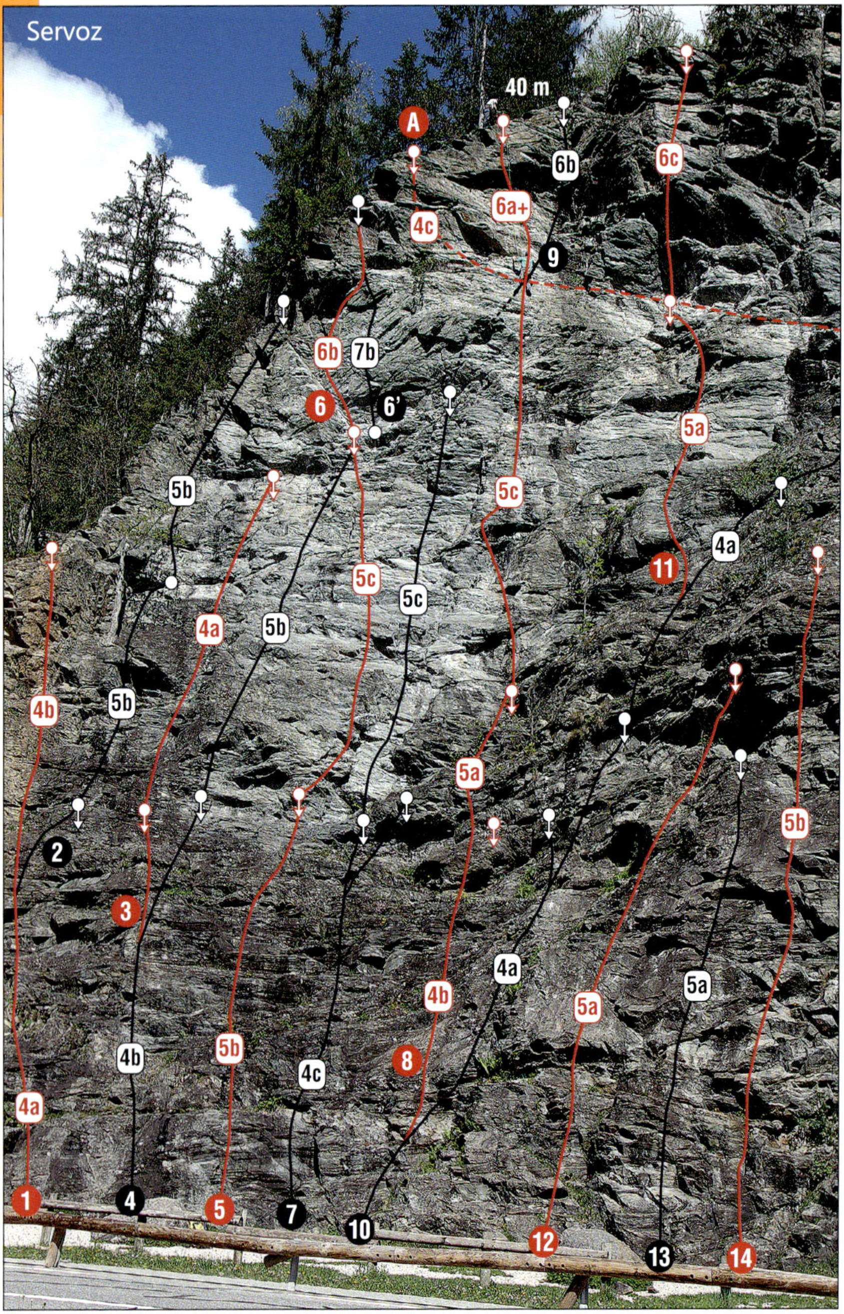
Servoz
40 m
A
4c
6a+
6b
6c
9
6b
7b
6
6'
5a
5b
5c
4a
11
1
4b
5b
4a
5b
5c
5c
2
3
5a
5b
4b
5b
4c
4b
8
4a
5a
5a
4a
4
5
7
10
12
13
14

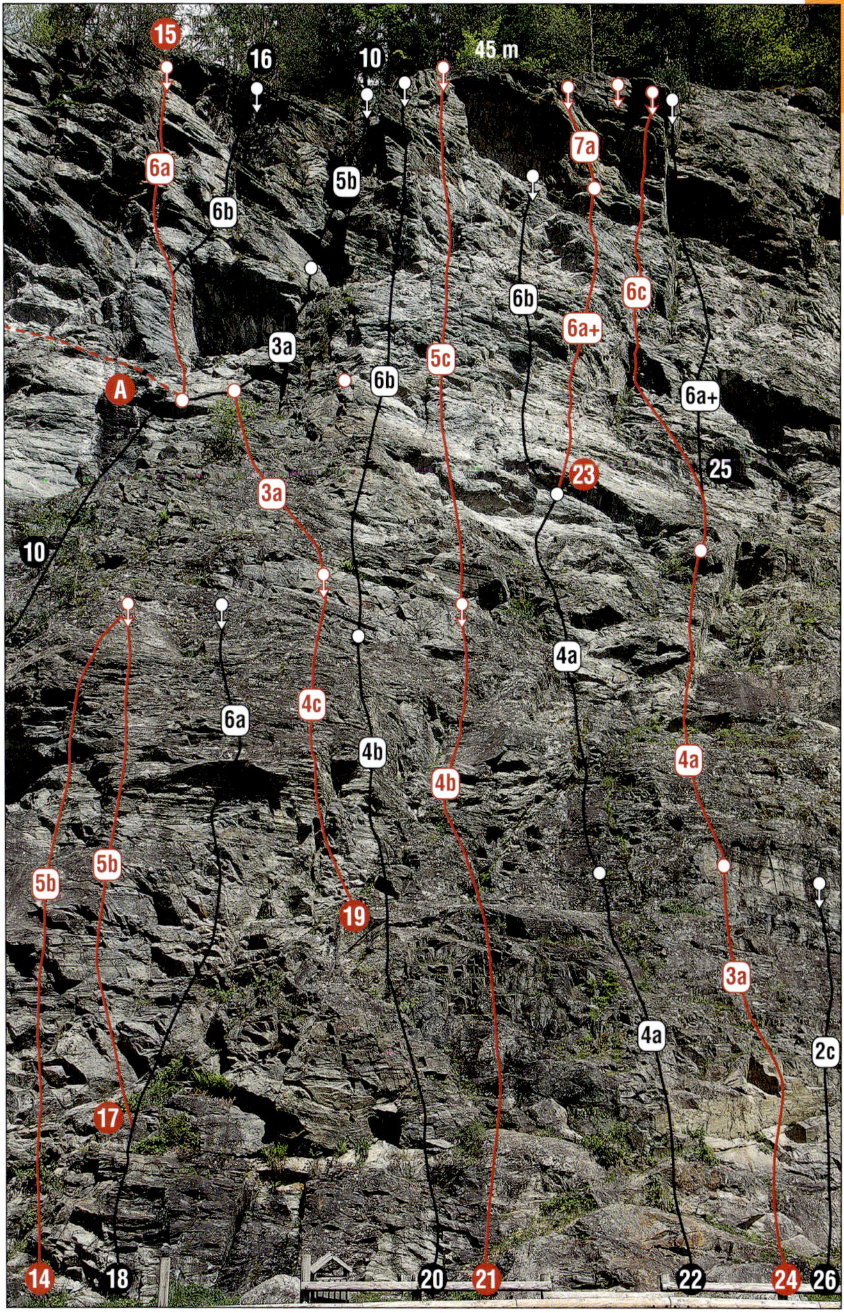
15
16
10
45 m
6a
6b
5b
7a
6b
6a+
6c
3a
5c
6b
A
6a+
25
23
3a
10
4a
4c
6a
4b
4b
4a
5b
5b
19
3a
4a
2c
17
14
18
20
21
22
24
26

La Paré

1450 m | W

60'

3

0 | 1 | 16 | 12 | 20 m

Perched on the west face of the Pormenaz summit, the Paré cliff dominates Servoz. With its endless and sustained vertical pitches, this interesting site will appeal to climbers who are comfortable in the 6c/7a grade. With fine views across to the impressive Fiz cliffs opposite, this cliff enjoys sunshine right into December. The final part of the approach route takes a very steep narrow trail which is equipped with hand-lines.

The cliff was equipped by Ilan and Jean-Sé Knoertzer in October 2008 (access route, first equipped route, cliff base clearance...) and most of the routes are credited to Ilan, Jean-Sé, Tristan and Léo Knoertzer , and Denis Poussin. Bruno and Olivier Sourzac, Toni Clarasso and François Burnier also put up routes. It's possible to bivvy in Ilan's Cabin (2-3 flat spots). Water can be found by going leftwards along the cliff base (fixed rope) to a ravine (5 mins).

A barbecue grill (belonging to our late friend Olivier Sourzac) is left in place for use next to the fire ring ("la salle à manger").

Rock : schist, the quality of which varies according to the different zones on the cliff, but which is cleaning up with climbing. Helmet recommended and care should be taken.

Equipment : 10mm and 12mm bolts. Belays equipped. 100m single rope required to lower off , but intermediate descent belays exist on the longest routes

Access : from Chamonix 16km. Take the N205 to Servoz, exit at the D13. At the entrance to the village take the D143 for 5km towards Le Mont.
At the fountain in this hamlet, go right on the road which leads to La Côte. After 500m there are several parking places next to the flash flood barrier. Altitude 981m.

Approach : from Servoz: 45 mins - 1h. Several false trails and tracks can cause confusion. It's important to aim for the cliff. The final part of the approach is equipped with hand-lines and leather gloves are advisable. From the parking walk down along the road for 100m then go left on a steep road which goes up to the hamlet of Fieugerand. Take the forest path signed to Barme Trappier. At the Souay river you have to get across one way or another. In high water go across barefoot or use the monkey bridge which is 20m up-stream. If you do this be sure to go back downhill for 20m on the far side of the river to get back on the right trail. Follow a flat path in the forest for 200m to a junction.

Go left into a dry stream-bed. Go up a huge tree trunk on the true left bank and cross a small rocky barrier to leave the stream (cairns) and to return to the forest. Follow the path to the fixed ropes which lead to the crag.

Soleil Levant

The first sector encountered on arrival at the crag.

1 - **Paresseux**: (common start with route 2), 6c, 45m, 18 quickdraws. A long and sustained journey on positive holds.

2 - **Paré fée de mode**: 6c+, 45m, 18 quickdraws. Compact rock.

3 - **La première de Lilou**: 6c+, 45m, 18 quickdraws. A consistent route on a nice face

4 - **Laura**: 7a, 45m, 18 quickdraws. A stamina route on the beautiful holes which typify this rock.

5 - **Mal Paré**: 6c+, 40m, 15 quickdraws. Great rock with holds of all shapes.

6 - **Paré sie**: 6c, 37m, 14 quickdraws. A wake-up call with a splendid finish.

7 - **Paré suze**: 6b+, 37m, 14 quickdraws. Careful route reading required to start this climb.

8 - **Paré Chirve**: 6b+, mediocre rock but great moves on small jugs.

***Lammergeier (a.k.a bearded eagle)**: nests in the Fis/Pormenaz cliff area. Contact Asters (organisation for wildlife protection) at: gypaete-barbu.com or call 0033 4 50 93 08 48 for info on access restriction and affected areas during nesting period (November 1st to July 31st).*

Soleil Levant
40 m
40 m
35 m
6c+
6c
7a
6c+
6c+
6c
6b+
6b+
1
2
3
4
5
6
7
8

Bouc

1 - **Par esthétique**: 6c+, 38m, 17 quickdraws, the most rightwards route of this sector with a technical section mid-route.

2 - **Souay disant**: 6b+, 38m, 17 quickdraws. Features an athletic section.

3 - **?**: 6b, 42m, 17 quickdraws. Three vertical walls to negotiate.

4 - **Paré-t-il?**: TD, 110m, 14 quickdraws plus belays. At the time of writing this is the most amenable of the multi-pitch routes on Le Paré. **P1**: 6a+, 25m; crack; **P2**: 6a+; 30m vertical wall; **P3**: 6a, traverse with steepenings, 23m; **P4**: 5b; long traverse with a final slab, 37m. Descent: abseil down the route. J-Sé Knoertzer and Denis Poussin.

Cabane

1 - **Val Paré**: 6c, 32m, 18 quickdraws. A sustained first part leads to a rest on the terrace. The upper part of the route dries slowly.

2 - **Passy ridicule**: 7a+, 20m, 7 quickdraws. Stamina with a long move.

3 - **Vanoise**: 6c, 20m. Positive holds. Joins route 2 at the last bolt.

4 - **L'Assise à plus**: 6b, 17m, 7 quickdraws. An overhanging section.

5 - **Un P'tit pas c'est Pare là**: 7a+, 40 m, 16 quickdraws. Tricky mantel at the finish.

6 - **Paré à Tonnerre**: 6c, 17 m, 8 quickdraws. Stamina.

7 - **Paré Xemple**: 6b+, 17 m, 8 quickdraws. Sequency section on sharp holds.

8 - **Paré li po pèt**: 6a+, 14 m 6 quickdraws. Sustained climbing on good holds.

9 - **Le Sarkopte**: 7a, 35 m, 14 quickdraws. A fine varied route with a sustained overhanging section.

10 - **Paré 7a molle**: ABO, J-Sé Knoertzer & Denis Poussin. 170m. **P1**: 7a+, 35m. **P2**: 7b, 12m. **P1+P2**: 7b+. **P3**: 7b, 28m. **P4**: 7a+, 28m. **P5**: 6C, 28m. **P6**: 7a+, 30m. Good compact rock.

11 - **Paré à virer**: 6b+, 46m, 18 quickdraws. Sustained. Intermediate belay at 35m.

12 - **Mac à Paré**: 6b+, 46m, 19 quickdraws (intermediate belay). The classic of the crag. A boulder move at the first overhang leads to stamina climbing to the top.

13 - **A Paré Yé**: 7b+, 25m, 12 quickdraws. A smooth section on small rounded holds requires concentration.

14 - **Paré Lé Haut**: 6c, 25m, 10 quickdraws. Sustained.

15 - **Antoine à Paré**: 6b+, 40m, 18 quickdraws. Warm-up.

16 - **Pilier d'Angle**: 6c, 30m, 14 quickdraws. Stamina with great ambiance.

Bouc, Cabane and Story Crack sectors

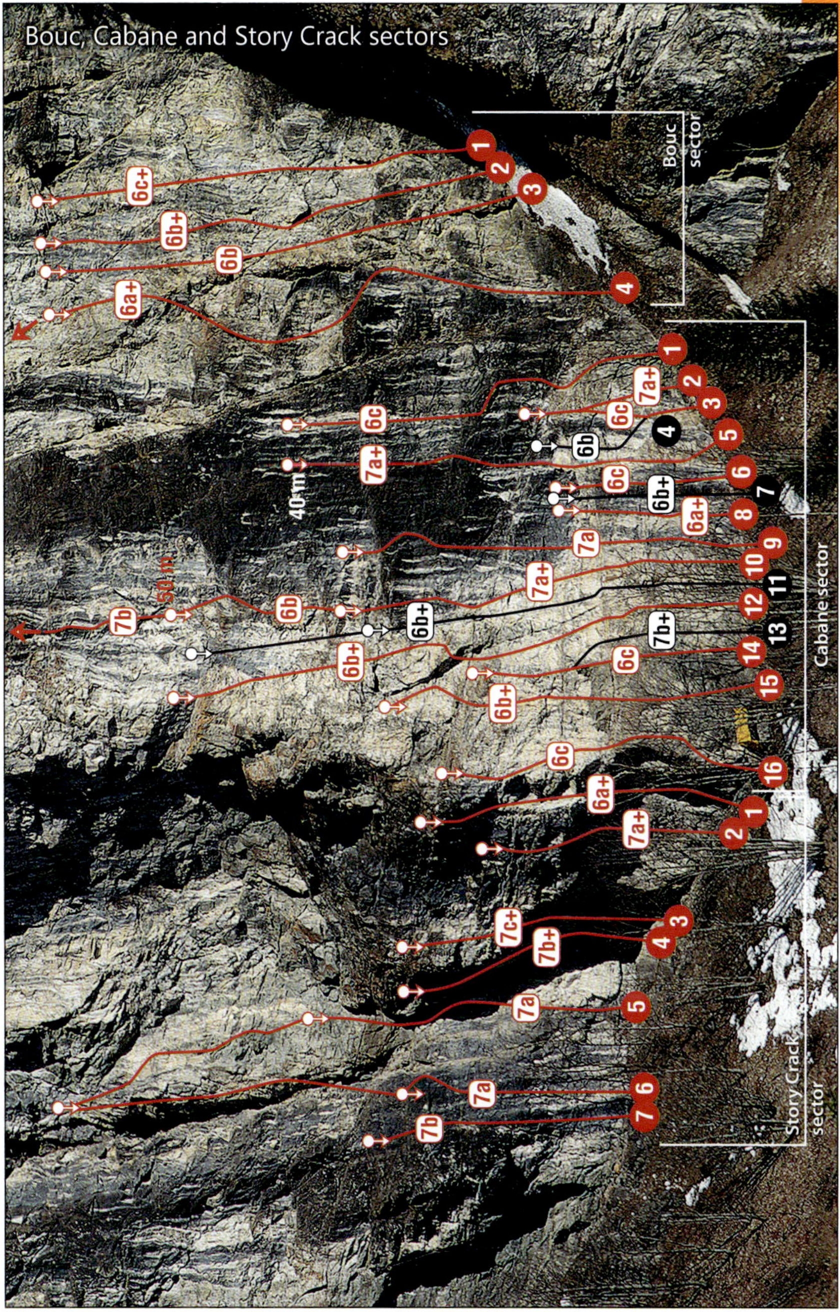

Story Crack

1 - **Athée Souay**: 6a+, 30m, 12 quickdraws. A good strenuous warm-up with a nice crack. Milk those rest points!

2 - **Faut pas réfléchir**: 7a+, 22m, 12 quickdraws. Some suspect flakes.

3 - **Paré story crack**: 7c+, 30m, 12 quickdraws. 8a without the two glued on holds. Two intense stamina boulder sections.

4 - **Ça Paré Drus**: 7b+, 30m, 12 quickdraws. A fine finger crack and a big overhang.

5 - **Juliette est Paré**: 7a, 25m + 25m, 19 quickdraws. Worth doing despite some suspect rock.

6 - **Manu memory**: **P1**: 7a, 30m; **P2**: 6c, 20m. Great moves up a vertical wall.

7 - **Black Rock**: 7b, 35m, 13 quickdraws. A splendid route on a steep black wall. A technical fingery boulder move leads to stamina on flat holds.

Ilan in "Ça Paré Drus", 7b+

Le Labo

1400 m SW

45'

3

0 0 9 8 30 m

An experimental movement laboratory! All the mind-bending moves you can think of are allowed to get up these enigmatic lines.

Rock : schist.

Climbing : athletic climbing.

Access : **1) From Servoz. By train**: Servoz station; then 40 mins to Montvauthier. Go through Servoz village center "Le Bouchet" then follow the sign to "Gorge de la Diosaz" and then by the "chemin de la Rossettaz" to Montvauthier. Car parking at the "Randonneurs" carpark.
2) From Les Houches. By train: Les Houches train station, follow the footpath for "Coupeau", "Le Bettey" and "La Flattière" (1h). **By car**: from Chamonix N205 take the 2nd exit to Les Houches. Turn off on the right towards Coupeau (4 km); do not take the next turning to the right for the Parc Merlet but continue up towards Le Bettey, La Flatière carpark.

Approach :
From Montvautier: (45 mins) At the entrance to the hamlet take the path that rises steeply on the left beside the aerial mast; and higher up follow the sign to "Grosses Pierres". The crag is situated about 100m further on past the chalet "Les Grosses Pierres". Go past the chalet and at the level of the bridge over the stream go up a small path which joins a forestry road 50m higher up. Access to the site is indicated by a yellow plaque "Le Labo".
From the "Le Bettey" carpark at La Flattière: 40/45 mins. Cross the hamlet to the end of the road and take the footpath on the right towards "Plan du Cry, Samoteux" and then on the left for "Samoteux". From there follow "Montvauthier par les Grosses Pierres". Cross the little bridge just before the chalet and to the right follow a small path up through the forest to join a forestry road. Look for a yellow plaque on a tree indicating "Le Labo". The crag is situated about 100m higher up from the chalet.

The routes

Several unfinished projects at the extreme left and right ends of the crag:

1 - **Faut pas y craindre**: 6b+, 20m.

2 - **Ultime la tome**: 7c?, 23m.

3 - **Guère de paix**: 7c?, 23m.

4 - **La force de Corio lisse**: 7c+?, 32m.

5 - **Obsolescence programmée**: 7a+, (7b without the blue hold) 32m.

6 - **CREA tine Phosphate**: 7B+?, 32m.

7 - **Le Théorème de ta Laisse**: 7b, 32m.

8 - **Bourre Moltès**: 7b, 23m.

9 - **Black Mamba**: 7a, 27m.

10 - **Nain faux man**: 6c+, 27m.

11 - **Bienvenue a la Nasa**: 7a, 28m.

12 - **La cage de Faradè**: 6b, 28m (start at the base of the big pine on the right).

13 - **?**: new route, 6c.

14 - **?**: new route, 6c.

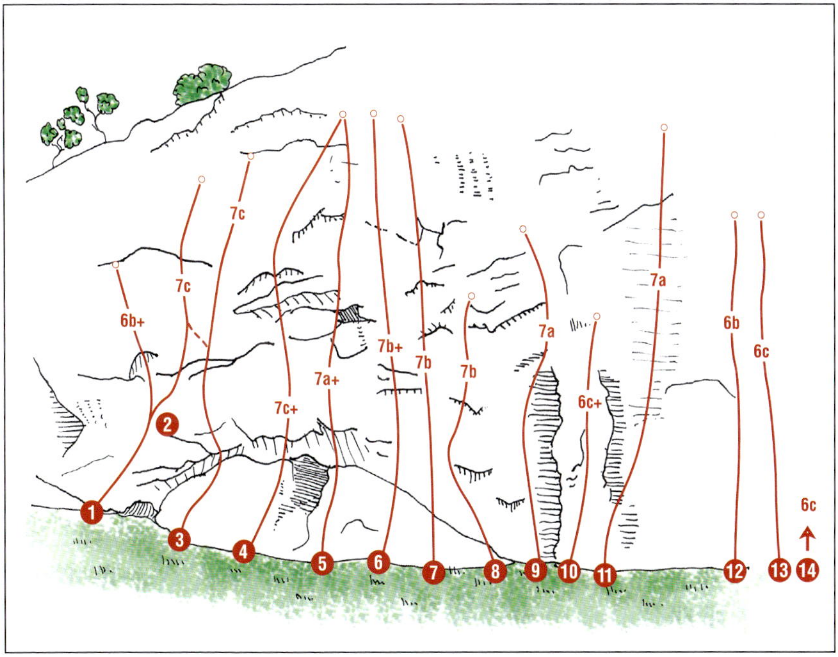

Les Chavants

950 m | W

5′

3 4

13 4 2 0 | 20 m

A very small crag, more interesting than it appears to be from the road.

Rock : easy routes on 20 metres high gneiss crag with lots of big holds; equipped with cemented-in ring bolts.

The site : an excellent beginners' crag in friendly surroundings. The location is easily accessible to non-climbers who may wish to accompany you, and is not dangerous for children. There is a pleasant picnic site on the banks of a small lake next to a botanical garden.

Access : **by car**: leave the N205 at the sign for Les Houches and go through the village towards the "Prarion telecabine". At the roundabout turn right. Large car-park next to the lake "lac des Chavants". **By bus**: from Chamonix, bus line 1. **By train**: stop at "Viaduc Sainte Marie" then 10 mins walk.

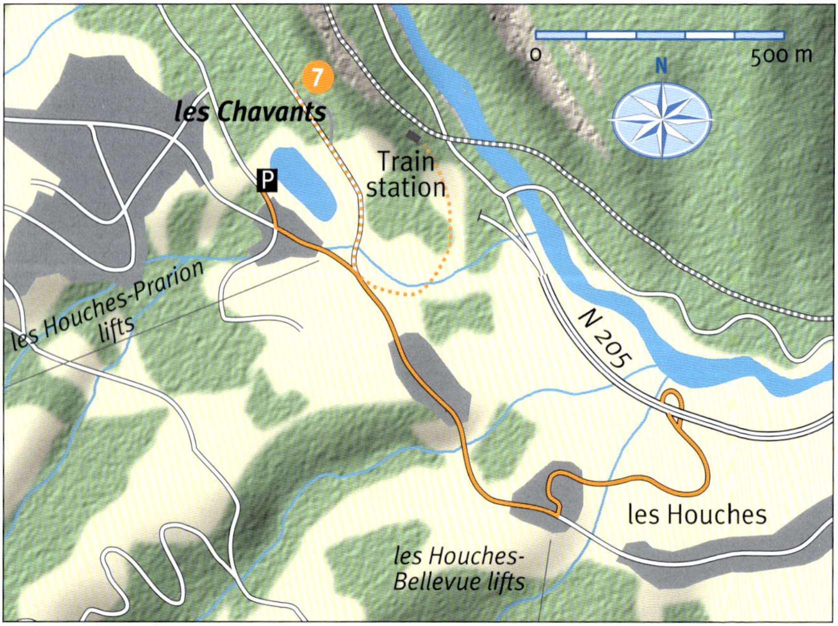

The routes

1 - **?**: 4c, 15 m. Often wet.

2 - **?**: 4c, 15 m. Start on a nice slab.

3 - 5a, 20 m. 12 quickdraws. A well protected wall

4 - 4a, 20 m. Climb left after the third point.

5 - 4b, 25 m. Start in route 4.

6 - 4a, 20 m. Nice route.

7 - 4a, 20 m.

8 - 5a, 20 m.

9 - Route «B+». 5c, 22 m.

10 - 4a, 22 m.

11 - 4c, 22 m. Good holds all the way.

12 - **Voie centrale**: 4c, 22 m, edge climbing on a slab.

13 - **Directe de l'arbre**: 4c, 22 m.

14 - 5c, 12 m. «B» at the start.

15 - 6a, 12 m. «C» at the start.

16 - 6a+, 10 m. «B» at the start.

17; 18; 19 - 4a, 10 m. Short routes (upper ledge)

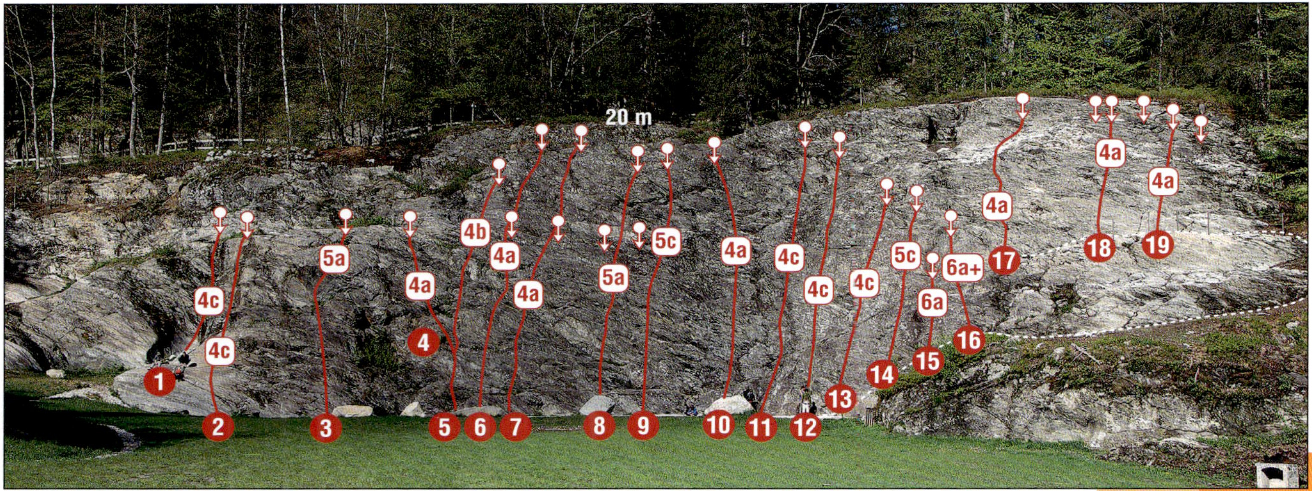

Coupeau

1300 m S

5'

3

4 4 15 2 15-20 m

This crag is in a shady, wooded setting, and is an ideal place to escape the summer heat.

Rocher : gneiss - a little friable in places.

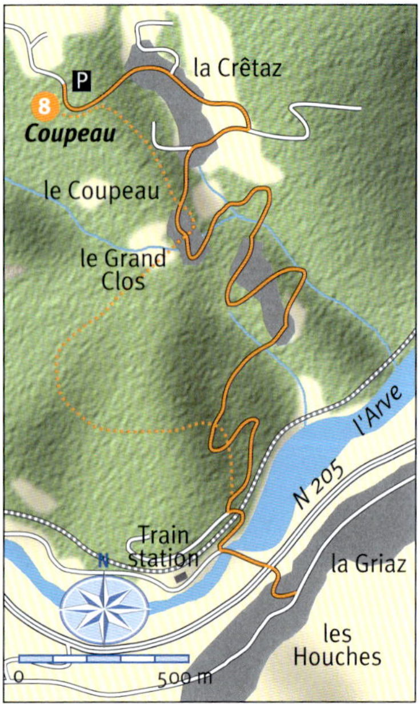

Climbing : this 15 metres wall is at least vertical all the way, and even has a short overhanging section in the middle. The climbing is fingery on small edges. The routes are in the shade and take a while to dry. 12 of the 16 routes are graded 6.

Equipment : 10mm bolts with hangers.

The site : basecamp is in a pleasant clearing at the top of the crag with a view over the Mont-Blanc and a park bench.

Access : **by train**: Les Houches train station, follow the foot- path to "Coupeau" then continue towards "La Flatière". The crag is left of the road at the last hairpin turn to the right before the village (1h). **By car**: coming from Chamonix , take N205 then the 2nd exit for Les Houches. Follow the road for "Le Coupeau" for 4 km. When you get to a crossroads, turn left towards "Bettey", "La Flatière". Drive another 250m and park your car after hairpin turn to the right (big boulders).

Approach : follow the path from the hairpin turn to the right and reach the top of the crag in 1 minute. To get to the foot of the routes, follow the path down on the left.

The routes

1 - **Cham n' cam**: 4c, 10m, 4 points, nice.

2 - **Eclipse-toi**: 5a, 10m, 3 bolts, warm up.

3 - **L'eau d'Issey de Chantal**: 5c, 11m, 3 bolts.

4 - **Petit Béru**: 6b, 15m, 5 bolts, one move.

5 - **Et 1, et 2 et 3/0**: 6b, 17m, 5 bolts, stamina.

6 - **Doigts de fée pour cœur de lion**: 7a+ (in the line of the bolts), 18m, 5 bolts.

7 - **Loupe pas le Bac**: 6c+, 18m, 6 bolts.

8 - **Un peu de toit, un peu de moi**: 6b, 18m, 6 bolts, stamina.

9 - **Si je le veux bien**: 6c, 17m, 7 bolts, a short hard move at the roof.

10 - **Guismo**: 6b, 16m, 7 bolts, idem.

11 - **Désir brûlant**: 6b, 16m, 7 bolts.

12 - **Moustique**: 6b, 16m, 7 bolts.

13 - **Banzaï**: 6a+, 16m, 6 bolts, same.

14 - **Boutch**: 6a+, 16m, 6 bolts, same.

15 - **Patita**: 6a.

16 - **Time is on my side**: 6b+, 16m, 6 bolts.

17 - **Pour toi Guilhem**: 6b+, 15m, 6 bolts.

18 - **Burnin' and lootin'**: 6b, 15m, 5 bolts. A lot of variation.

Lucien Boucansaud in "Si je le veux bien", 6c

19 - **La haine**: 7a+, 15m, 5 bolts. 7 moves on vertical edges.

20 - **Craféron**: 6a+.

21 - **Cétacé**: 5a.

22 - **Hailine**: 5b.

23 - **Peorsène**: 4c.

24 - **Noéma**: 4a.

25 - **Crocolino**: 3c.

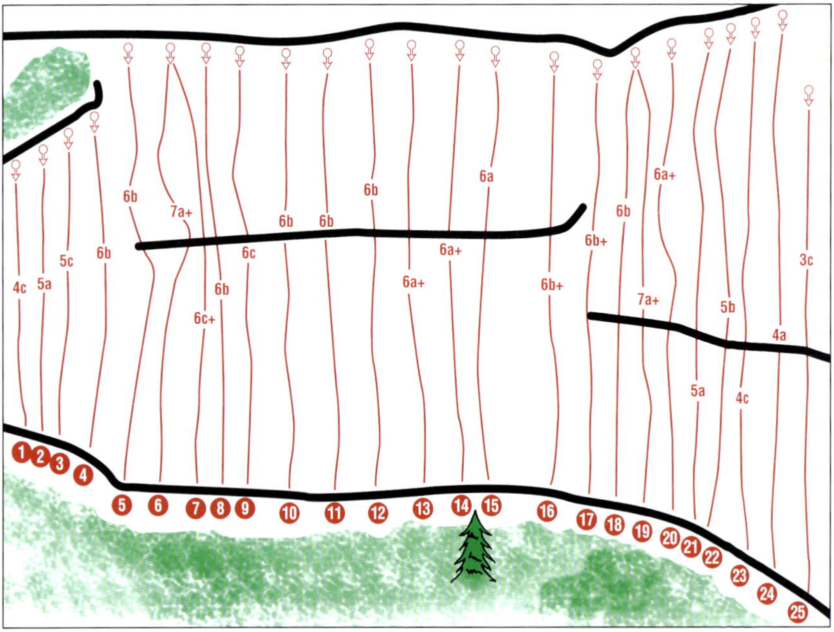

COMPAGNIE DES GUIDES
1821
Mont-Blanc
CHAMONIX
LA MONTAGNE VERSANT SAUVAGE
MORE
WILD.
WWW.CHAMONIX-GUIDES.COM - #MOREWILD

AREA 02 **ROC DÉMENT**

9

Roc Dément

1450 m | S

20′

3

0 0 5 8 15-35 m

At first glance this crag is not very appealing but Thierry Renault has managed to put up some fine lines on the left side of the crag which make this a very worthwhile venue.

Rock : gneiss and schist.

Climbing : vertical or slightly overhanging walls on featured rock with good holds. Some lines are a little close together and this can cause a bit of confusion, but on the other hand it gives numerous possibilities for combinations.

Equipment : 10mm bolts and hangers. Belays equipped for lowering. 70m single rope.

Access : **by train**: Les Houches station then 40 min walk toward P2. **By car**: coming from Chamonix, take the second exit for Les Houches. Follow the road for "Le Coupeau" for 4km then "parc Merlet". Car park at P2.

Approach : 20 mins. At the very top end of the carpark take a footpath which goes down through the forest; partially blocked by a mound of earth at about 100m. Carry on in the same direction and find the path marked with cairns which leads you to a clearing where you will see a feeding manger for large animals. (A wood cut was taking place at the time of writing this guide). Continue in easterly direction. There is a passage on steep terrain (fixed rope) before arriving at the site.

Mehdi Bidault in Korigan, 6c+

The routes

1 - **Shéma**: 6c+, 35m. 20 quickdraws. Start in the corner. Traverse to the left after 10m: a crack and a tricky slab.

2 - **La Félure**: 6c, 35m. 20 quickdraws. Same start than 1. Demanding crack at the end.

3 - **Too old to rock and Roll**: 7a, 35m, Kong hangers. 15 quickdraws. Start as for route 2. The higher you climb the harder it gets!

4 - **Too young to die...** : 6b, 25m, 12 quickdraws, Fixe hangers. Cracks leading to a final wall. Good warm-up.

4'- **?**

5 - **Lègue à Lyse**: 7a, 22m, Kong hangers. Start on the edge of the pillar.

6 - **Korigan**: 6c+, 30m, Kong hangers. Steep wall, one of the best routes on the cliff. Variation: 6c+, 30m, Fixe hangers.

7 - **Merleterie**: 7a+, 30m, 12 quick-draws, Fixe and Petzl hangers. Superb climb on sharp holds and cracks.

8 - **Gratton Labeur**: 30m, 7a+, Kong hangers.

9 - **Noire Désir**: 7b, 25m. Fixe hangers.

10 - **Mine de rien**: 7b+, 25m, Kong hangers. Steep fingers wall.

11 - **Grise mines**: 7b+, 20m, Series of boulder moves.

12 - **Sicamou**: 7b+, 18m, Fingery section in a fine yellow wall.

13 - **Totem cam**: 7c+, 20m. Without using the route 12 holds. Several quickdraws are already in place.

14 - Project.

15 - **Lego**: 6b+ ? .

Jonathan Charlet in Noire Désir, 7b

35 m
Roc Dément
6c+
6c
7a
4'
1
6b
7a
7a+
6c+
?
2
3
4
5
6
7
14

6c+
1
7a
6c
6b
7a+
7a
6c+
7b
2
3
7a+
4
7b+
7b+
7b
7c+
5
6
7
9
10
8
11
12
13

Roc des Os

1250 m — S

40'

0 1 8 0 — 15-20 m

This small cliff, discovered by Thierry Renault, provides largely trad routes where only the belays are equipped, with a few fixed points on the slabs.
There are a dozen crack routes which can be well-protected with nuts and cams; Climbers unused to this type of climbing should aim a little below their level because placing gear requires a certain experience.

Rock : good gneiss.

Gear : take a full rack of cams and nuts for all the routes. Tips
- Rack a full range of gear on your harness.
- Place gear as soon as possible, before the hard moves.
- Don't push gear too far into the cracks.
- The second should carry a nut key to remove gear.

Getting gear whilst lowering down can be dangerous if the route doesn't go straight up. In this case it's much better if the second gets the gear out whilst climbing.

Access : from Chamonix:
- **By car**: 2.5km. Take the D743 road west of Chamonix towards Les Bossons for 2km. Pass the Montquarts round-about then go right along the Chemin des Epinettes for 50m. Park by the footbridge.
- **By train**: get off at Les Bossons station and go past the Montquarts round-about, taking the Chemin des Epinettes on the right for 50m to reach the footbridge.
- **By bike/on foot**: take the road to Les Gaillands and follow the bike track westwards.

Approach : 40-50 mins: 15 mins on tracks and 25-30 mins on paths. Cross the bridge to reach the bike track. Follow this leftwards for 1.5km until just beyond a yellow marker with the number 153. 50m further along a first big cairn is passed on the edge of the track and 50m more leads to a smaller cairn next to a path going off right. Take this path through vegetation to a scree slope. The path steepens and goes into the forest - go right at a junction. A hand-line gives access to the climbs.

The routes

1 - **Logos**: 6a+, 18m. Vertical crack.

2 - **Molosse**: 6c, 18m. 3 bolts at the start. Thin crack.

3 - **Raspa populos**: 6a+, 18m. Nice hand crack.

4 - **Osso Buco**: 6b, 18m. Sustained vertical climbing.

5 - **Ostralopithèque**: 6a, 25m. Difficult to strip when lowering.

6 - **Ostralopithèque variante**: Direct: 6c, 30m. 3 bolts at the finish. Difficult to strip when lowering.

7 - **Pathos**: 6c, 25m. Difficult to strip when lowering.

8 - **Ostrogoth**: 6a+, 25m. Difficult to strip when lowering.

9 - **Vamos**: 5c/6a, 25m. Difficult to strip when lowering.

Roc des Os
6c
6c
6
7
6a+
6a
6a
6a+
6b
6c
6a+
1
2
3
4
5
8
9

Area 03

Les Bossons
Les Gaillands

Les Bossons

1100 m

5'

24 23 25 47 2-8 m

The Songenaz forest is scattered with boulders of all sizes that ended their journey here many millenia ago. At the end of the 90s, twenty or so of them were cleaned and opened by Fabrice Judenne, Romain Desgranges and the young climbers of the Chamonix climbing club.

Rock : granite blocks, compact with cracks, 2-10 metres in height. Most are around 4 metres high.

Climbing : 120 problems have been numbered and marked with arrows. There is a huge variety of levels on offer - everyone can find something to suit them here. This site is particularly good for children (lower boulders) but is used more by experts - so many of the yellow and green problems are mossy. There are five circuits: yellow (children), green (4), blue (5), red (6), black (7 and above). Some of the markings are no longer visible and there are some bad holds.

The site : cool even in the middle of summer, especially towards the end of the day. It is possible to get a drink and a snack at the Cerro buvette that overlooks the Bossons glacier by hiking up 20 minutes.

Access : from Chamonix take the RN 505 towards Geneva. Take the "les Bossons" exit. Go over the bridge that crosses the main road and go straight on. Go past the Crèmerie du Glacier on your left and go over a small bridge.

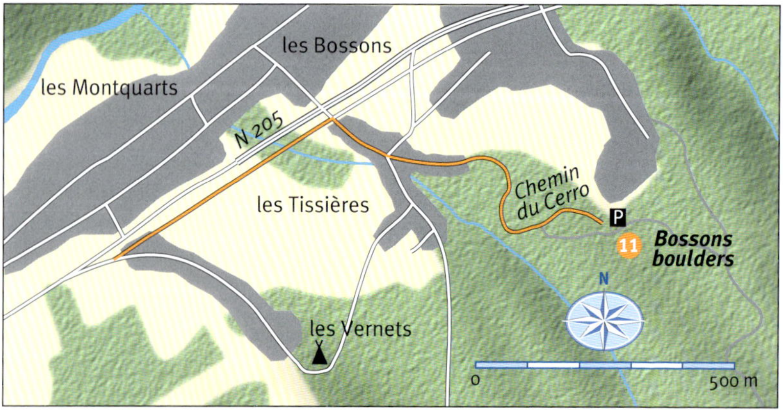

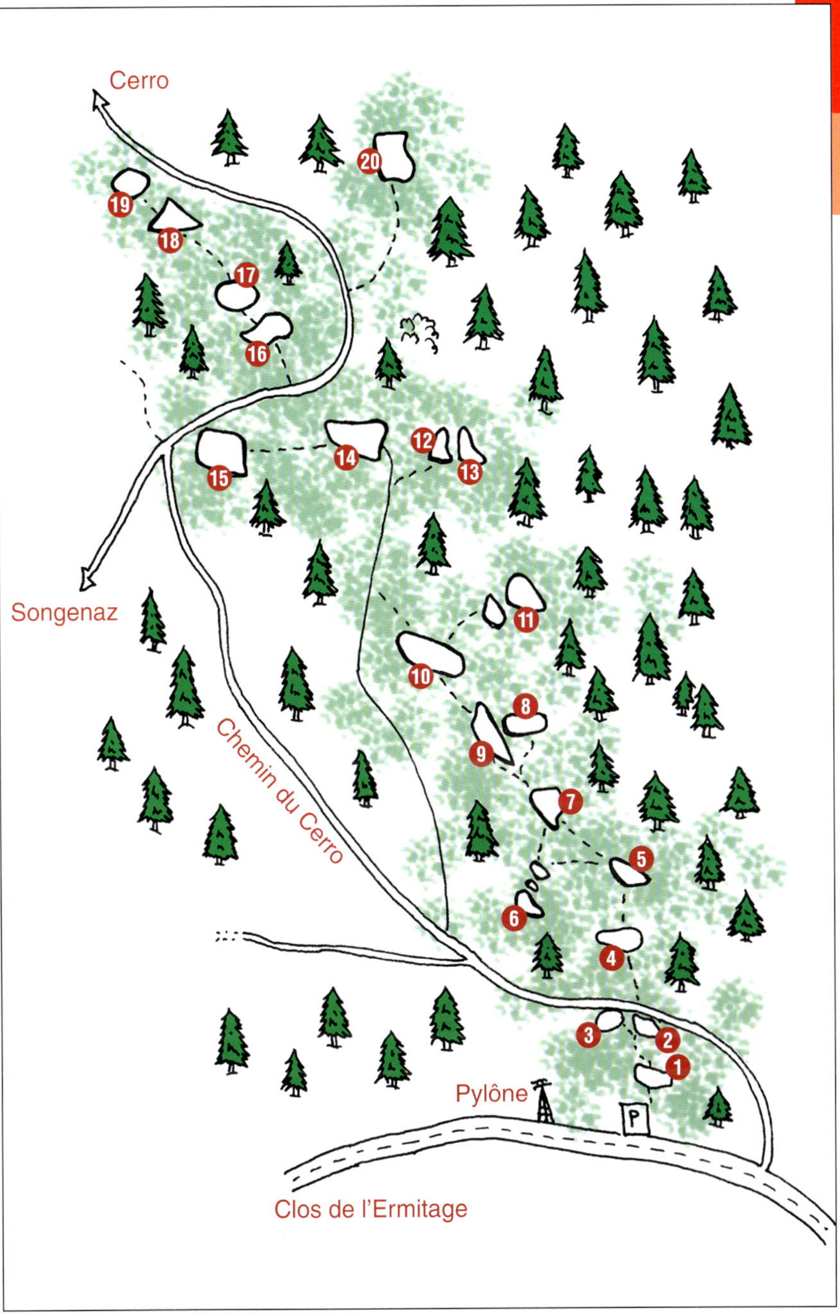
Cerro
Songenaz
Chemin du Cerro
Pylône
P
Clos de l'Ermitage
1
2
3
4
5
6
7
8
9
10
11
12
13
14
15
16
17
18
19
20

Turn left and immediately right - route du Cerro. Follow this road for four bends and park on the right before the electric pylon. From les Houches take the RN 505 towards Chamonix, "les Bossons" exit. Go over the bridge that crosses the main road and go straight on. Go past the Crèmerie du Glacier on your left and go over a small bridge. Turn left and immediately right - route du Cerro. Follow this road for four bends and park on the right before the electric pylon.

Safety : bring a bouldering mat and a watchful partner for spotting. For the higher boulders we would recommend checking the descent route. It could also be a good idea to have a brush to clean some of the problems - moss and lichen grow very quickly here.

Parking : 45°54'13"N, 6°50'45"E. There are ten parking spaces just before the end of the road that goes to the Clos de l'Ermitage, before the electric pylon. Please respect private property. The first boulder is 50 metres uphill, in the forest.

Yellow circuit

From 3a - 4a. Great for kids, most of the routes are no more than 3 metres high. Unfortunately some of the less used problems are moss covered. 26 problems.

Boulder 1 : (cube shaped), problems 1 & 2, 3a***, good slab, south facing, 2m.

Boulder 2 : 6, 3c, exit needs cleaning, arrow no longer visible. 7, 3c.

Boulder 3 : 3, 3b. 4, 3b. 5, 3a.

Boulder 5 : (3 m, mossy) 8, 3a, sloping slab. 9, 3a.

Boulder 7 : 10, 3a***, getting mossy. 11, 3a ***, interesting overhang. 12, 3c. 13, 3c.

Boulder 8 : (needs cleaning) 14, 3b. 15, 3a.

Boulder 9 : 16, 3c.

Boulder 10 : 17, 3c, smearing with precision. 18, 3b. 19, 3c. 20, 4b. 21, 3b*** (without leaning on the tree).

Boulder 11 : (good 4m slab, needs some cleaning) 22, 3b. 23 et 24, 3c, compact slab.

Boulder 12 : 25, 3a. 26, 3a, wall.

Green circuit

Problems from 4a to 4c.

Boulder 1 : 1, 4b, good wall, 3 m. 2, 4c***, small moves.

Boulder 3 : 3, 3c, moss.

Boulder 4 : (mossy at the finish) 4, 4c.

Boulder 7 : (4 m) 5, 5a, NE facing. Start next to the tree. Arrow worn off.

Boulder 9 : 6, 4a***. 7, 4c***. 7', 4a, traverse from left to right.

Boulder 10 : (very nice small slab, needs cleaning) 8, 5a. 9, 4c.

Boulder 11 : 10, 4a. 11, 5a. 12, 4c. 13, 4a. 14, 4c.

Boulder 12 : (4 m): 15, 4a. 16, 4c. 17, 4a.

Boulder 13 : (3 m): 18, 4a. 19, 4a.

Boulder 14 : 20, 4a. 21, 4a.

Boulder 16 : (arrows worn off; mossy) 22, 4a. 23, 4a.

Boulder 17 : 24, 5a. 25, 4a.

Boulder 18 : 26, 5a.

Boulder 19 : (3 m, nice slab, get your brushes out...) 27, 4c. 28, 4c.

Blue and Red circuits

(the gradings are a bit tight)

Boulder 1 : **B (blue)** 1, 5b, wall, look for the exit holds. B2, 5b, at an angle. B3, 5b, short. **R (red)**1**, 5c, almost like the green, finish a bit exposed - check from the top. R2***, 6a+, start sitting at an angle: use your ankles.

Boulder 2 : (precision and nerves of steel needed on this nice slab, 4 m) R3, 6a+***, place precisely, finish a bit exposed - best checked out from the top. R4, 6a***, great, play with inverted moves, finish in line with the arrow. 6a+, without the two finger pocket.

Boulder 3 : (3-4m, south, arrows barely visible): R6, 6a+***, physical at the exit. 6b start seated next to the fir tree. R7, 6a. 6b seated start (inverted left hand).

Boulder 4 : (climb 50m above the path. Path. Boulder a bit neglected): B5, 5b, strong pull-up. R8, 6c+, 2.5m crimps, pull up to finish.

Boulder 6 : (2m, at the NE point of a group of 3 boulders): B6, 5b. B7, 5b. R9, 6a, all with pull-up moves.

Boulder 7 : (looks like a cat's head, not often climbed, mossy): R10, 6a. Seated start.

Boulder 8 : (2m) R11, 6b, traverse. Start from the tree.

Boulder 10 : (4 m) B8, 5b. R12, 6a***, traverse, seated start, from the corner. R13, 6a, a bit short. R14, 6a.

Boulder 11 : (2 boulders side by side) R15, 6a, explosive block. R16, 6a.

Boulder 13 : B9, 5c. R17, 6a+. R18, 6a+.

Boulder 14 : (the "cube", 4m at its highest. One of the most interesting. Slightly tricky descent) B10, 5b. B11, 5b. B12, 5b, on the pillar. B13a, 5c**, from one crimp to the other. B13b, 6a***, technical slab, no arrow, start with the left hand on the lefthand ridge. R19, 6b***, rising traverse, mossy. R20, 6a, mossy. R21, 6a, compact rock. R22, 6a.

Boulder 15 : (the "big block", the biggest of the site on the side of the Cerro path. 10m high. Moss has invaded the exits on the north and west faces). R23, 6b+, energetic bulge. R24, 6c, short pull-up. R25, 6a, same. R26, 6b+***, line up the dyno/lunge. R27, 6b, on the pillar, active smear. R28, 6c, 8m, slab, needs to be cleaned, + steel nerves. Possible top rope (go up via R27 !).

Boulder 16 : (boulders 16-20, follow a small path above the Cerro path): NE face is in the best condition. Arrows worn off. B14, 5c. B15, 5b, block. B16, 5b, slab. B17, 5c. R29, 6a+, small crimp on quartz.

Boulder 17 : (interesting) B18, 5b, 3 m. B19, 5b, wall. B20, 5c, short overhang. R33, 6a. R34, 5c, short pull up.

Boulder 18 : B21, 5b. B22, 5c. R35, 6a+.

Boulder 19 : B23, 5b, 4m, near by the tree. B24, 5b. B25, 5c.

Boulder 20 : R30, 6a. R31, 6b.

1
1
1
A
2
B
2
1
Boulder 1

5
4
Boulder 2

7
6
Boulder 3

16
7
6
Boulder 9

21
20
4
13b
13a
Boulder 14

7
27
26
6
8
28
Boulder 15

■ Black circuit

Boulder 1 : 1, 7a***, long traverse to the right of green 1, open hands, finish after the tree.

Boulder 10 : 2, 7b+, traverse.

Boulder 11 : 3, 6c.

Boulder 14 : 4, 6c, seated start.

Boulder 15 : (le "grand bloc") 5, 7a ***, needs cleaning. 6, 7a+, seated start with two finger pocket. 7, 7b***, two finger move, left hand crimp, pull up onto flat. No arrow, start to the right of 6 black. 8, 8a, overhang. 8b, seated start by Anthony Lamiche, not repeated since. 9, 7a, high slab exposed, mossy.

Boulder 17 : 12, 7b+***, long traverse, to the right near the edge. 13, 7a+ seated start.

Boulder 18 : 14, 7a+. 15, 7a. 16, ?. 17, 6c***, seated start, left shoulder move.

Boulder 20 : (5m the best boulder in the zone according to the connaisseurs. Finish needs cleaning. Double crashpad welcome) 10, 7c. 11, 7b+***.

14
Boulder 18

10
31
11
30
Boulder 20

Les Gaillands

1000 m | SW - SE

1' - 5'

In the 1930s, Alfred Couttet, known as "La Colaude", put up the first routes on this crag, with the intention of creating a place where alpinists could learn to climb. He was soon joined by Roger Frison-Roche in this project, considered at the time to be revolutionary. "Les Rochers des Gaillands" are equipped and maintained by the Chamonix guides' company, which has helped to turn this crag into a "mythical" place..

Rock : a compact gneiss

Climbing : offers varied climbing; slabs, cracks, overhangs... with 60% of the routes graded lower than 5+. Routes are equipped with strong cemented-in bolts. However, in some places these are rather spaced out (risk of dangerous falls). 12 to 15 quick-draws.

Access : the crag is located 2km from Chamonix town centre. **By car**: from Chamonix center, follow the direction "Les Gaillands"; the crag is beside the road. Large car park. **By bus**: line 1. **By train**: les Pélerins Train station, then 5 mins walk.

The site : despite being somewhat overcrowded, Les Gaillands is still a nice place to climb, thanks to its lakeside situation and the stunning views over Mont-Blanc and the Aiguilles de Chamonix. It is an ideal place for a family outing; there are lakes, a nature trail, a fitness track, and bars with terraces close by.

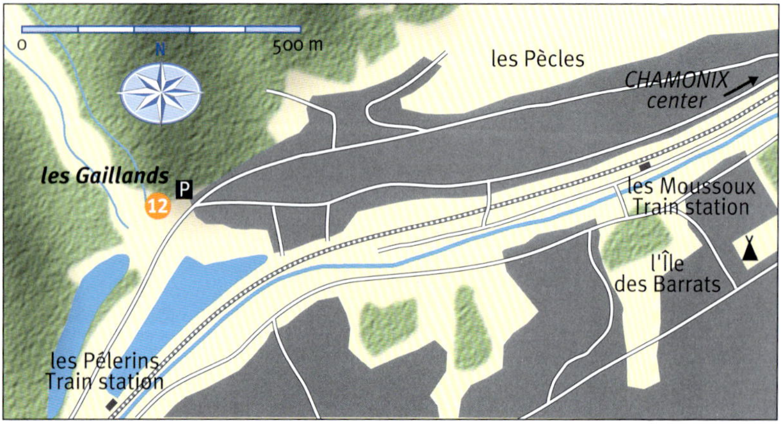

The areas

1 - **LE PETIT GAILLAND**
Maximum height of the face: 45m. Some nice, but polished, slabs and overhangs graded in the sixes. Equipped, but not very suitable for top roping.

2 - **L'ECHELLE**
Good to practise lead-climbing, (50m rope).

3 - **LE GRAND GAILLAND**
70 m high, this small face offers lots of middle grade, multi-pitch routes. Descent on foot is strongly recommended. Equipped.

4 - **LES VIPERES**
Height: 70m, an interesting beginners' section.

5 - **LES FORESTIERS**
Height: 60m, 25 middle grade pitches, (5b, 5c). 60m rope needed for top roping on the left. Bolted.

6 - **LES CHASSEURS**
Height: 25m. Some nice, athletic pitches at around 6b/c. Bolted.

7 - **SECTEUR FRENDO**
Height: 60m. A superb little wall of less polished rock. Bolted.

8 - **SECTEUR PICSOU**
Height: 10m. From 4 to 6b. Short routes suitable for group instruction.

Le Petit Gailland

1000 m S

3′

3

9 13 14 3 45 m

The routes

Warning: many routes here do not lend themselves to top roping or lowering off, as they are too long.

1 - **L'Y**: 5c.

1′ - 6a.

2 - **Sur le fil**: delicate... 6c.

3 - **La voie du golot directe**: balance and precision, 6b+.

4 - **La voie du golot gauche**: nice finishing move, 6a.

5 - **La Franco**: 5c+.

6 - **La Franco directe**: 6b.

7 - **Directe aux guides**: strange layback... 6b.

8 - **Les Lézards**: one explosive move, 7a.

9 - **Le surplomb Martinetti**: it's jamming time, 6c.

10 - **Ecailles directe**: 6a+, 20m. Nice but a little bit polish.

11 - **Les écailles**: 6a, 30m. A good route with a finger move.

12 - **Variante du dièdre**: 5c, 40m. A succession of short athletic sections.

13 - **La centrale**: 5b, 40m. A classic.

13′ - **Variation**: 6c, 10m. A hard short wall with chipped hold.

14 - **La plaque rouge**: 5c, 40m. A good one. Start in route 13.

15 - **La Diagonale**: 4c, 45m. **P1**: 3b, 30m; **P2**: 4c, 15m. Possible descent on foot.

15′ - **?**: 5c, 10m.

15″ - **?**: 4a. Climb the chimney.

16 - **Directe à L'arbre**: 5c, 20m. Slightly committed finish.

17 to 21 - 30 m. Five nice and well protected routes.

22 - **?**: **P1**: 4a, 25 m; **P2**: 6b, 15m. A short difficult slab move.

23 and 24 - 3c, 25m. Very well protected, routes to learn lead climbing.

25 to 27 - 20m, 3b. Good terrain for beginners.

28 - **Le pilier rouge**: 6a, 20m. Aesthetic one.

29 - **La directe Lachenal**: 5c, 20m.

30 - **Le fin pilier**: 6c, 20m. Tricky.

31 - **Dièdre Terray**: 6a, 35m. A beautiful classic.

32 - **?**: 7a, 15 m. Poor protection.

33 - **Le toit**: **P1**: 5b; **P2**: 6a+. A nice one.

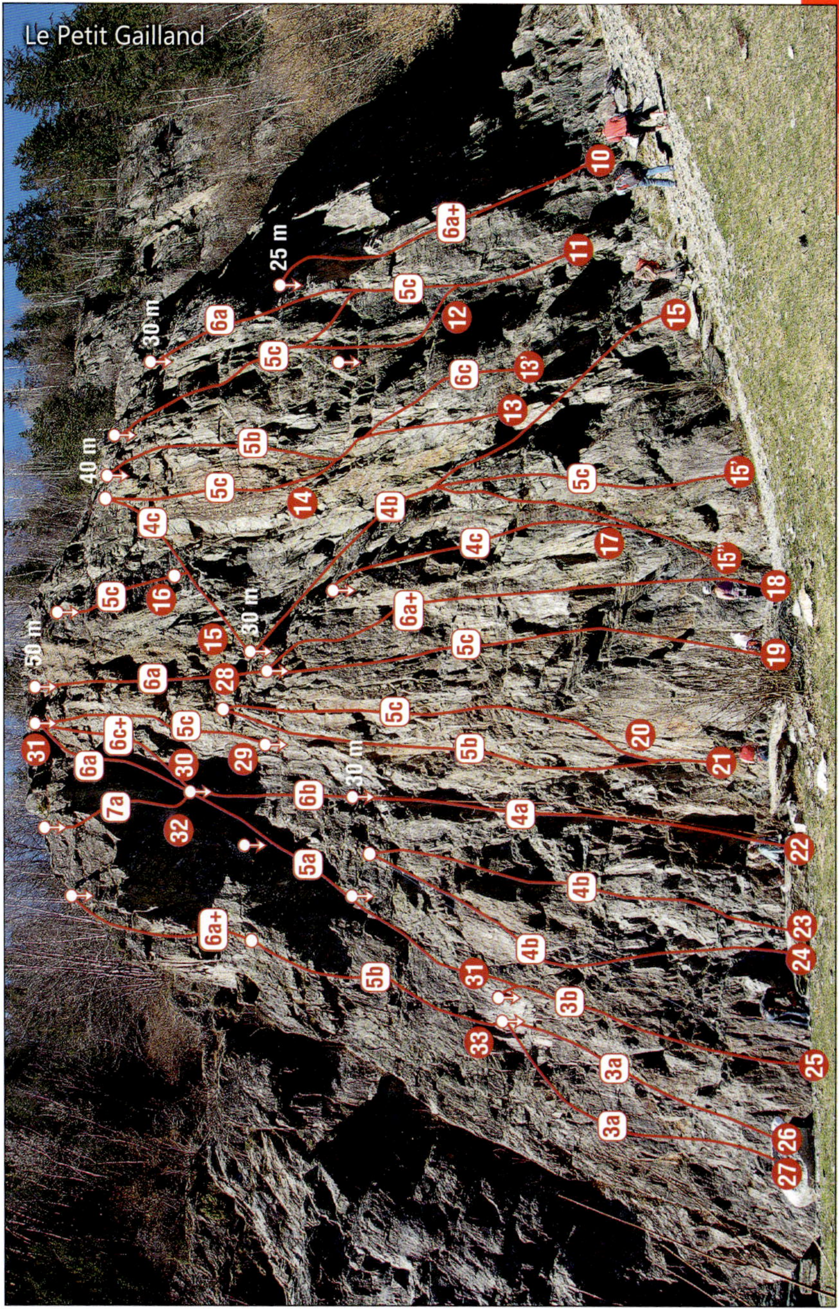
Le Petit Gailland

Le Petit Gailland
right-hand side
40 m
30 m
5c
6a
7a
6b
6c
6a+
12
11
10
9
8
7

6b
6a
6c
7a
6a
5c
1'
5
4
6
5
1
3
2
Le Petit Gailland
far right

Echelle area

1000 m S

1'

3 4

8 8 3 0 15-40 m

The routes

Interesting area, well equipped and a good place to practise lead-climbing.

1 - **Le dessert des Tatares**: 5a, 20 m. Crack climb.

2 - **La double fissure de l'ingratitude**: 6a, 20 m.

3 - **La compagnie des Indes**: 6b, 20 m. Jam session to start.

4 - **Cheikh en blanc**: 6a, 20 m. A nice crack route.

5 - **Le toit direct**: One move of 6a+.

6 - **Le toit**: Excellent holds at the end, 5c+.

7 to 11 - Nice slabs with short steep sections.

12 - **Voie la plus facile**: 3c. The easiest route, up a small corner.

13 to 16 - Four routes on more polished slabs.

17 - **Pilier des Monchus**: 4a. 2 pitches. Only belays are equipped.

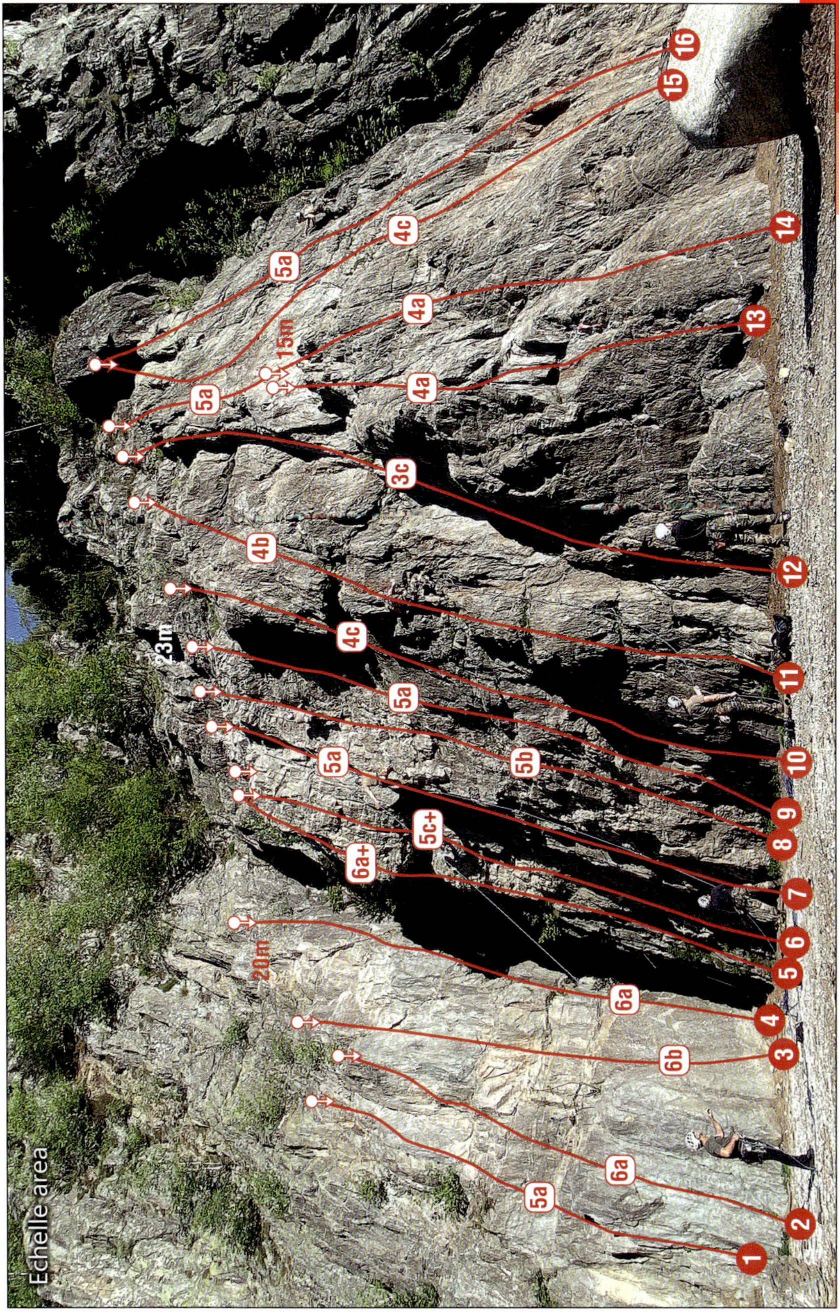

Echelle area
1
5a
2
6a
3
6b
4
6a
20m
5
6a+
6
5c+
7
5a
8
5b
9
5a
10
4c
23m
11
4b
12
3c
13
4a
14
4a
15m
15
4c
5a
16
5a

Grand Gailland

1000 m | S

2′

3 | 4

10 | 8 | 8 | 1 | 15-70 m

The routes

Given the huge number of routes on this crag, it is easy to climb a selection going from one route to another on the different ledges. The suggested link-ups are logical and classic combinations. Take 15 quickdraws to be safe. Walking off is advised on busy days - traverse left and go down a series of ladders.

1 - **La Directissime**: 75m, TD. **P1**: 3c; **P2**: 6a+, delicate wall with vertical holds; **P3**: 6a.

2 - **La Cheminée des guides**: finish on the pillar, 50m, D. **P1**: 3c; **P2**: (go right of the overhang) 5a; **P3**: (finish on the pillar) 4c.

3 - **Le petit surplomb**: 5c, 15m. Left of the roof. Just athletic enough.

4 - **Arête Frison**: 5b, 70m. **P1**: 5b; **P2**: 5a; **P3**: 6a.

5 - **Dièdre Rouge**: 6a, 20m. Polished crag. A classic one.

6 - **La plaque**: 15m, 7a glancing the ridge, 7c staying in line with the bolts.

7 - **Pilier de la Plaque**: 5c, 20m. Interesting, graded generously.

8 - **La Savonnette + la Colaude + petit mur**: 70m, TD-. **P1**: 5c (dalle Terray); **P2**: 5a; **P3**: 6a. Brown rings.

9 - **Pilier de gauche**: **P1**: 4a, 15m; **P2**: 6a. Pink rings, magnificent.

10 - **La Directe**: 6a+, 20m, gold rings. Thin inverted crack. Technical.

11 - **AD**: **P1**: 5b; **P2**: 5a. Good pockets.

12 - **Le Dièdre Gris**: 5a, 20m. The Gaillands classic.

13 - **Le pilier Gris**: 4a, 15m.

14 - **Voie Normale**: 70m, Gold bolts at the start. **P1**: 3a; **P2**: 3c; **P3**: 3b. Follows the weaknesses in the rock.

15 - **Les Rings Argentés**: 70m, AD. **P1**: 4a; **P2**: 4a; **P3**: 5a.

16 - **La Cheminée**: 3b, 20m. Variant of the normal route.

17 - **La Venger**: 40m. **P1**: 3b; **P2**: 5b. Small overhang on the left.

18 - **?**. 40m. Short pitches: **P1**: 4a; **P2**: 5a; **P3**: 4c, good for learning.

18′ - **?**. 3c.

19 - **La Braco**: 50m. **P1**: 4a; **P2**: 4c; **P3**: 5a. A good line.

20 - **L'arête intégrale**: 30m. **P1**: 5c; **P2**: 6a. Follow the brown bolts.

21 - **L'arête**: 5a, 15m. A slice of history, aerial.

22 - **La Bérardini**: 6a+, 10m. Good slab.

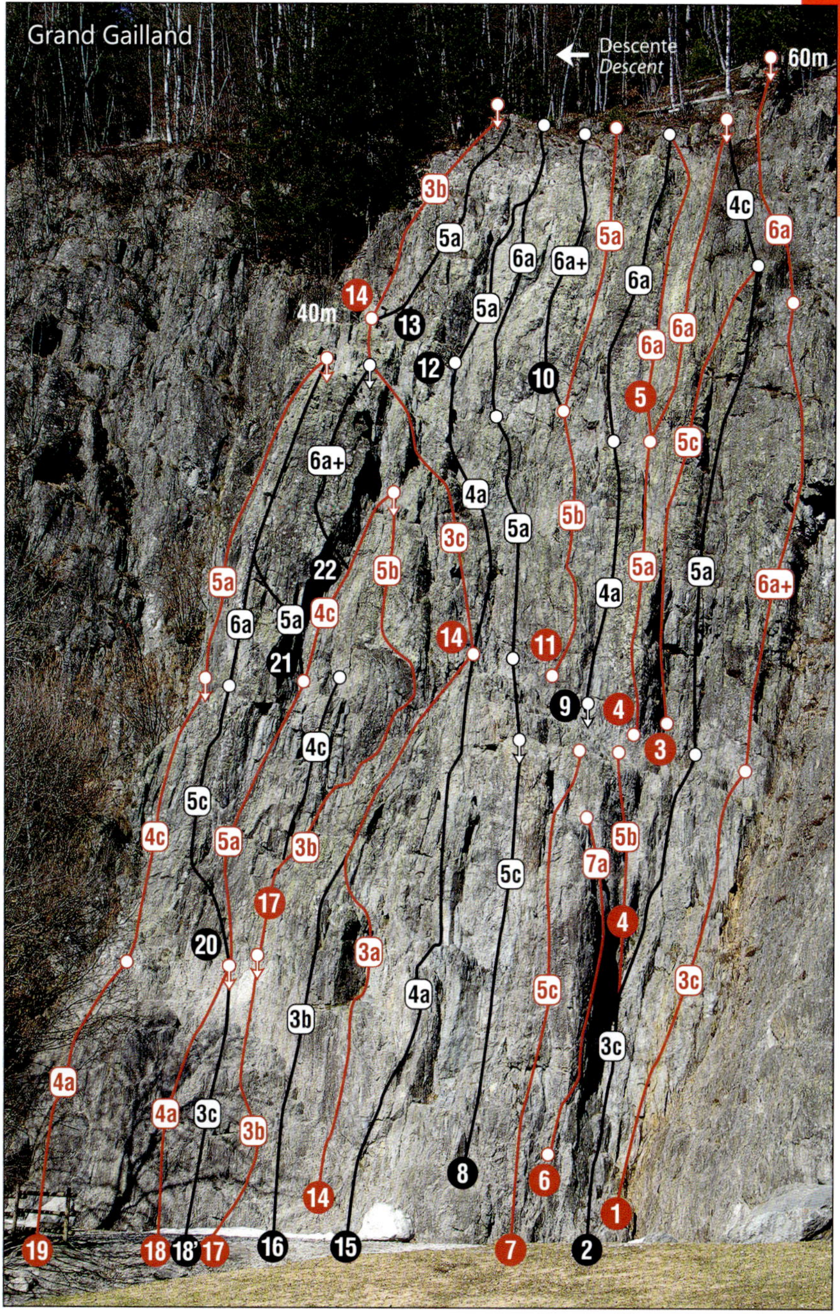
Grand Gailland
Descente
Descent
60m
40m
19
18
18'
17
16
15
14
7
2
8
6
1
20
21
22
13
12
10
11
9
4
3
5

Vipères sector

1000 m | S

3'

3 | 4

10 | 0 | 0 | 0 | 12-70 m

The routes

This is a very good area for beginners.

1 - **?**: 3c, 10m.

2 - **?**: 3c, 10m.

3 - **La Saintous**: **P1**: 3c; **P2**: 3b; lichen is back...

4 - **Rattles Nakes**: **P1**: 3c; **P2**: 4a.

5 - **Dièdre des Pompons**: **P1**: 3c; **P2**: 4a; **P3**: 3c. 60m.

6 - **L'aspic**: **P1**: 3b.

7 - **?**: 4a.

8 - **Les Terrassiers**: **P1**: 3c; **P2**: 3c, 45m.

9 - **?**: 3c.

10 - **?**: 3c.

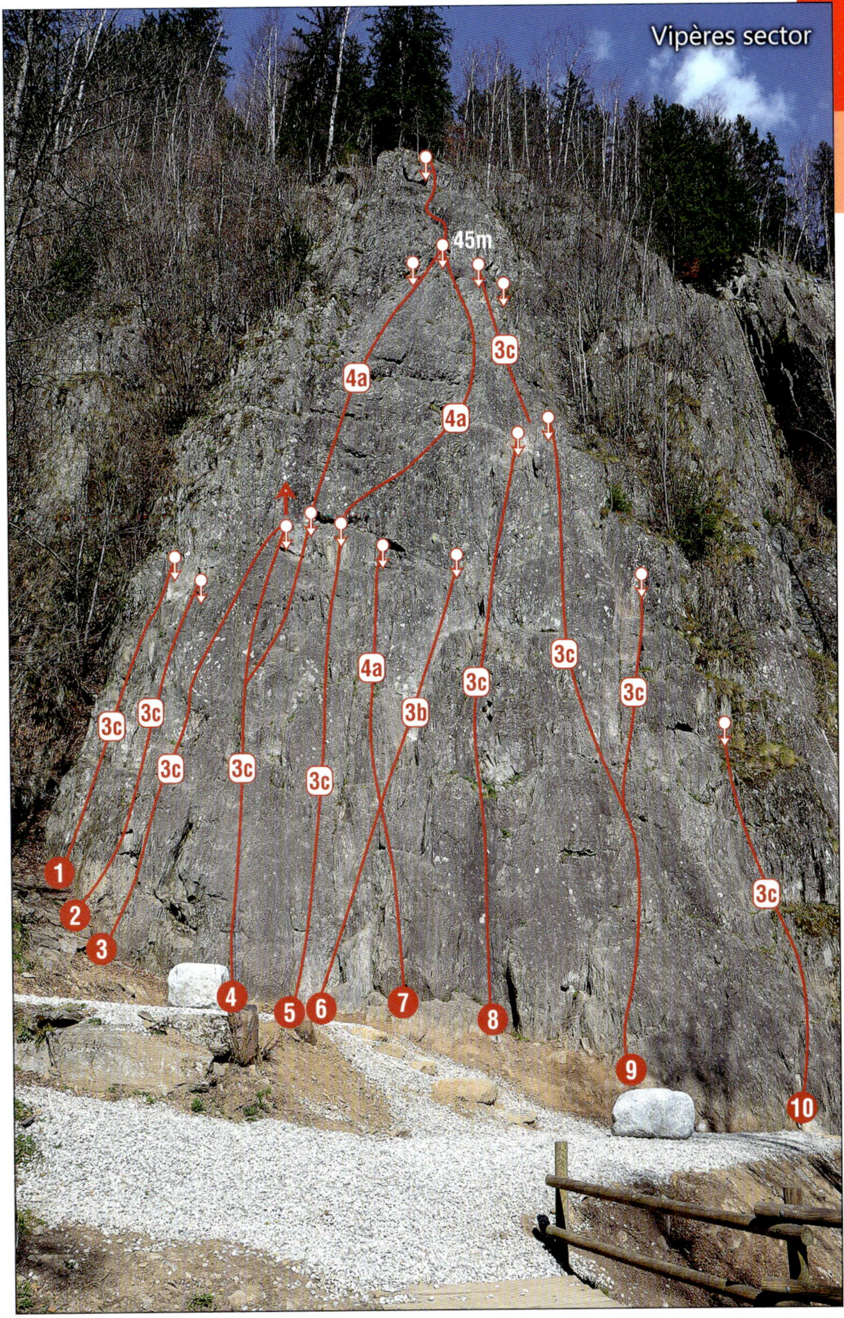
Vipères sector
45m
4a
4a
3c
3c
3c
3c
3c
3c
3c
4a
3b
3c
3c
3c
3c
1
2
3
4
5
6
7
8
9
10

Forestiers

AREA 03 **FORESTIERS**

1000 m | S

5′

3 | 4

11 | 17 | 9 | 0 | 15-60 m

An interesting and sometimes quite crowded area, but there is a wide space at the base. 30 pitches of average difficulty (5b/5c). Make sure to use a 60m rope for top roping on the left-hand section, and 80m on the right.

Far left

1 - **L'arête des bûcherons**: 5c, 25m. Overhanging start, but on good holds.

2 - **La libérable**: 5b, 30m. Same kind of start.

2′ - **Variante de droite**: 5c, if you keep to the right more athletic.

3 - **Nouvelle voie**: with gold-coloured rings, 4c, with an easy overhang at the start.

La Libérable, 5b

Far left

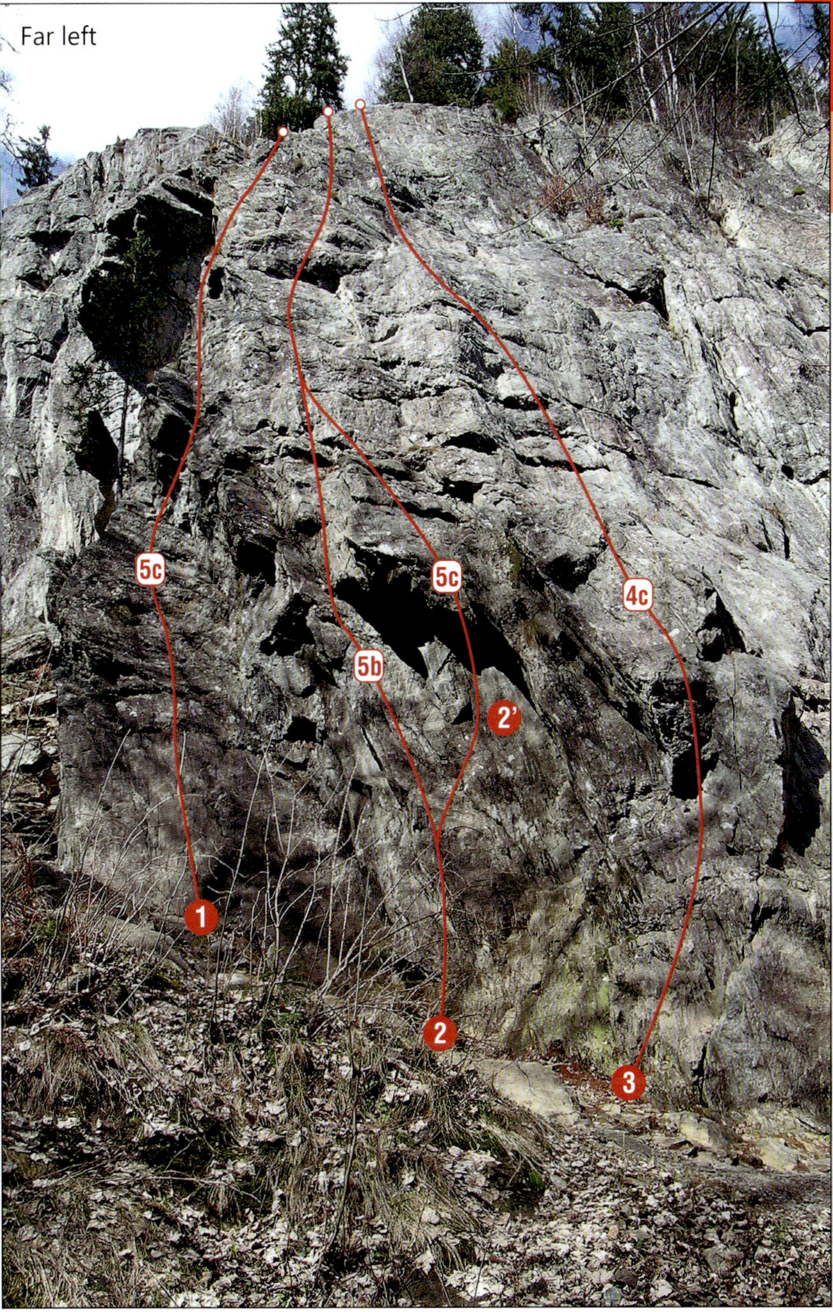

Forestiers
Central section

4 - **Moustikul**: 4c, 27m. Nice pitch on big pockets.

5 - **La Daïlle à Dédé**: 4c, 27m. Same.

6 - **La Forestière**: **P1**: 5b, 35m, dubious flakes; **P2**: 5b, 15m. Nice finish up an airy pillar.

7 - 6a+, 30m. Follow the stainless steel rings.

8 - **La D**: 5b, 30m. Nice finishing crack/corner. Possible start via route 7.

9 - **La Michoquo**: **P1**: 6a, 30m. Start... Petzl rings. **P2**: 5c, 20m. A superb route.

10 - **La Vipérine**: 5c, 30m. A demanding corner, needing balance and precise footwork. More exposed than other routes.

11 - 5a, 35m. A delicate start, then keep to the arête.

12 - **La Petite Marie**: **P1**: 4c, 30m. Steep wall, with the holds in the right places. **P2**: 5c, 20m.

13 - 6a, 30m. One tricky slab move.

14 - **Le Compas**: **P1**: 4c, 30m; **P2**: 4b, 30m. Dubious rock.

15, 16, 17 - Three interesting alternative ends.

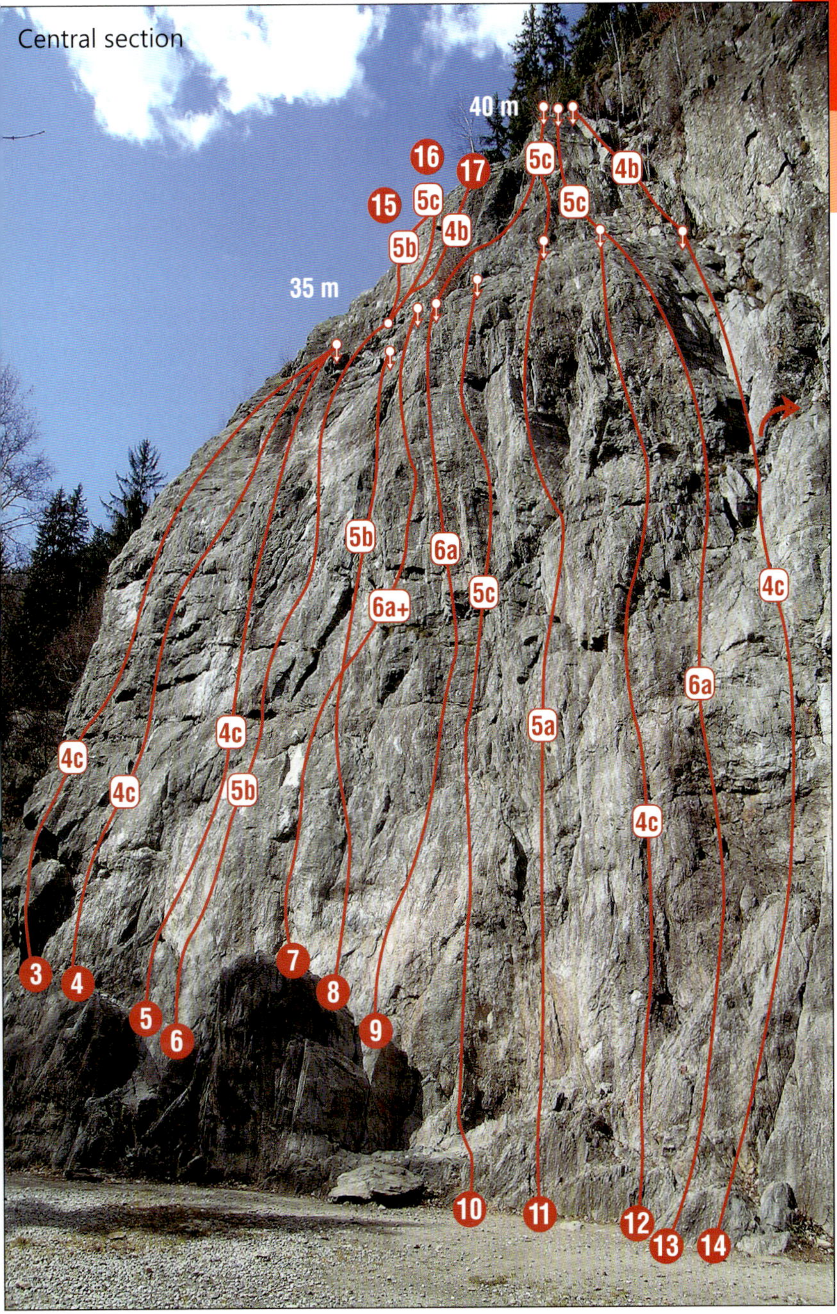
Central section
40 m
35 m
16
17
15
5c
5b
4b
5c
4b
5c
5b
6a
6a+
5c
4c
6a
5a
4c
4c
4c
5b
4c
3
4
5
6
7
8
9
10
11
12
13
14

Forestiers right-hand section

An 80m rope is requested for top roping.

1 - **L'éperon Claret**: 50m. **P1**: 5c, 10m; **P2**: 5b; **P3**: 5b, 15m. A beautiful finishing stance. **P1+P2**: 28m.

2 - **?**: 6a, 10m. Delicate slab.

3 - **?**: 5c, 10m. Same.

4 - **Le Sorbier**: 50m. **P1**: 4c, 10m; **P2**: 5b. Bolts are spaced; **P3**: 5b+, 15m. Corner with a tricky finish. Bolts and rock have the same color.

5 - **Le Marteau**: **P1**: 4c, 10m; **P2**: 30m, one slabby section (6a), then a very athletic overhang (6b+). A 6a alternative on the right.

6 - **?**: 4b, 10 m.

7 - **La Polytechnique**: 6a, 30m, athletic finish.

7' - **Connection link**: 5c.

8 - **La Bastoche**: 5c, 15m.

9 - **Les liaisons dangereuses**: **P1**: 5b Short crossing to the right. **P2**: 5b Same finish than 10.

10 - **Trait d'union**: 6b.

Right-hand section
50 m
5b+
5b
6a
5b
6b+
6b
6a
7'
10
5b
5c
5b
9
6a
5c
7
6a
8
4b
6a
5c
4c
4c
5c
1
2
3
4
5
6

Chasseurs

1000 m W

5'

2 3

0 2 5 4 25 m

Barracuda, 6c+

The routes

Some nice, athletic pitches at arounc 6b/c. Bolted

1 - **La Bollonaire**: 7a, 25m, interestinc overhanging corner.

2 - **La Spitre**: 7a, 25m, needs determination and decisiveness!.

3 - **Couscous**: 6c, 20m.

4 - **Jypsckey**: 6a+, than 6b (doubtfu flakes), 27m.

5 - **Le surplomb à Zian**: **P1**: 6a; **P2** 6b+. **P1+P2**: 25m.

6 - **La Ckésia**: **P1**: 5a; **P2**: 6a+. **P1+P2**: 27m.

7 - **Petite fleur des champs**: 27m, 5a then 7a, two wild roofs, some doubt about the solidity of the second....

8 - **Barracuda**: 6c+, 22m, technical wall.

9 - **Finies les vacances**: 5b/5c, 20m, slab.

10 - **La cheminée des chasseurs**: 5b, classic Chamonix crack.

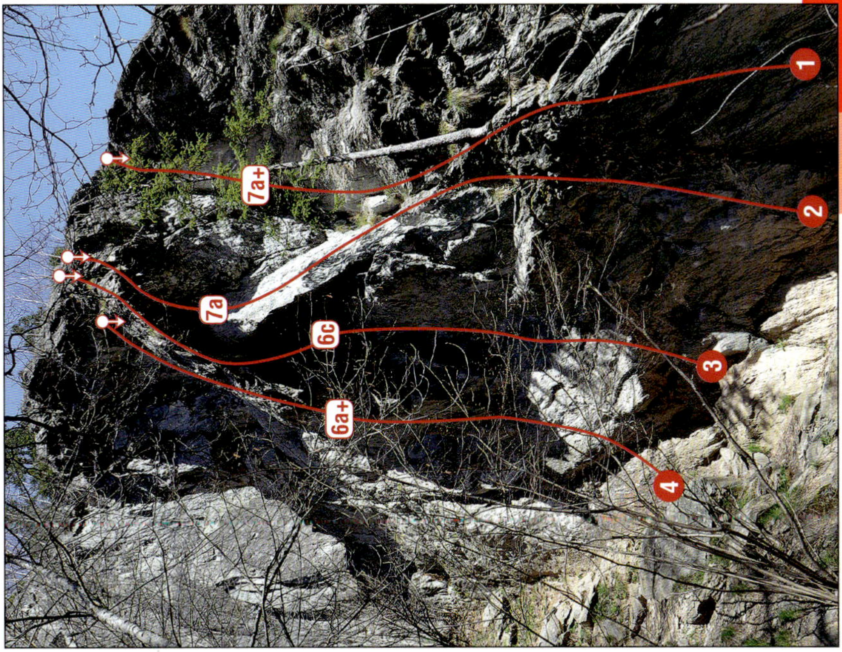
1
2
3
4
7a+
7a
6c
6a+

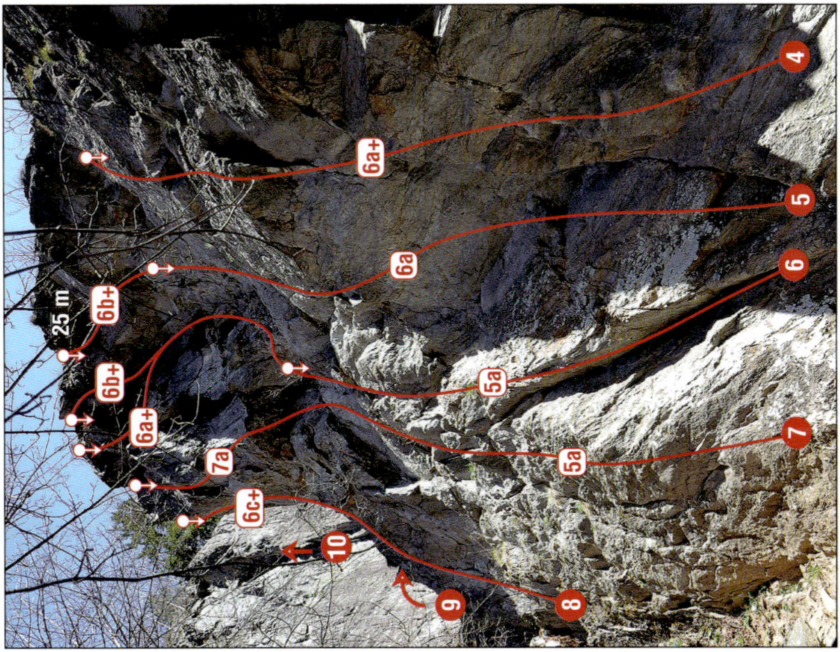
4
5
6
7
8
9
10
6a+
6a
6b+
25 m
6b+
6a+
7a
6c+
5a
5a

Frendo area

1000 m S

7'

2 3

7 12 17 1 60 m

The routes

A great area with a 60 metre-high wall of superb rock. Well equipped.

1 - **Grattons laveurs**: 6a+, 10m.

2 - **Eperon d'Anna**: 5c, 18m.

3 - **Un géranium dans le dos**: 5b, 25m, wide corner.

4 - **La raflée**: 6b, 32m, a good, technical route on sidepulls.

4'- **Dark Totor**: 5c, exposed ridge.

5 - **Le dièdre Frendo**: 5c,32m, historical.

6 - **La Batson**: **P1**: 6b; **P2**: 6a+.

7 - **Lame de rasoir**: 6a, the bolts are not in the right places.

8 - **La reprise**: 4b.

9 - **La Sylvanair**: **P1**: 5c; **P2**: 6c. "Petzl" hangers. Name written at the start.

10 - **La Virofrêney**: **P1**: 4c; **P2**: 5a; **P3**: 6b; **P4**: 5a.

11 - **La Puce**: 5c, interesting variation at the top of the corner, to the left.

12 - **Dix-huit berges**: **P1**: 4c; **P2**: 5c; **P3**: 6b; with a 5b variation in P3.

13 - **Maladie d'amour sexuel**: slab climb, 5b, 6b. Very technical slab.

13' - **Toutounet attitude**: "Fixe" gold-coloured hangers, delicate crack, 6b+.

14 - **Sein et sauf**: 6a+.

15 - **Tangente de X**: 6a+, a small overhang and a thin crack.

16 - **L'insoutenable légèreté de ma mère**: 5b, a wide corner.

17 - **Gertrude**: **P1**: 5c; **P2**: 5b; an impressive but easy overhang.

18 - **L'arête**: **P1**: 6a; **P2**: 5c; one of the nicest climbs in the area.

18' - **Variante**: 5b, 12m. Fingers crack. Well protected.

19 - **La Liscot junior**: 4b.

20 - **Princesse Hortence**: 5c.

Routes 21, 22, 23: 12m. Short beginners routes.

24 - **Petits poids**: 6c+. Commited climb.

DIÈDRE RAVANEL (see page 93)

25 - **Dièdre Ravanel**: **P1**: 5a; **P2**: 6a+.

26 - **Fissure Roche-toon**: **P1**: 4c; **P2**: 6a+.

27 - **Fissure à l'ours**: 6c, a superb crack.

28 - **Le gastounet au taquet**: inox bolts, 6b+. One hard movement.

29 - **Rouge sang**: 7a, slab.

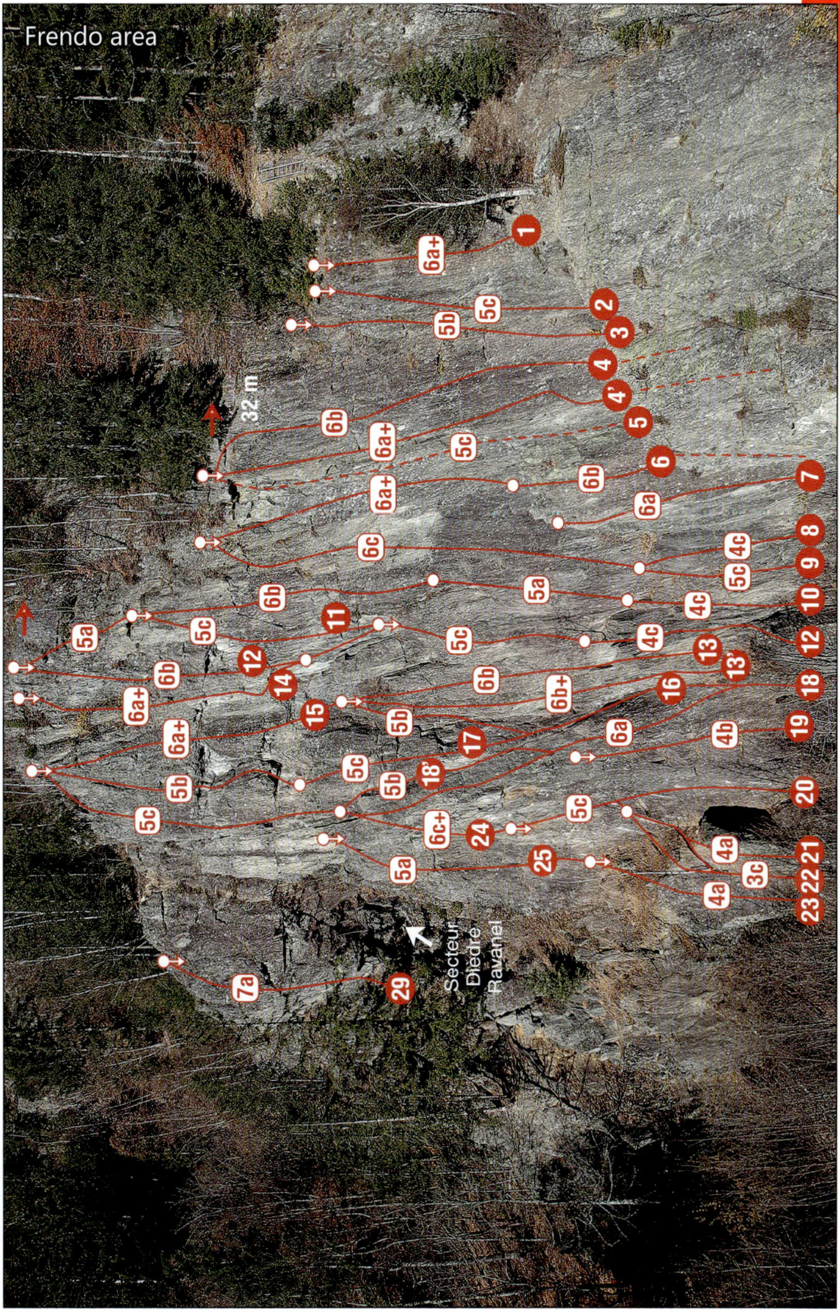
Frendo area
32 m
Secteur Dièdre Ravanel

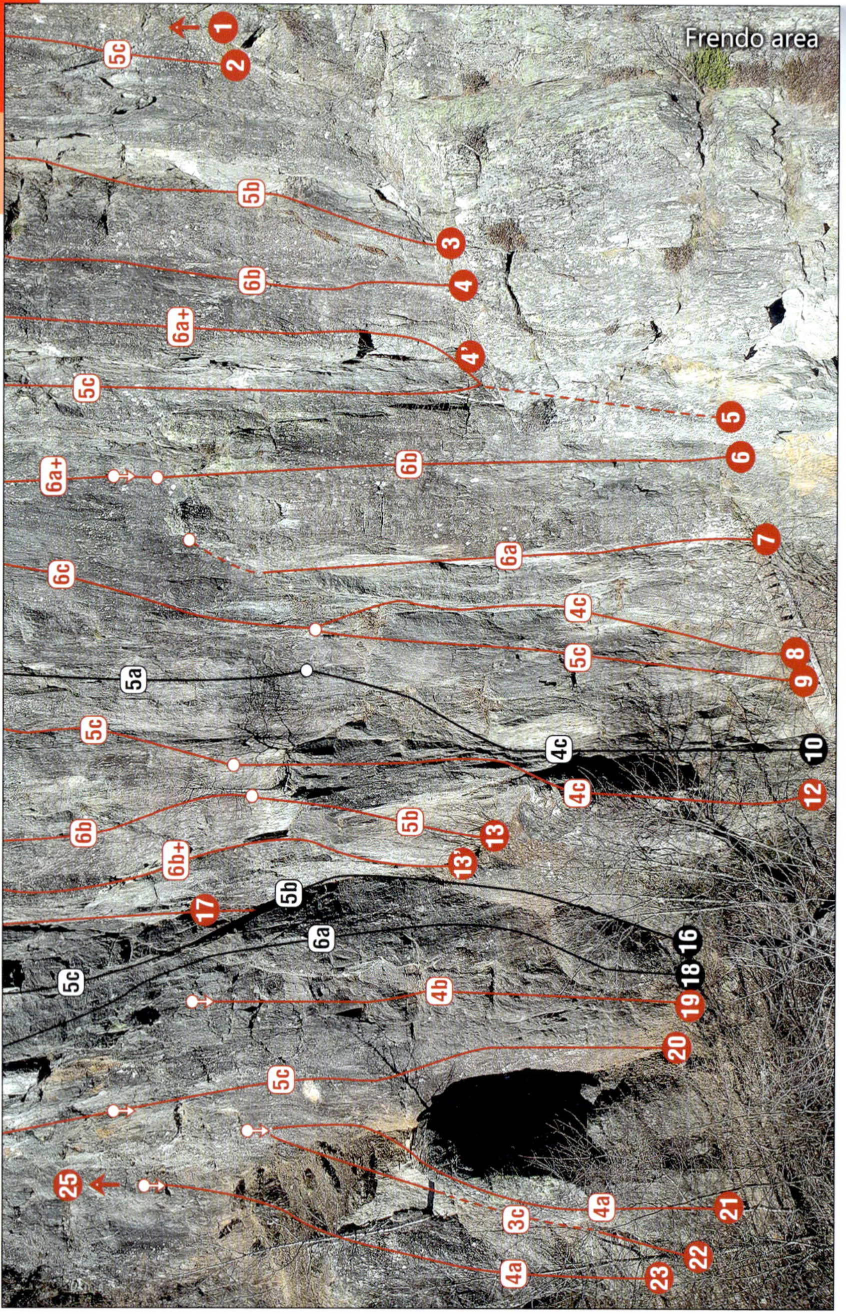
Frendo area

Dièdre Ravanel

La Sylvanair, 5c

Picsou

1000 m | S

7'

3

6 | 3 | 3 | 0 | 10 m

50m left of Frendo area.

The routes

1 - **Riri**: 3c, small corner, very mossy.

2 - **Fifi**: 3c, mossy.

3 - **Loulou**: 4a, interesting slab.

4 - **Donald**: 4b, a small spur.

5 - **Daisy**: 5a, on the crest.

6 - **Dingo**: 6a, boulder move.

7 - **Pluto**: 5c, spaced holds.

8 - **Géo**: 6a, unbalancing layback.

9 - **Mickey**: 6a, vertical slab, dubious rock.

10 - **Minnie**: 5c, nice pitch, very mossy.

11 - **Gontrand**: 4b, easily angled, very mossy.

12 - **Rappetous**: 3c, easily angled, very mossy.

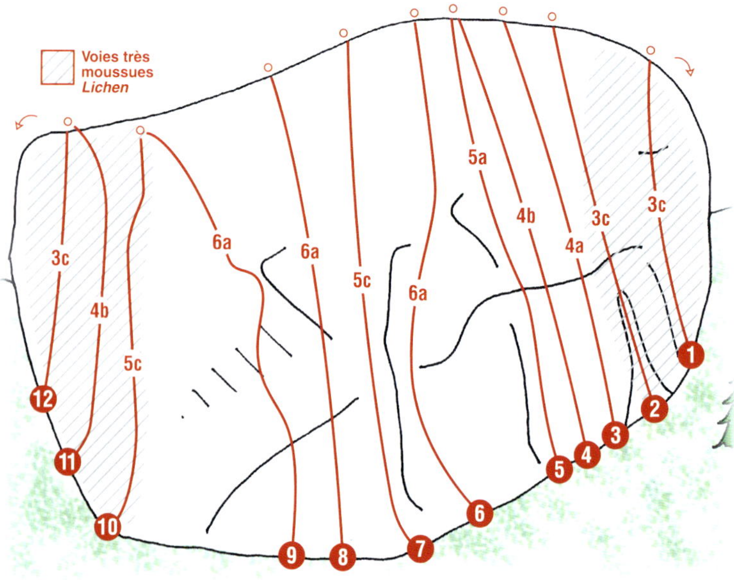

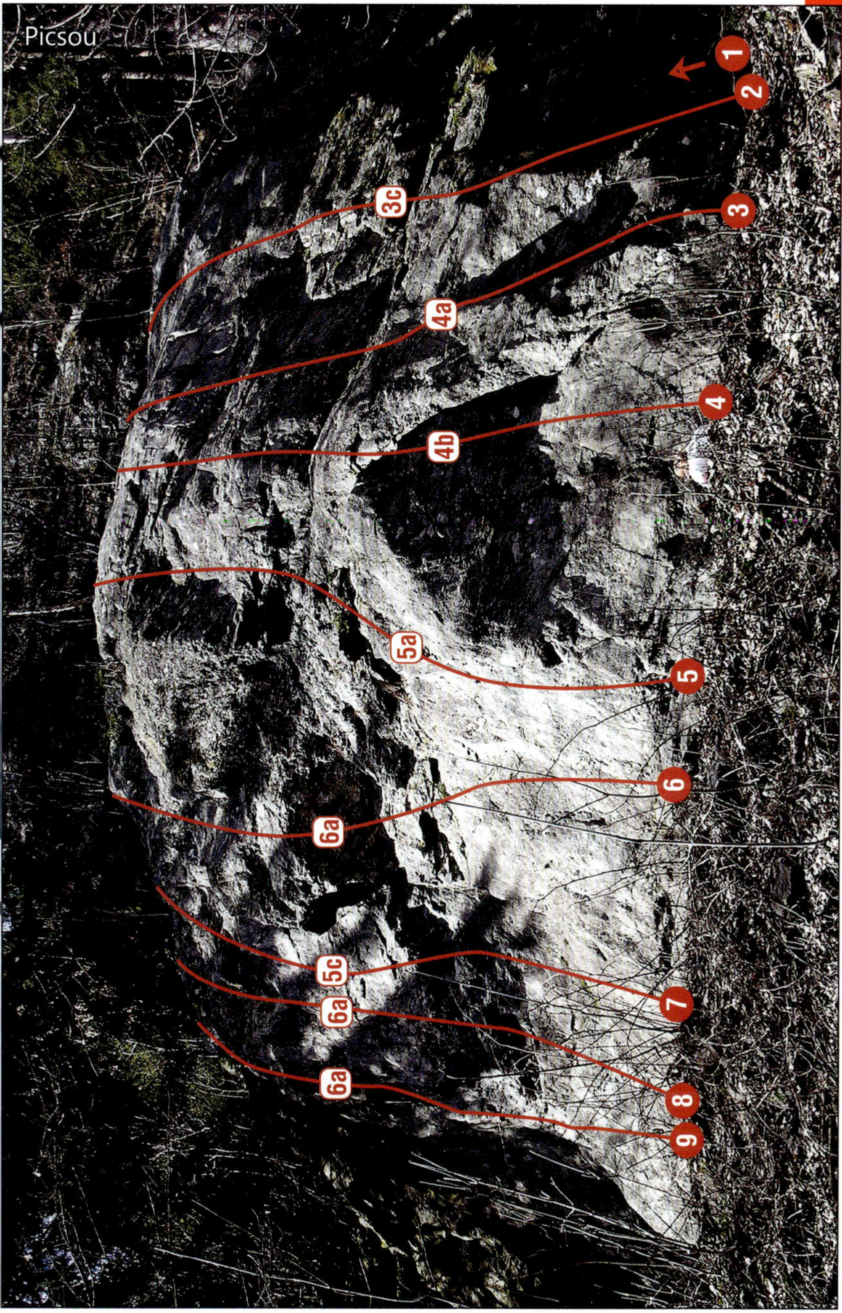
Picsou
1
2
3c
3
4a
4
4b
5a
5
6
6a
5c
7
6a
8
6a
9

Area **04**

Le Brévent
La Soulire
La Flégère

Les Plaques du Brévent

2400 m E

5′

3 4

2 9 25 2 20-30 m

The Brévent slabs, situated at an altitude of 2450m, facing Mont-Blanc, are a quiet, pleasant place to climb, easily accessible from the top of the Brévent cablecar.

Rock : compact gneiss.

Climbing : the rock offers predominantly slabby climbing, but there are some good crack lines. The crag layout can be divided into two sections by the "Brêche du Brévent".

The site : rocky and mountainous (scree, boulders…), but the site is nevertheless easily accessible to non-climbers and the views over the Mont-Blanc range are breathtaking.

Access : from Chamonix, take the Brévent cablecar to the summit.

Approach : follow the obvious path which leads down to the "Brèche du Brévent" (5 mins). It is also possible to reach the crag from Planpraz (the cablecar mid-station): follow the path (ski run) towards Le Brévent (45 mins).

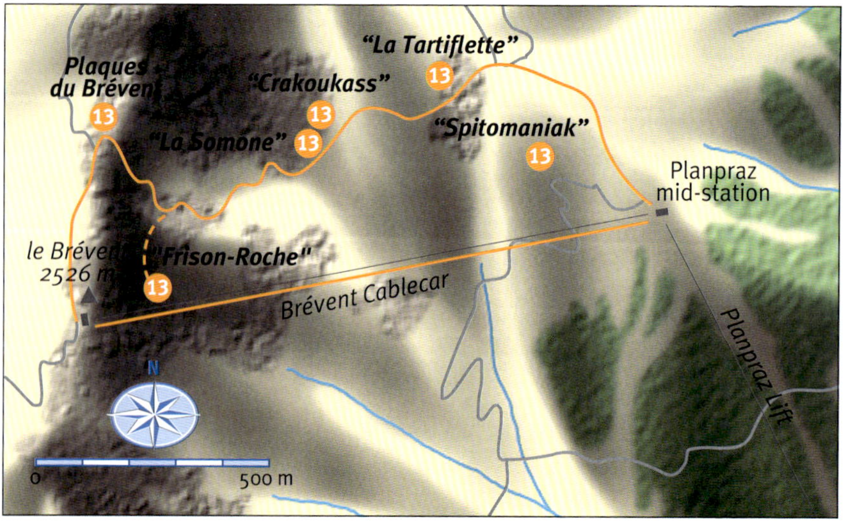

To the left of the "Brèche"

These routes are generally not as good as those situated to the right of the breach, where the rock is sounder.

1 - **Falling in love**: 6b. Technical slab.

2 - **Liaison fatale**: 6b, 30m. Committed.

3 - ?: 6b+, starts with boulder move.

4 - **Alters et... go**: 6c+/7a, falling here could be very unpleasant.

5 - ?: 6b+ the most interesting route.

6 - ?: 6a, 25m. Nice technical slab.

7 - ?: 5c, 25m.

8 - **Le quatrième tiers**: 5a.

9 - **Rêve de cornichon**: 5b.

8 - **TMB**: 4b, variante S.

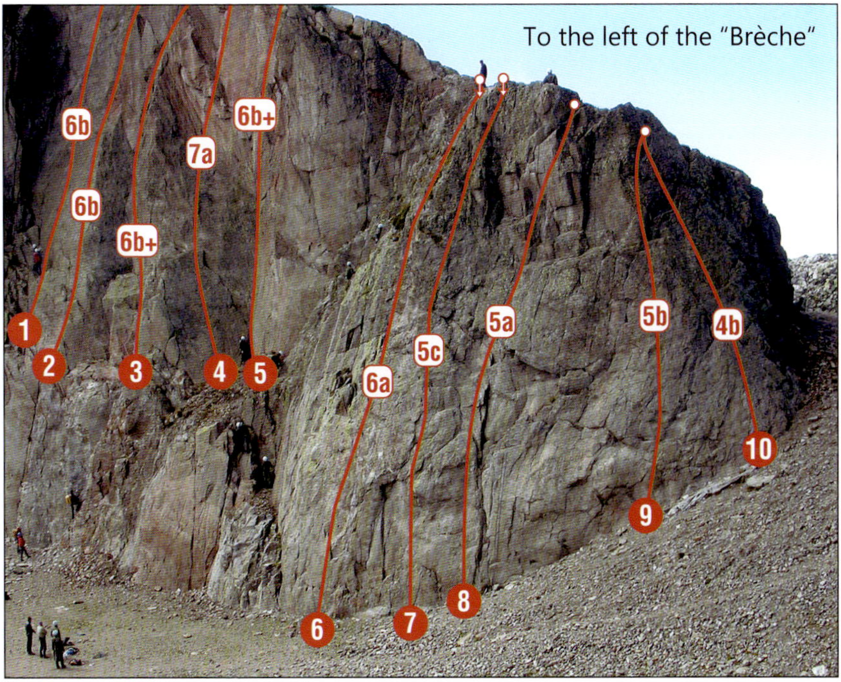

To the right of the "Brèche"

There is always an access to the top of the route to set up top ropes.

1 - **Défense d'user**: 7a. Short aggressive pitch. Loose rock.

2 - **Un porc ex-porc**: 6c. Technical start.

3 - **Touche pas à mon spot**: 6b. Idem.

4 - **C'est après coup que ça fait mal**: 6a+.

5 - **Attention à la marche!** 6c.

6 - **Tiroir caisse**: 6b.

7 - **?**: 6a, technical climb.

8 - **?**: 6a+.

9 - **?**: 6b on the crest. One of the nicest lines.

10 - **?**: 6c.

11 - **?**: 6b.

12 - **Les sorcières de Salem**: right hand finish, 6a

13 - **La belle et la benne**: 6a+.

14 - **Poil dans la main**: 6a.

15 - **A bout de souffle**: 6b.

16 - **Trop belle pour toit**: 6b.

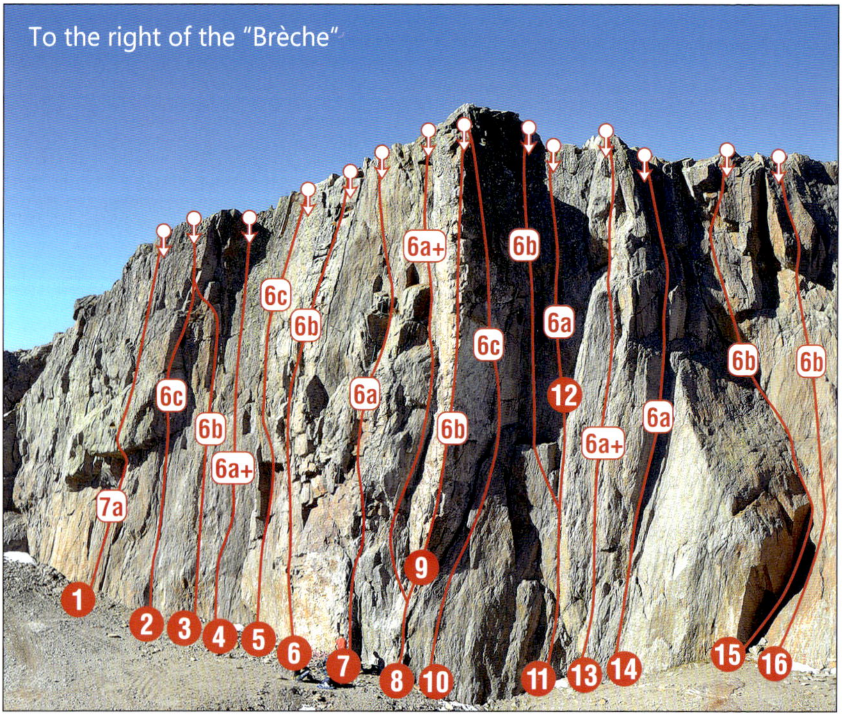

To the right of the "Brèche"

17 - **Les ailes du désir**: 5a.

18 - **Demi-lune**: 4c (an old classic).

19 - **Sérieux s'abstenir**: 5a.

20 - **Enfant de la lune**: 5c. Committing start.

21 - **Lolita nie en bloc**: 6b. Committing.

22 - **L'homme est rare**: 5c.

23 - **Rappelle-moi ton nom**. 6a.

24 - **Viol sans visibilité**: 6a+.

25 - 26 - **Salutation au soleil**: 6c.

27 - **T'as pas tout lu...** 6b, beautiful open book.

28 - **?**: 6b.

29 - **Follow the line**: 6b (Layback hold).

30 - **Monsieur propre**: 6b.

31 - **Capate for ever**: 6b.

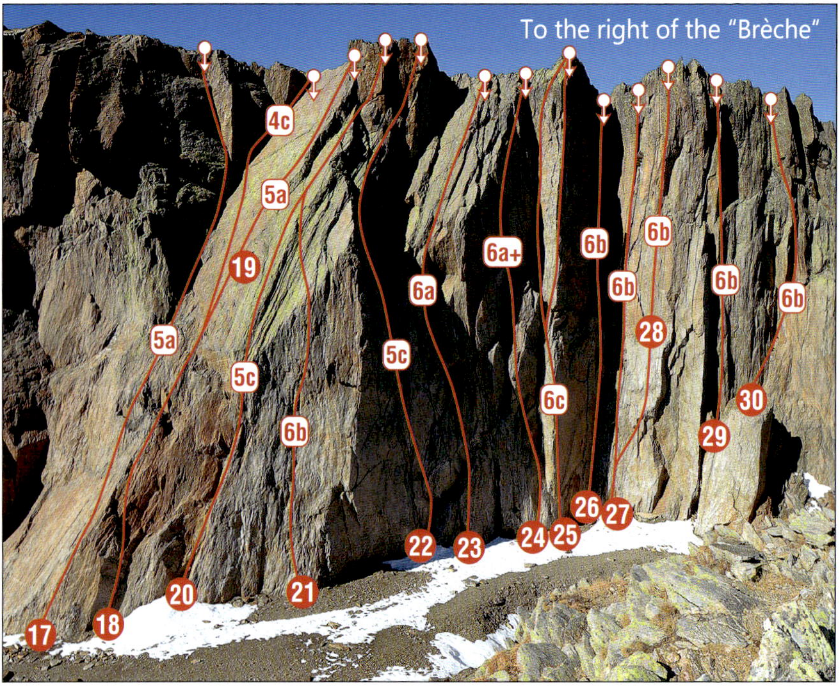

"Frison-Roche" Route

2400 m S

15'

3

0 1 0 0 220 m

The south-east face of the Brévent had been neglected for almost 50 years, due to poor quality rock, until the Chamonix Guides' Company set up this route.

Rock : good quality gneiss, but with a few short, loose sections.

Climbing : the climbing is varied (slabs and cracks) and protected by 10mm bolts. There may be some danger of stonefall on busy days.

Access : (15 mins) from the top of the Brévent cablecar take the path which leads down to the "Brêche du Brévent". Continue along this path until after the second corner and then leave it rightwards, heading towards the face. Cross a slope covered in boulders to reach a steep gully and then follow the vague path to the foot of the route.

Gear : 12 quickdraws, 50 metres rope(s), slings. Crampons are necessary if there is still snow in the gully.

Route description : (first ascent by Michel Arizzi, Yves Ancrenaz, Alain et Georges Payot, Didier Chenevoy - 07/08/2000). Length: 220m, 6 pitches.

Grade : 6a (slab), unavoidable moves of 5c.

P1 : 5b (6a if you keep to the arete).

P2 : 5b, rising traverse rightwards.

P3 : 5c, short wall, the start is steep.

P4 : 6a (5c unavoidable), athletic climbing at the start and finish.

P5 : traverse to the left along the ledge for 30m.

P6 : lovely corner to finish, 5b/5c.

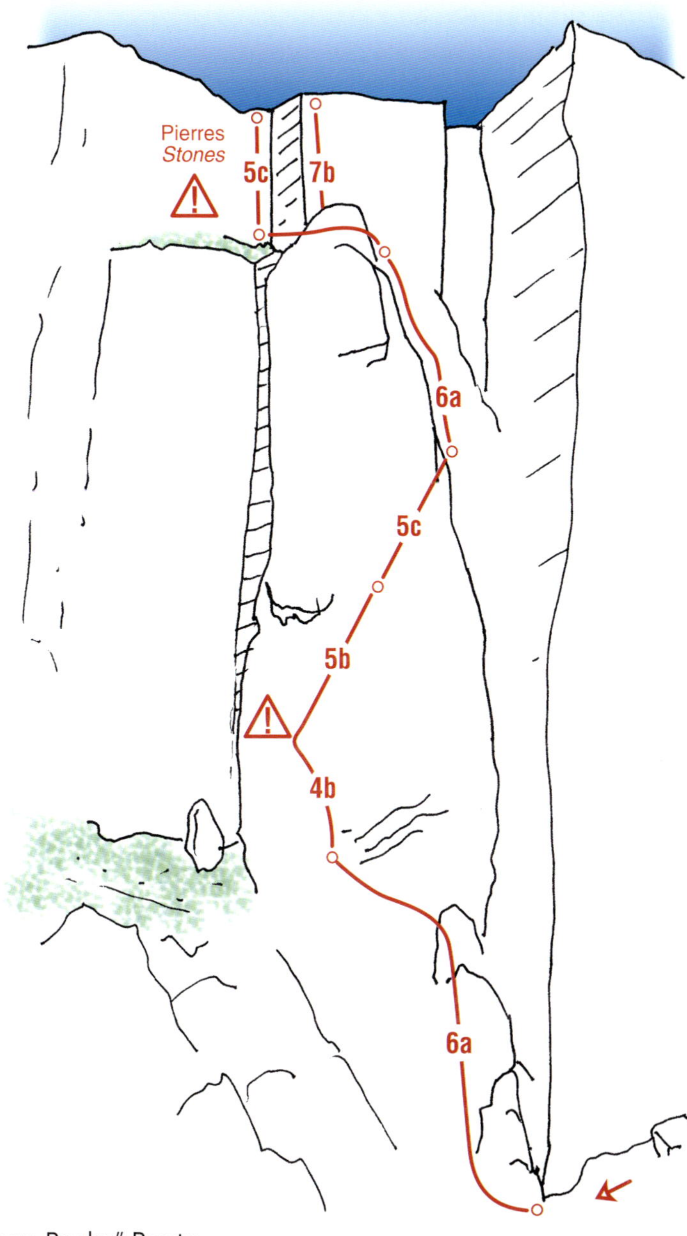

"Frison-Roche" Route

"La Somone"

2200 m S

25'

3

0 1 0 0 200 m

A succession of nice easy steps.

Rock : fractured gneiss.

Climbing : slabs and fluted rock.

Access : Brévent cablecar (take a return ticket).

Approach : from the top of Brévent, follow the "Charles Bozon" ski-run, go through the breach and continue towards Planpraz. Reach the bottom of the route accross a scree slope, at the base of a small pillar (sling at the start). 25 mins.

Equipment : 10 quickdraws. 30m rope. Equipped with bolts and hangers. It is possible to use some medium-size stoppers.

Route : was opened on August 13th and 14th, 2001 by Manu Méot, Morgan and Jérémy Franc. 200m, 7 pitches.

Difficulty : AD+, homogenous, unavoidable 4c.

Return : go back to the top of Brévent (a few minutes).

P1 : 25m dalle, 4b.

P2 : 20m very nice fluting. Stoppers school, 4c.

P3 : 30m slab and then thin crest, 4a.

P4 : 25m superb slab leading to the top of the gendarme, 5a. 10m. Abseil. Cross the scree slope on 30m.

P5 : 30m fluting, 5a. Go down towards the path and follow the base of the Brévent climbing school (left-hand sector). Pass between a big boulder and the rock-face to find the start of the last two pitches.

P6 : 30m, 4c.

P7 : 25m, 4b.

Gneiss

"La Somone"

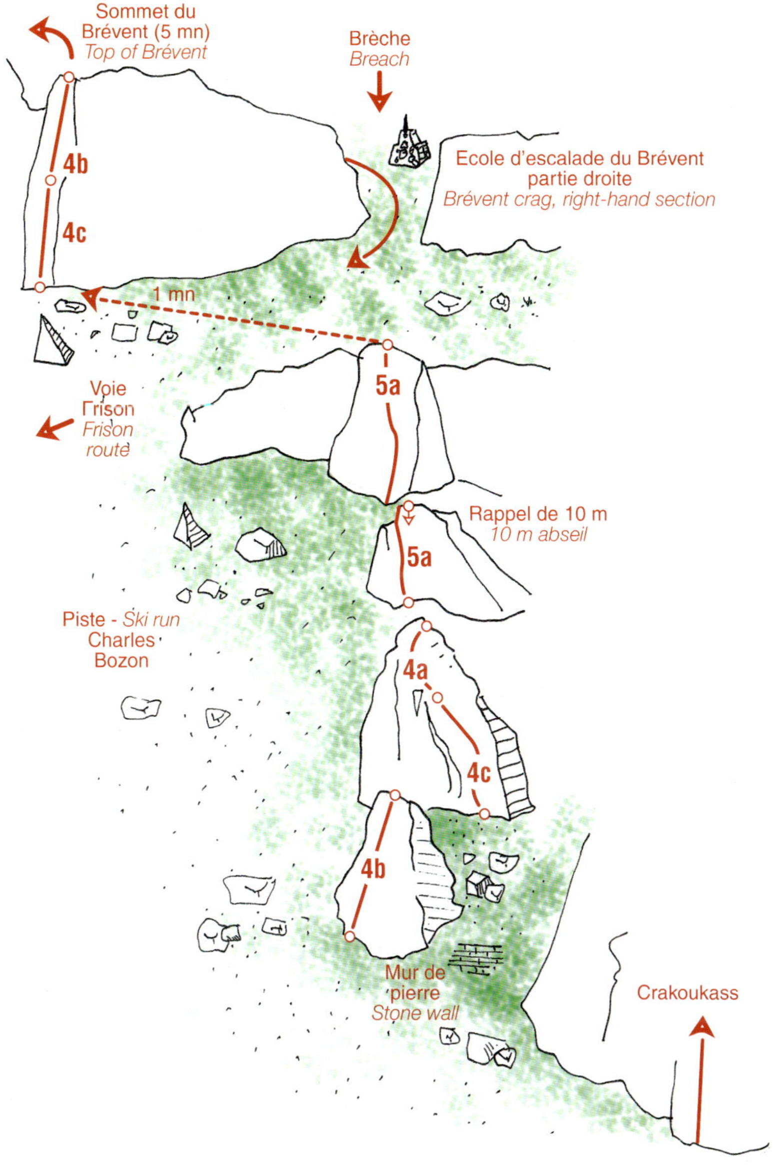
Sommet du
Brévent (5 mn)
Top of Brévent
Brèche
Breach
4b
4c
Ecole d'escalade du Brévent
partie droite
Brévent crag, right-hand section
1 mn
5a
Voie
Frison
Frison
route
Rappel de 10 m
10 m abseil
5a
Piste - *Ski run*
Charles
Bozon
4a
4c
4b
Mur de
pierre
Stone wall
Crakoukass

"Crakoukass"

2150 m — S

25'

3

0 1 0 0 — 240 m

A good route, already well-known, not too committing and well-equipped.

Rock : broken gneiss, generally wholesome, with some dubious flakes. Is advisable to wear a helmet.

Climbing : varied climbing, slabs, spur, chimney, crack...

Access : Brévent cablecar (take a return ticket).

Approach : from the top of Brévent, follow the "Charles Bozon" ski-run, go through a breach to get back to the Chamonix side and get to the bottom of the crag (25 mins). The path brings you 50m below the starting pillar.

Equipment : 10 quickdraws. 45m rope, a few slings.

Route : was opened in July 2000 by Julie Balmat, Patrice Manrart and Manu Meot. 240m, 9 pitches. It has two parts with a few variants.

Difficulty : D. Unavoidable 5b.

Return : walk back to the top of the Brévent, 10 mins.

P1 : 30m. If you start on the left of the pillar, nice fluted cracks; 4c. If you start on the right, slab, some dubious flakes, 5b.

P2 : 30m. Start in the diedre then follow the crest of the arete.

P3 : 15m. Go up towards a chimney, then climb the monolith and abseil down (10 m) or unclimb (easier), 5a.

P4 : 15m. Diedre. Belay at the top on the small spur. 5b. P4 variation: traverse on a ridge to the left to avoid the "Gendarme". A shortcut to reach the last two pinacles.

P5 : either continue on the arete for two pitches, 6b, missing hangers, or traverse to the left on easy terrain, climb up a small pillar, then traverse to the left to climb the west side of the gendarme, 5c. 20m abseil in the west face.

Scramble up the scree slope on 100m to get to the great gendarme of the Brévent. Start on the left of the face.

P1 : 30m, slab and crack, 5a.

P2 : 30m, finishing stance on the crest of the arete, 4c.

Go down the couloir between the two points and climb the second gendarme, 35m, 5b.

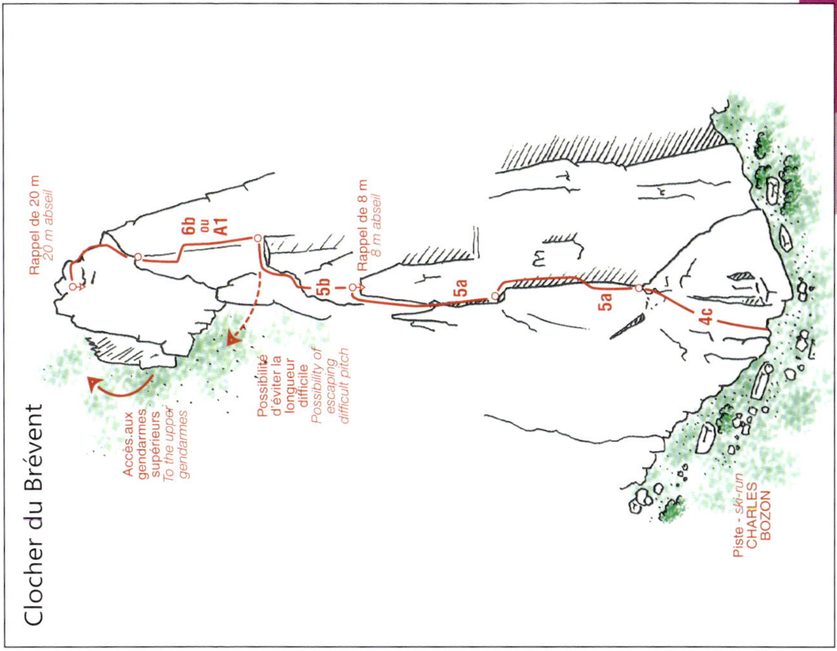
Clocher du Brévent
Rappel de 20 m
20 m abseil
6b
ou
A1
Rappel de 8 m
8 m abseil
5b
5a
5a
4c
Accès aux gendarmes supérieurs
To the upper gendarmes
Possibilité d'éviter la longueur difficile
Possibility of escaping difficult pitch
Piste - ski-run
CHARLES BOZON

Clocher du Brévent
Upper gendarmes
Grand Gendarme
6b
a1
5b
5a
5a
4c
Piste Charles Bozon
5b
4c
5a

"Spitomaniak"

1800 m · S

10'

3

0 1 0 0 · 280 m

This route takes the rocky outcrops on the East edge of the Brévent Couloir.

Rock : good grippy gneiss.

Climbing : pleasant climbing, making clever use of walls and slabs between ledges and terraces, opposite the most beautiful view in the world!

Access : the Plan Praz cable car - mid-station of the Brévent.

Approach : go up the ski piste / track towards the Brévent for 500m, then take a path on the left which descends the Brévent cwm (just after the take-off point for the parapentes). Go down about 100m and, after a few zigzags, the path passes near a track. Look for a flat area under the initial slab.

Gear : 10 quickdraws plus belays; 50m single rope.

Route : D, 280m. Manu and Sacha Méot, Arthur Romano, summer 2013. 11 pitches, south facing.

P1 : 35m, 5b. Slab.

P2 : 30m, 5b. Short wall, 1 move.

P3 : 45m, 5b. Nice steeper wall on good holds.

P4 : 25m, 5a. Traverse a ledge rightwards.

P5 : 35m, 5c+. Tricky finish on slopers.

P6 : 25m, 5a. Short technical section.

P7 : 40m, 3b. Easy-angled.

P8 : 35m, 4a. Belay above the yellow pipe.

P9 : 30m, 3. Horizontal traverse.

P10 : 35m, 5b. Final wall.

P11 : 35m, 3b.

"Spitomaniak"
3b
5b
3a
4a
3b
5a
5c+
5a
5b
5b
5b

"La Tartiflette!"

2200 m		S
15'		
		3
0 1 0 0		150 m

An interesting climbing garden on the western side of the "pentes de l'hôtel".

Rock : gneiss. Pitches are surrounded with growth but the rock is superb. The climbing is varied: slabs, diedres, aretes...

Access : Brévent cablecar. Stop at the midstation (Planpraz).

Approach : from Planpraz, follow the ski run towards Brévent, go through a breach and walk up on your right towards the base of the rocky slabs. 15 mins.

Equipment : 10 quickdraws. 40m rope, slings. Leave the rucksack at the start.

The route : was opened on August 3rd, 2003 by Manu Méot and Eric Mathieu. 150m. 6 pitches.

Difficulty : D. Unavoidable 5b.

"La Tartiflette!"

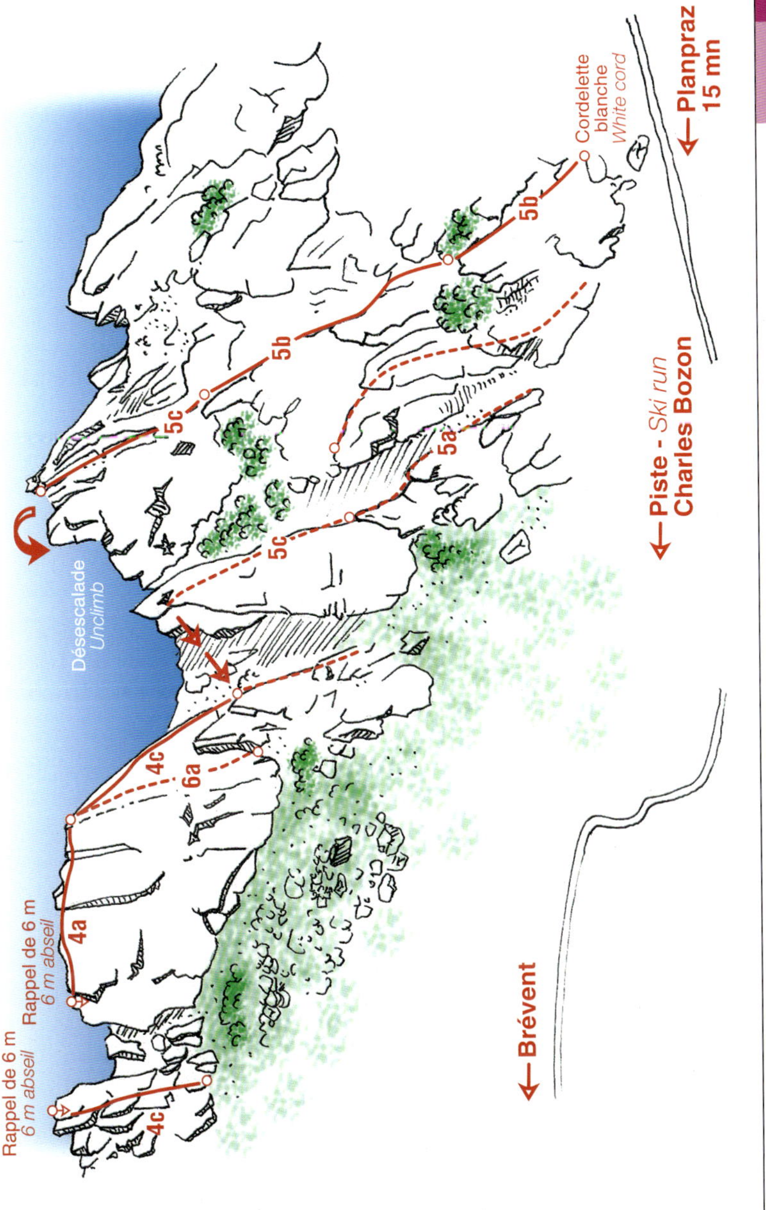

14

AREA 04 **LA SOULIRE**

La Soulire

1150 m — SE

20'

3

0 5 8 0 — 30-55 m

A new little crag closed of the valley.

Rock : gneiss.

Climbing : slabs interlaced with steeper passages with several cracks. Some passages on fragile rock require a more cautious climb. Wearing a helmet is strongly advised. Most of the routes have the name written at the base.

Equipment : cemented anchors and stud plate system; a few starts where the first point may be at some distance.

The site : south-easterly exposure, easily accessible, the crag has a dozen climbing routes of middle difficulty. Close to the "Paradis des Praz" children's play area.

Access : **by train**: Flégère train station 30 mins. Join the road "route du Golf des Praz de Chamonix". **By bus**: bus line 1, la Flégère bus stop ; bus line 2, les Bois bus stop. Join the "route du Golf des Praz" de Chamonix. 25 mins. **By car**: from Chamonix RD 1506 direction Argentière, 4.5 km. Join the "route du Golf" and the "Paradis des Praz" car-park. 20 mins.

Approach : from the golf course car-park follow the direction of the "Paradis des Praz". Once at the park follow to the left the sign to "Balcon Sud". After about 10 mins walk join the large track which runs parallel to the Telecabine line. Follow along for 200m and turn right - easterly direction - le Balcon Sud footpath. Again walk for about 5 mins and you will find the rock face situated above a scree; a cairn marks the path leading to the base of the wall.

The routes

1 - **Le chevreau**: 6a, 30m, 10 quick-draws. Easy slab and an athletic crack.

2 - **Marie.net**: 6a+, 30m, 11 quick-draws. Climb the flakes at the end. Few long slings to prevent rope friction.

3 - **Demi-siècle**: 6a+, 35m, 11 quick-draws. Probably the best.

4 - **Inshector**: 6a+. Same start then route 3.

5 - **Anesthé Zian**: 5b+, 30m, 10 quick-draws. An athletic start.

6 - **?**: 6c, 20m, 7 quickdraws, Two bolts not connected at the belay. Short finery mov to start.

7 - **Le duc**: 6a, 30m, 10 quickdraws. a few loose rock sections.

8 - **Guidos**: 6a, 30m, 10 quickdraws. Climb cautiously, fragile flakes.

9 - **Octobra**: 5c, 30m, 11 quickdraws. Nice climbing.

10 - **Croc Mignon**: 5c, 30m, 11 quick-draws. Slab climbing on a pillar.

11 - **Fils sûr**: 5a, 30m, 11 quickdraws.

12 - **Prise de Dent**: 6b/c, 55m. The route Start 50 m to the right of route 11. **P1**: 3c; **P2**: 6b+. A good wall with an athletic finish.

La Flégère

2000 m S

8′

3 4

0 4 10 1 20-30 m

Located a ten-minute walk from the lift station, this climbing site, facing one of the most beautiful panoramas in the world seems to have all the assets to seduce. However, the steep access corridor as well as the level of the routes, reserved it for experienced climbers.

Rock : gneiss and schist sometime loose. Helmet use is recommended.

Climbing : slab and crack, with short harder sections.

Equipment : resin anchor. Well protected climb.

The site : facing Mont Blanc range.

Access :
- **by train**: stop at Les Praz de Chamonix station.
- **by bus**: stop at la Flégère lift station.
- **by car**: take RD 1506 toward Argentière for 4km. Car park at the Flégère lift station.

Approach : 10 mins. Take the lift to the mid-station. Walk down to the Flégère hut, then east direction for 100m. Reach the meadow to the right. Follow the path to the steep couloir.

The routes

1 - **Le Louis dort**: 6c, 30m, quickdraws. Crux on the final ridge. One of the nicest.

2 - **Anne So fit la belle**: 7a, 32m, 15 quickdraws. Boulder problem.

3 - **Magali du hatu**: 6a, 30m, 13 quickdraws. Final crack sound hollow.

4 - **De beau rat**: 6c, 32m, 15 quickdraws. Several shot hard sections.

5 - **Y'a Anne**: 5c. **P1**: nice slab climbing; **P2**: crack, loose rock.

6 - **La Marie au soleil**: 6a+. On the ride, the tree is welcome.

7 -**?**: 6a, 30m. Slab and crack.

8 - **So fit les compte**: 6c (A0). 28m, 14 quickdraws. Very hard final slab. Exit is possible in route 9.

9 - **Mitch à Rizz**: 5c, 30m, 15 quickdraws. Slabs between grassy terrain.

10 - **Jeannot de la jungle**: 5c, 28m, 12 quickdraws. On the pillar. Tree is helpfull.

11 - **Celle y a**: 5c+, 28m, 9 quickdraws. Rock sometime loose.

12 - **L'eau rance**: 5c, 25m, 11 quickdraws. Broken rocks.

13 - **Magali du haut**: 6a+.

14 - **Flore et sens**: 6b.

La Flégère
La Flégère hut
1
2
3
4
5
6
7
8
9
10
11
12
13
14
6c
7a
6a
6c
6a+
6b
5c
6a
6c
6a
5c
6a
5c
5c
5c+
5c
6a+
6b

Area 05

Le Montenvers
Les Mottets
La Pierre d'Orthaz
Les Dalles de l'Arveyron
Le Chapeau

Le Montenvers

With the Grandes Jorasses in the background, the Drus in the foreground and the diminishing Mer de Glace below - which has retreated 150 metres since the first edition of this guide in 1989, the climbing routes are shared between two sectors: "les echelles" (the ladders) and "les dalles du Montenvers" (Montenvers slabs) - the latter with several new routes of 280 metres.

Rock : granite polished by the glacier over the millenia.

Climbing : slab climbing with small holds and edges. More balancy than physical.

Altitude : 1600 - 1800 metres.

Aspect : east facing. The site gets sun early in the morning. Possible to climb here up to October.

Access : take the train to the Montenvers. Check return times as there are fewer trains in the off season (June, October, November). There is a hiking path from Chamonix, which takes about 1 and a half to 2 hours, plus 15 - 30 minutes from the train station, depending on which sector you are heading to.

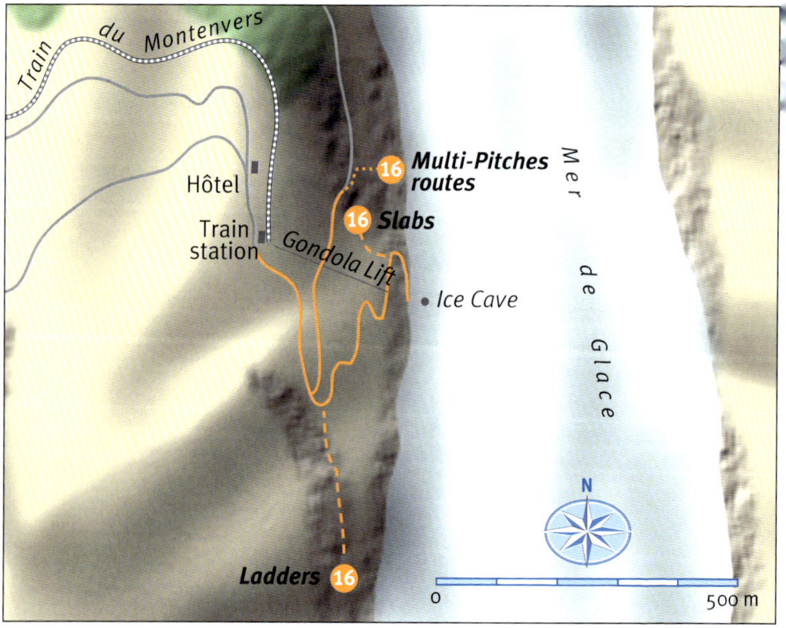

Ladders Sector

1900 m E

15′

3 4

8 27 12 2 110 m

Equipped in the 1980s by Frederic Bozon, this lovely granite slab has been unjustly forgotten. Michel Piola has given it a serious facelift by putting up seven new routes, all well equipped and carefully cleaned.

Climbing : 40 or so pitches, half of them new, equipped with cemented bolts, grade 5. Ideal for starting lead climbing. The older routes are recognisable by the ugly bolt hangers covered in synthetic cement. The routes are often covered in lichen as they are rarely used.

The site : a ledge overlooking one of the most beautiful panoramas in the world. It is possible to go down to the Mer de Glace, a hundred metres lower, via a series of ladders. Although the ledge is comfortable it is potentially dangerous for children.

Equipment : 80m rope, or 2x50 metre abseil ropes. 12-15 quickdraws (for the most recent routes).

Approach : 15 mins. From the station follow the wide path to the south that goes down to the ice cave at the Mer de Glace. Leave the path after 100 metres after a large left hand bend, taking the path on the right marked "refuges de haute montagne". Go down the first set of ladders, then go to the right: two short ladders lead to the ledge for the routes (the new track to the glacier goes via the ledge).

Michel Piola routes

From left to right

1 - **La Grand Echelle**: D, 5a compulsory, sealed bolts, nice line, comfortable belays.

2 - **Adieu Sibérie**: D+, 4c compulsory. Nice consistent route.

3 - **Le Palais des Glaces**: D-, 4c compulsory, 100m.

4 - **Vertical Tango**: 6b+, 45m. Joins route 5. Technical. Fixe brand bolts.

5 - **Buddha-bar**: TD, 5c, 110m. Three fabulous pitches on great rock.

6 - **Aspirant Sunrise**: D-, 4c mandatory, 110m (P3 with 2 points). **P1**: 4a; **P2**: 4c; **P3**: 4c. "Reumer" rings. A nice route. Pleasant climbing.

7 - **La commedia dell'arte**: D, 4c mandatory, 110m. Fixe brand rings. **P1**: 5a; **P2**: 3a; **P3**: 5a/5c. Variation on the right, 5c on third pitch.

Buddha-bar, P3: 5c

Michel Piola routes
1
5a
5b
5a
2
5b
5b
5a
3
4c
3a
5a
4
6b+
5
6
7
5c
6a
5c
4a
5a
4c
4c
3a
5b

Frédéric Bozon routes

From right to the left

8 - **Ziquemur**: 50m, 6b stay in the line of the bolts.

9 - **Danton**: 50m. **P1**: 5c; **P2**: 6a+. Small overhang, good but slightly dirty rock.

10 - **Sostene et CalAREA**: 50m, **P1**: 4c; **P2**: 4c. Consistent. Slightly mossy.

11 - **Pilier des Rossignols**: 50m, **P1**: 5c; **P2**: 5b. Mainly cracks.

12 - **Mésomolécules**: 5c, 25m. Slabs and flakes.

13 - **Glace-nost**: **P1**: 5c; **P2**: 5c.

14 - **A la Bastille**: **P1**: 6a; **P2**: 6c. Compact rock.

15 - **Ah dur-dur! P1**: 6b; **P2**: 7a+. Compact rock, in need of a clean.

16 - **La Directe**: **P1**: 6b; **P2**: 7b. Polish and compact rock.

17 - **L'arandelar**: **P1**: 5b; **P2**: 6a. Sympa.

18 - **Fils de la glisse**: **P1**: 6c+; **P2**: 5b. Good slab pitch.

19 - **Acide Lactique**: **P1**: 6a; **P2**: 6a. Good, slightly dirty.

20 - **La Plage Blanche**: **P1**: 5b+; **P2**: 5b. A bit committing.

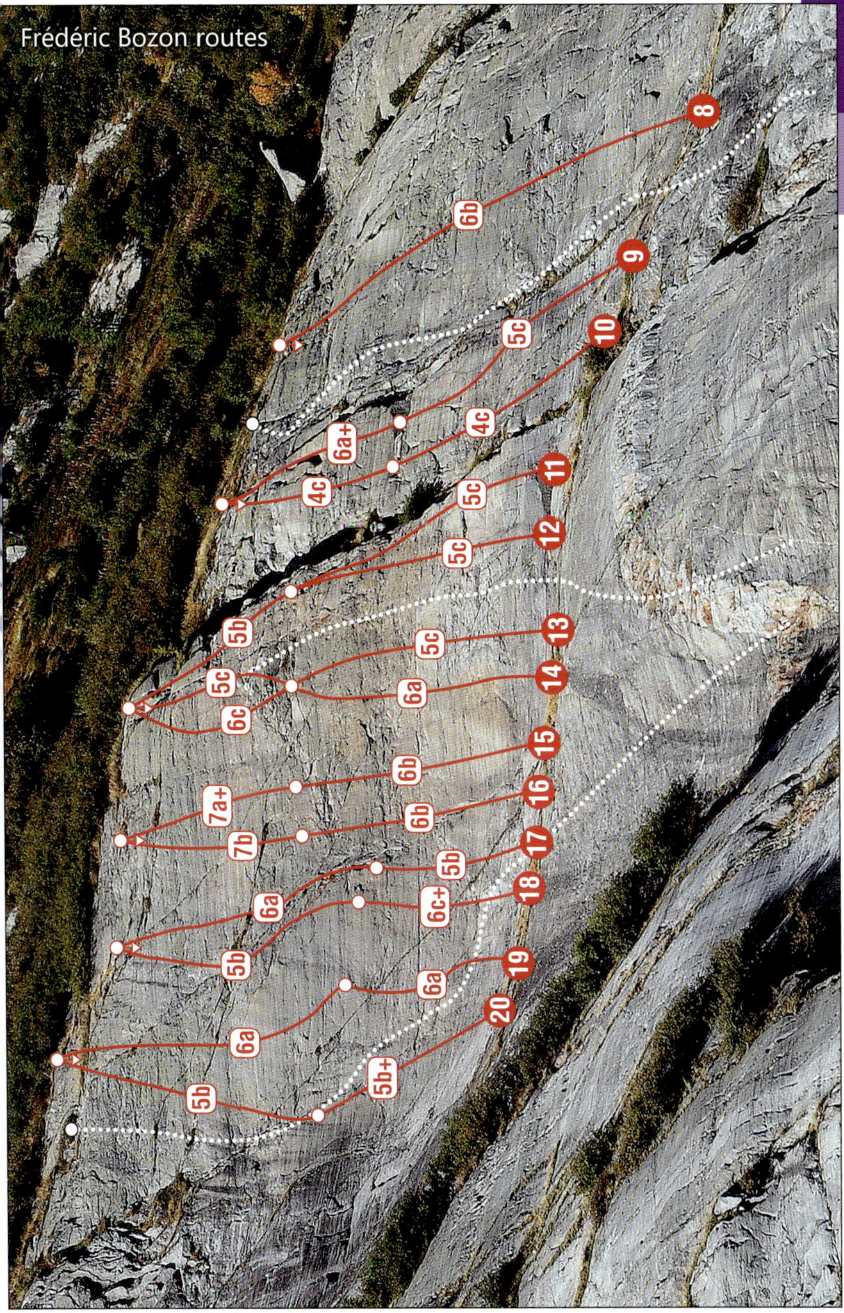
Frédéric Bozon routes
8
6b
9
5c
6a+
10
4c
4c
11
5c
12
5c
5b
13
5c
5c
14
6a
6c
15
6b
7a+
16
6b
7b
17
5b
6a
18
6c+
5b
19
6a
6a
20
5b+
5b

Montenvers slabes sector

1900 m E

20' - 30'

3

0 12 17 0 25-60 m

A beautiful climbing garden reserved for the happy few who know of its existence - crowds of tourists are only a hundred metres away. These routes were opened in 1989 by Frederic Bozon, Stephane Balmat and Eric Mariaud. Since then the Chamonix Guides Bureau has re-equipped forty or so pitches with sealed bolts.

Climbing : half of the routes are grade 5, 45-70 metres long. They are often two pitch routes. The climbing is predominantly slab with some steep protruding knobs. Small holds.

The site : the climbing starts on the ledges that run across the last third of the face. The left hand wall is relatively accessible and comfortable; the right hand wall is just as interesting but slightly uncomfortable. It is reached by a long slab traverse (grade 3) which is equipped with bolts, but exposed. The alternative is to abseil down two pitches from the geodesic sign.

Gear : 70m rope or 2x50m abseil ropes. 15 quick draws, more for P1 +P2 (45 metres, left hand section).

Access :

Approach for the Montenvers left hand slabe : from the station, follow the path that goes down to the Mer de Glace ice Cave as far as the top Mer de Glace lift station. Then descent the metallic stairs to reach a wooden house. Go behind this building along the rock. Follow a path, than cables and yellow marks to reach a wide ledge.

Approach for the Montenvers right hand slabe and the multi-pitches routes (20 mins) : from the station, follow the path that goes down to the Mer de Glace Ice cave. Leave this path on the left to follow the one indicate le "Rocher des Mottets". Follow the path until directly underneath the Hotel du Montenvers. A bit further the path starts to go downhill - climb onto the bank on the right to find a narrow path. Follow it for 50 metres, parallel to the main path. Go down another narrow path to the right through the rhododendrons, then left, and you will reach the top of the slabs. Find the geodesic point (metal structure): the abseil chain for the multi-pitches routes is on the slab. The abseil chain for the right hand section is 30 metres to the right of the sign (facing the Mer de Glace).

Left hand section

First belay is situated 15 metres uphill from the "camp de base" ledge. Short pitch (3a, 2 bolts) to reach it.

1 - **Birdy**: 6c, 30m, an excellent pitch; several small sidepulls below a jug which you can see coming... hope it's a good one!

2 - **Free**: 6b, 30m.

3 - **Rousse-fraise**: 6a, 25m, a name to give you a thirst on a route that is a desert of holds.

4 - **Ciao Tympan**: 5c, 25m, a good introduction to this section.

5 - **Corto Maltese**: 5b, 25m.

6 - **Brune-Cass**: 6a, 45m, magnificent.

7 - **Encorp**: 6a+, 45m, crafty.

8 - **Dimanche à la plage**: 6c, 54m: the "purple passage" of the crag, brilliant, but as smooth as glass. Awaits a "mutant" for a free ascent... 6c with two points of aid...

9 - **Fissure velue**: 5b/5c, 45m, very pleasant,.

10 - **«T'Choucas»**: 6b.

11 - **Dalle Tome**: 6a+, 45m, beautiful.

12 - **Roc dream**: 5c/6a, 45m, a dream...

13 - **Vol sans escale**: 5b, 45m.

Left hand section

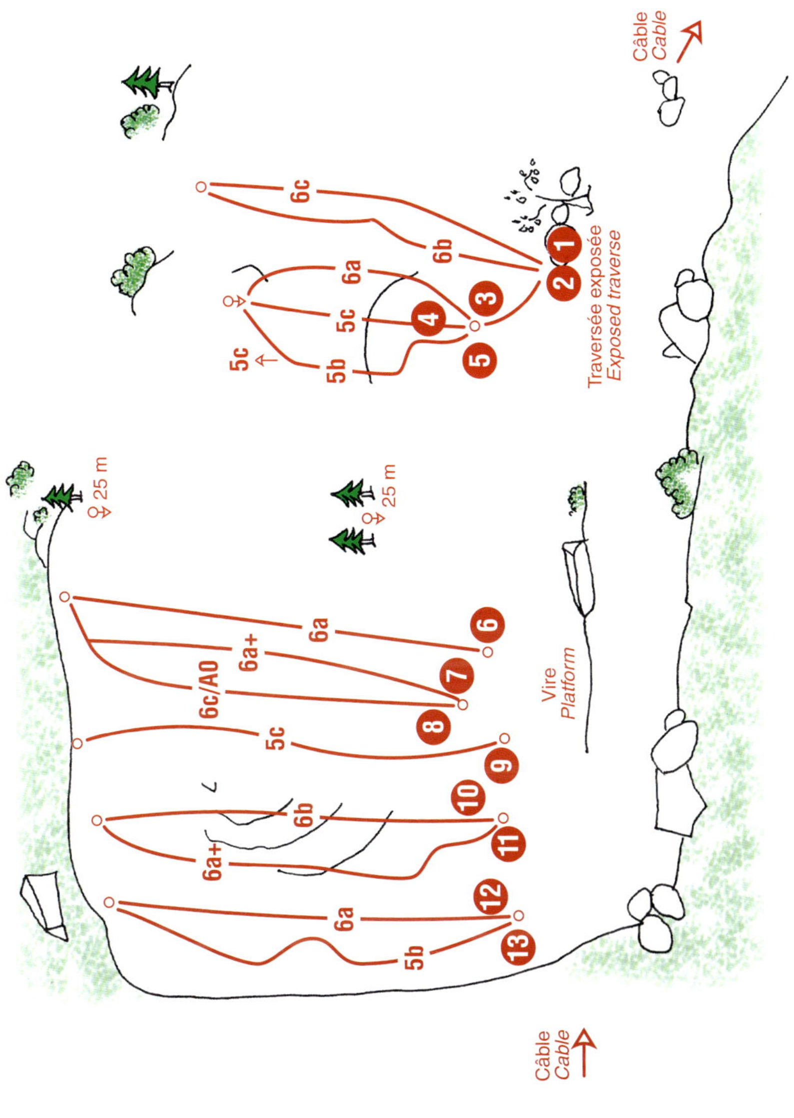

Right hand section

Names of routes are generally written at the bottom.

1 - **Les dorifores**: 60m, 2 two bolted pitches; **P1**: bulging 6b; **P2**: 5c.

2 - **Si les cons volaient**: 6a+.

3 - **Joshua Free**: a strange feeling of insecurity... 6b/6b+.

4 - **The end**: 6b.

5 - **Y'a des jours sans**: 5b.

6 - **Paradise Bird**: 5c.

7 - **Le Toune**: 5b.

8 - **Boréal de Madrid**: pleasant, 5c.

9 - **La Romaine**: very nice, 6a+.

10 - **Le Ciel serait kaki**: nothing there... 6a.

11 - **Crédit Horticole**: 6a.

12 - **La source**: 6a+.

13 - **On ekeep cool**: 5b.

14 - **El maestro**: 5c.

15 - **Yesterday**: nice slab to finish, 4c.

16 - **Paul et Mique**: 5b.

Right hand section

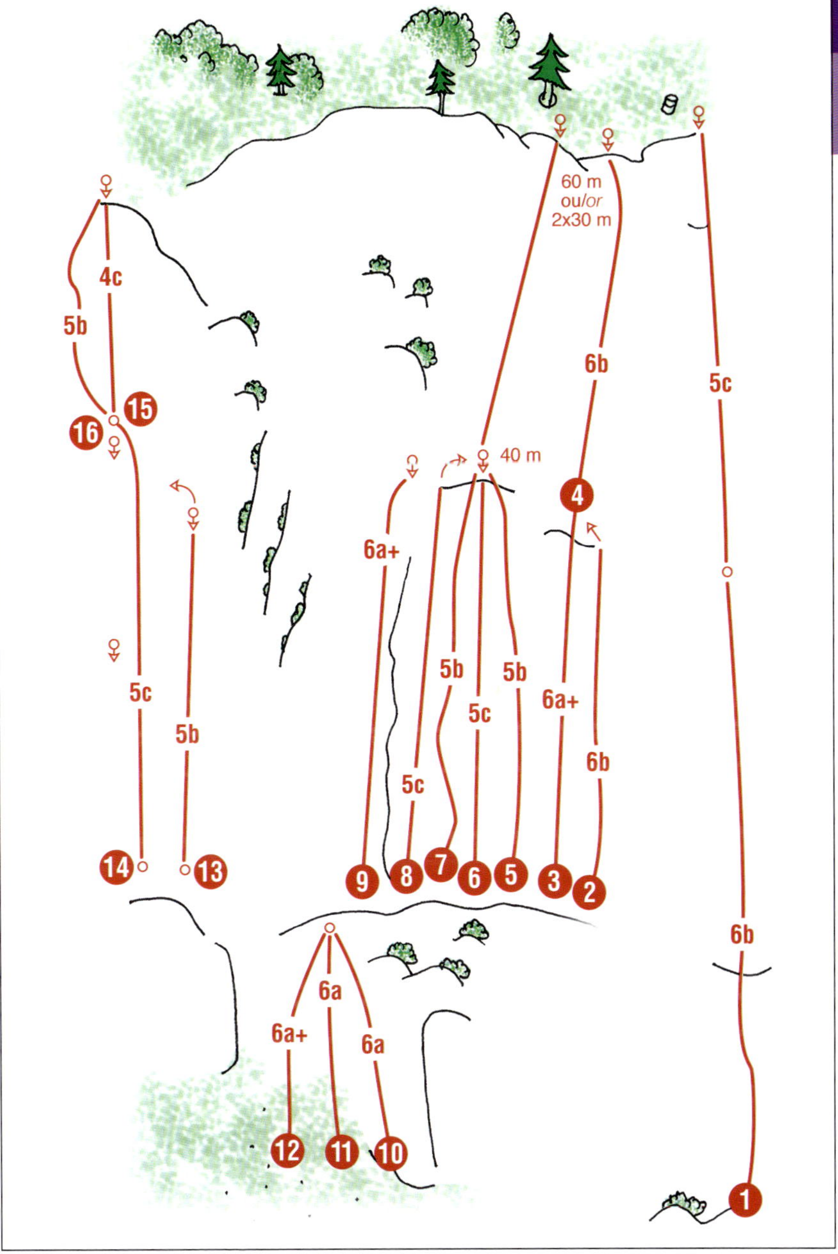

Multi-Pitches routes

1800 m E

30′

3

0	1	3	0	220 m

Untill 2008 those routes were accessible from the glacier, but with the ice melting of the glacier it is no longer possible.

Access : abseil belay bellow the geodesic signal. 5 abseils.

Gear : 12 quick-draws. 2x50m ropes.

The routes

1 - **Coup de boule**: AD+. 220m. 5b. Michel Fontes, Laurent Collignon, 25 juillet 2006. The route follows the weaklesses in the rock face. Grade 4 for most of the pitches, except the before last one (5b mandatory). From the last ledge traverse left to reach the start of the route.

2 - **Pérou fils**: TD+. 220m. 6b mandatory. Michel Arizzi, Jonathan Arizzi, J. Grand Clément June 27th 2008. **P1**: 5b, 35m, slab; **P2**: 30m, 6c (6b mandatory), steep wall; **P3**: 25m, one move 5c; **P4**: 25m, 5c; **P5**: 25m, 5a, good "removable" holds; **P6**: 20m, 6b+ (6a+ mandatory).

3 - **Voie Josiane**: D. 220m. 5b mandatory. J. Grand Clément, M. Arizzi, 2006 8th and 9th july, 5b mandatory. **P1**: 30m, 4c/5a, friction climbing; **P2**: 35m, 5a; **P3**: 35m, 5c/6a (5b mandatory), a nice pillar; **P4**: 30m, 4c, dalle; **P5**: 25m, 5b, slabe; **P6**: 30m, 6a, a little bit steeper; **P7**: 5c; **P8**: 2.

4 - **La ligne Blanche**: start 10m to the right of "Josiane" route nearby a big boulder. D+. 220m. 5c mandatory. Forest Franck, Saudemont Pascal, Wiss Nadine, August 2018, 25th, 26th, 28th and 30th. **P1**: 4b, slab; **P2**: 4a, slab, traverse 5m to the left on the grassy ledge; **P3**: 6a+, (A0/5c), 45m. A beautiful pitch, along a quartz crack; **P4**: 4a, traverse to the left. Be careful with the loose rock!; **P5**: 5c, slab; **P6**: 4c, climb left direction to reach "Josiane" route nearby a larch tree.

Multi-Pitches routes

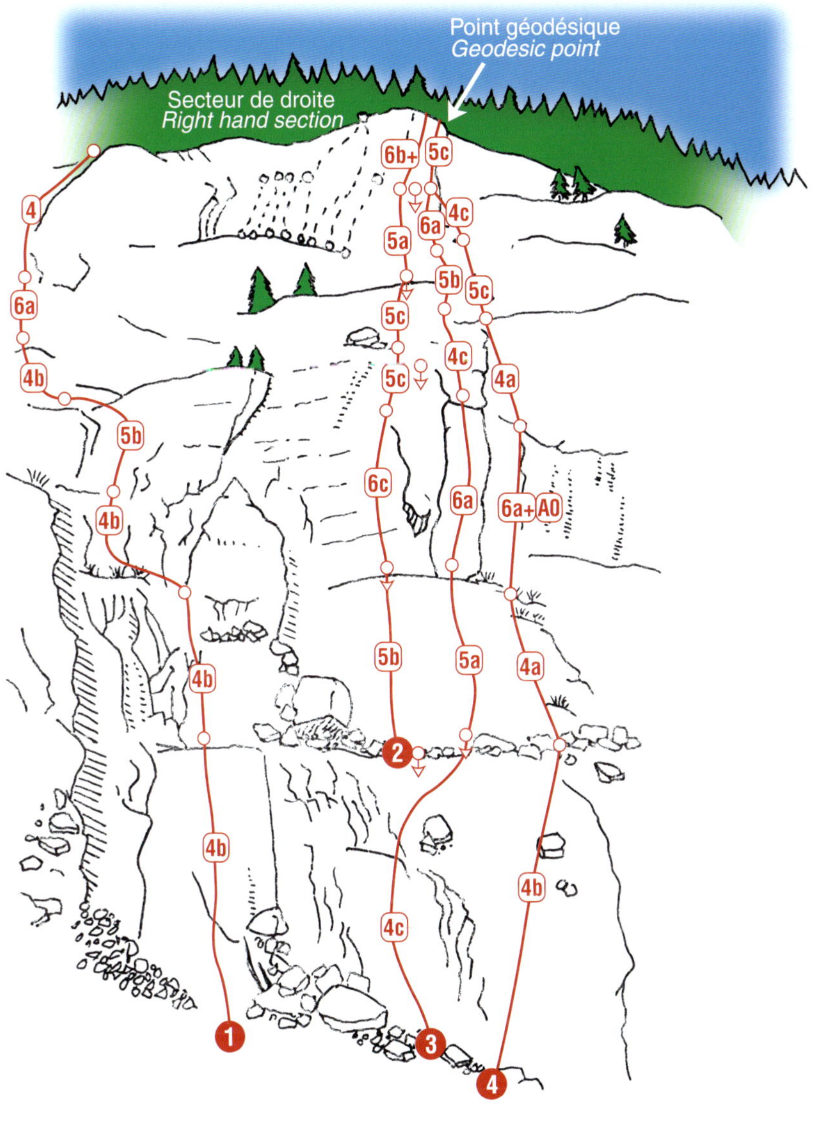

Les Mottets

1500 m | E-SW

40' - 60'

3

2 | 1 | 3 | 0 | 180-470 m

This newly developed sector is on the left bank of the Arveyron Gorge. To this day, three 180 to 250m high routes have been equipped.

Rock : sound smooth granite, with flakes in some places.

Climbing : the climbing is mostly frictiony on superb knobbly rock, with a few vertical pitches (not as sound).

Equipment : 10 mm bolts and hangers, rather spaced out, requiring a certain amount of confidence, so keep slightly below your competence to tackle difficulties more serenely.

Aspect : East, South-East. In early summer, it takes the sun until about 3pm. It is advised to avoid the site in stormy conditions.

The site : near the lower part of the "Mer de Glace" glacier. The site is superb and should develop greatly in the next few years.

Access : Montenvers railway.

Approach : (IGN map TOP 25 3531 ET). 35 mins from the Montenvers top station. In the vicinity of Hotel du Montenvers, take the path marked "Chamonix" and follow it for 15 minutes. You will find a track on your right, signposted "Les Mottets" and leading to a small refreshment stall. On the left of the bar, take a track marked with cairns and follow it for about 5 mins, then take to the right down a scree slope (cairns), and you will find the abseil line of "La Chorale" (four abseil pitches on slabs).

Return : get back up to the bar and walk down to Chamonix on a good path (45 mins).

The routes

1 - **"La Chorale"**: Serge and Franck Trésamini, Jean-Pierre Albinoni, September 2004. D. Unavoidable 5c. Four pitches of 40 to 50m. 10mm bolts. 10 quickdraws, 2x50m abseil rope. Slab climbing on small edges. Still a few chippings. **P1**: 5a; **P2**: 5c; **P3**: 6a; **P4**: 5c.

2 - **"La Voix des Ténors"**: (follow the cairns on the scree slope). Serge Trésamini, Jean-Pierre Albinoni, Lionel Pernollet, Septembre 2004. D. Unavoidable 5c, 220m. This route follows the crest of the nice red pillar. 10mm bolts. 12 quickdraws. 2x50m rope. **P1**: 40m, 5c. Quite delicate on a steep wall. **P2**, **P3** and **P4**: homogenous difficulty 5b/c. Mostly friction. Spaced up equipment in the less angled sections.

Les Mottets
5c
6a
5b
6a
6a
5b
5c
5c
4c
6b
5c
3c
4
5a
1
5c
5c
2
5c
3

3 - **"Schap'aux Mottets"**: first climb on the lower part, Serge Trésamini and Lionel Pernollet, July 2001. Equipped by Lionel Pernollet and Pierre Schapira, September 2004. TD-. Unavoidable 6a. 220m. This route goes up the second crag which is steeper. Varied climbing on slabs and cracks. 12 quickdraws, 2x50m rope. **P1**: 40m, 5c, steep wall; **P2**: 5c, belay on the pillar; **P3**: 3c, pitch on a flattened slab; **P4**: 6b, crack; **P5**: 6a.

4 - **"Les fleurs des Mottets"**: Mick Johnson and Ed Grindley, 2nd August 2006.

La Voix des Ténors, 5c

Via Corda Alpina
Sur les sentes des chamois

A 600m vertical-height route goes up the Mottets crag. Climbing on a succession of small crags not exceeding 3c, separated by ledges. It is an interesting route for this level of difficulty as the terrain has little angle and is quite reassuring. At the top, the Mottets refreshment stall is a good surprise to quench one's thirst (snacks and omelettes). Allow for 3h 30mins climbing.

Access : **by train**: Flégère train station. **By bus**: bus line 2 : Arveyon bus stop. **By car**: from Chamonix take the RD 1506 direction Argentière for 1.5 km and then a small road on the right Pierre d'Orthaz, hotel de l'Aveyron. Carpark.

Approach : **by train**: (20 mins) cross over at the railway crossing and follow the route des Gaudenays for 500 m, go right onto the road for the heliport and continue to the bridge on the Arveyron. Cross over and on the left the "chemin des Carrières". (See approach by car to continue).

By bus: go through the small underpass under the train track, follow the path for 100m, turn right over the bridge of the Arveyron and then left onto the chemin d'Orthaz. (See approach by car to continue).

By car: (20 mins) walk along the left bank of the Arveyron on the chemin d'Orthaz (go past the electric power plant) and the "chemin des Carrières". Follow the nordic ski trail in the same direction, north-east. Leave the "Monte de Pépé" to the right. As the path bends to the left you find a sign post for "la Norvège". The via Corda Alpina begins just behind a small spur. Cairns.

Route : follow the cairns and the bolts. Also look for cut off branches. Take time and look around as the route is not straightforward. Around the middle a long left-hand traverse leads to some rolling slabs.

Return : (45 mins). From the bar, use the return path from the Vallée Blanche in the direction od Chamonix. After 15 mins, take to the right in the direction of "Les Bois". You will meet the approach itinerary from Orthaz, at the level of the farm. If you came via "Les Bois", take to the right to go back to the bridge on the river.

Equipment : (Sabine, Serge and Frank) 10mm bolts and hangers, rather spaced up but placed at strategic places. 40m rope. 7 quickdraws. Comfortable rock-shoes or even tennis shoes with good sticky soles.

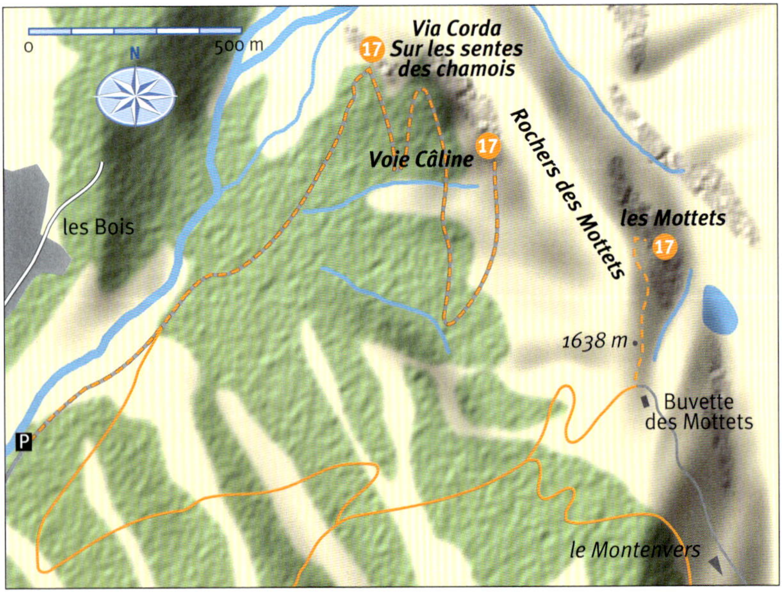

Les Mottets buvette

Via Corda "Sur les sentes des Chamois"

Voie Câline

"Voie Câline": 350m. AD-. 3c. 19 short pitches. A long and pleasant route; some exposed parts. Beautiful view over the Chamonix valley.

Gear : 10 quick draws. 40m rope.

Advice : same way as via Corda Alpine. Avoid during stormy weather. 3 to 4 hours climbing and an hour to get down. Nice buvette at the top. Jean-Pierre Albinoni, René Bouchard, Jean-Paul Démarchi, Serge and Frank Trésamini. June 2009.

Access : 1 hour. Altitude gain: 570m. Same way as via corda Alpine. From the "Norvège", follow the main path right up to the EDF cable car station. You will pass a stream then the path gets narrow. Just before some rock fall, go to the right ("voie Câline" sighn post). Climb a few flights of metal steps to the bottom of the route.

The route : **P1**: 15m, 3a; **P2**: 15m, 3b; **P3**: 15m, 3c; **P4**: 20m across to the right, 2; **P5**: to the right, 15m, 2c; **P6**: 15m, 3c; **P7**, **P8**, **P9**: 2 gentle slab; **P10**: 3a; **P11**, **P12**: 2a; **P13**: 20m, 4a; **P14**: 10m, 3b; **P15**: 15m, 3b; **P16**: 15m, 3b; **P17**: 30m, 4a, then 2a; **P18**: to reach the last spur. Good granite; **P19**: 20m, 4a.

Descent : same way as via Corda Alpine.

4a
4a
3b
4a
2a
3a
2
3c
2
2c
3c
3b
3a
Voie Câline

La Pierre d'Orthaz

1000 m | W

5'

0 3 9 6 | 5 m

A famous lump of rock, which has seen all the major legendary alpinists pass under its overhangs. It sits imposingly in the middle of a clearing, which, not too long ago, served as a camp site for young, hard up alpinists. Its overhanging west face has about 15 lines, with some fairly complicated traverses.

Rock : rough and/or polished granite.

Climbing : the problems are between 3 and 5 metres high and the landings are generally good. The climbing is powerful on small edges and rounded holds.

Access : from Chamonix, by bus: line 2, "Arveyon" bus stop. **By train**: "Les Praz de Chamonix" station. **By car**: from Chamonix take the RD 1506 for Argentière (1.5 km) and then take a small road on the right direction Hotel de l'Arveyron. Carpark.

Approach : **by bus and by train:** 10 mins. **By car**: from the car park, follow the path through the forest for 150m until you come to a clearing where the sacred stone awaits.

The site : the boulder is in a pleasant meadow and is ideal for family outings. It is also a meeting place, somewhere to find a climbing partner for the next day. In spring however, the rock is directly in the line of a sizeable avalanche gully...

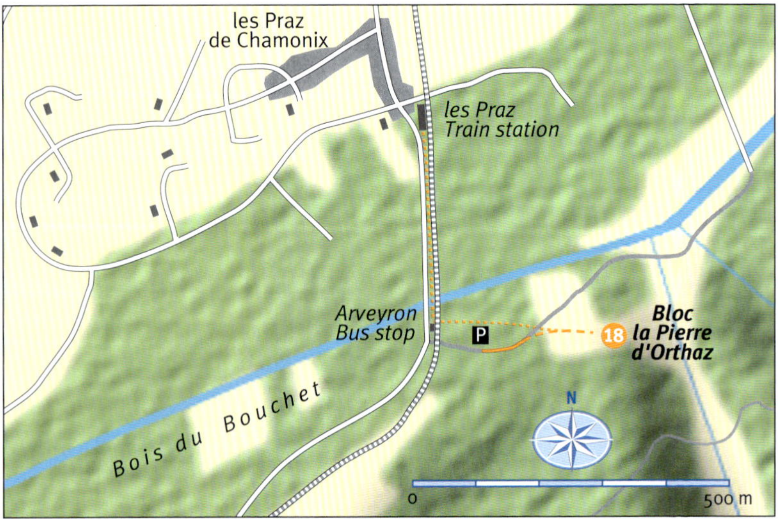

In the good old days...

Right side

1 - **Le château**: 6b, rising traverse on the crenellated arete, bad landing.

2 - **L'arête de droite**: 6b, or "rocking chair": enigmatic start.

3 - **L'astragale par l'arête**: 7b, on reaching the jug for the left hand, traverse right.

3 bis - **L'astragale**: 7c+, start in the corner, the arete for the right hand is allowed.

4 - **Les francs-tireurs**: 6a, start by using the ramp, then direct: the higher you get, the better the holds. At the top, pull up using a jug, far to the left.

5 - **Traversée du haut**: 6b, good stamina training if you "take a return ticket".

6 - **Les francs-jeteurs**: 7b.

7 - **La chaise-longue**: 6c+, shorties may have to dyno from the large sloping ledge to a good left hand hold.

8 - **L'arête** (or "le vide-ordure"): 6b+, with or without the feet.

9 - **L'unijambiste**: 6c+, a succession of precarious holds, athletic; start below the overhang with a small hold for the left hand.

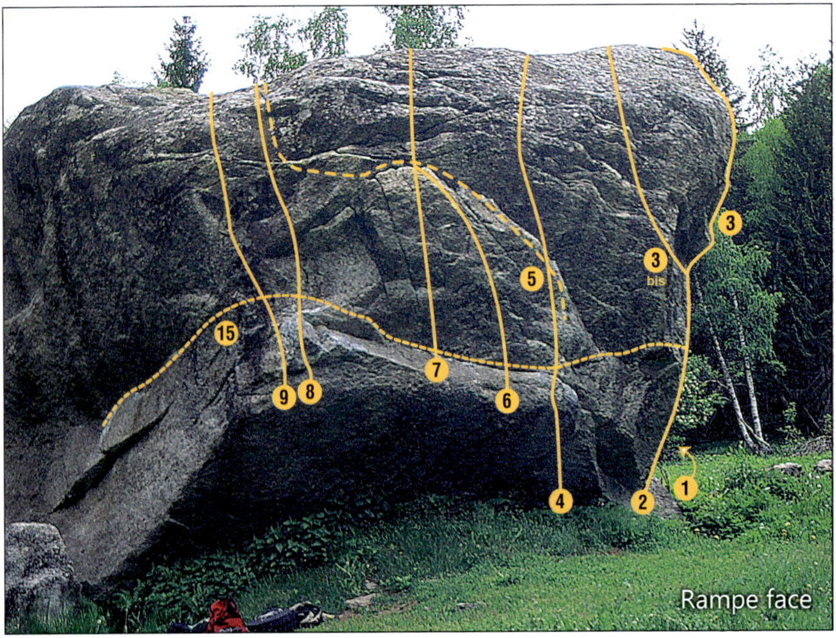

Left side

10 - Many stars have worked on this one, without success...

11 - **L'araignée**: 6a+, take a deep breath at the end...

12 - **L'araignée directe** or la **«balançoire»**: 7a+, tricky finish.

13 - **Variante de droite**: 6c+, at the top, put your foot where your hand is...

14 - **Voie normale**: 5b, reach for big holds.

15 - **Traversée Gary**: 8a, to the right hand corner, otherwise 7b.

16 - **Equilibriste**: 5c+, friction.

17 - **L'extrême gauche**: 5c, athletic overhang.

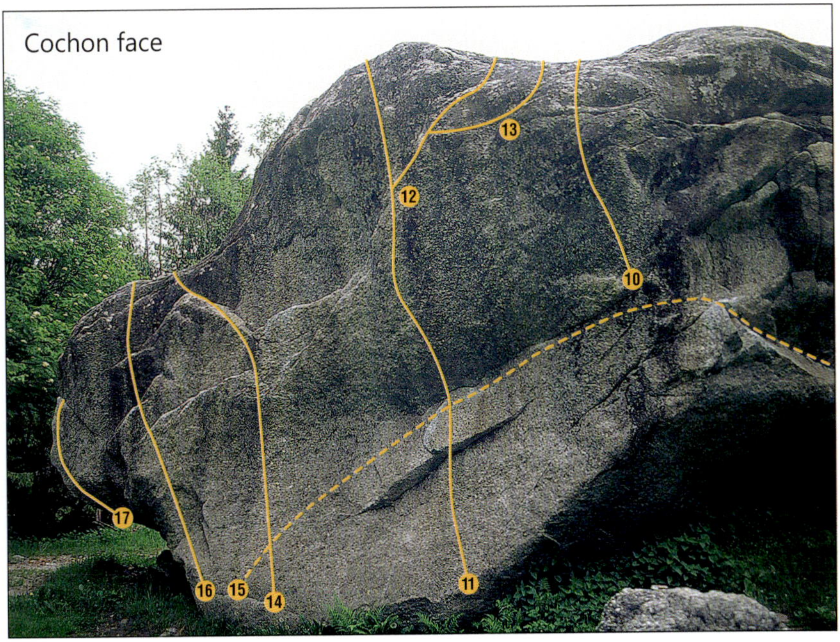

Les Dalles de l'Arveyron

1300 m SW

15' to 40'

2 3

3 5 16 4 60 m

These glacier polished slabs remain relatively quiet. They offer a wide spectrum of difficulties and there is something for the 4th grade and 7th grade climber alike.

Rock : the granite is smooth and sound and covered in small edges, but there are also some nice cracks.

Climbing : the crag is 60m high and has 18 routes. The climber must rely on friction and precise footwork. The harder routes are fairly short. The first pitches are mostly frictiony, the second ones steeper and more technical.

Aspect : South facing. In summer, this means climbing early in the morning, to avoid roasting your toes in your rock boots! On the other hand, it also means that climbing is possible here until very late in the season.

The site : the crag is on the path which leads to the "Source de l'Arveyron". (5 mins away). There is a large flat area at the bottom of the routes.

Access : **by bus**: bus line 1 or 2, "les Tines" bus stop. **By train**: "Les Tines" station. **By car**: from Chamonix, take the main road (RD 1506) towards Argentière. After 7km, just before the avalanche barrier, turn right towards Le Lavancher. Go through the village to the end of the made-up road and continue another 500m on a good track. Carpark.

Approach : **by bus and by train**: from the station at Les Tines or the bus stop 40 mins. Take the little road in the forest signed Le Lavancher and Sources de l'Aveyron. **By car**: from the Lavancher carpark: follow the path for the snack bar "la buvette du Chapeau" then turn right downhill following the sign to "Sources de l'Arveyron". Le climbing site is by the side of the path

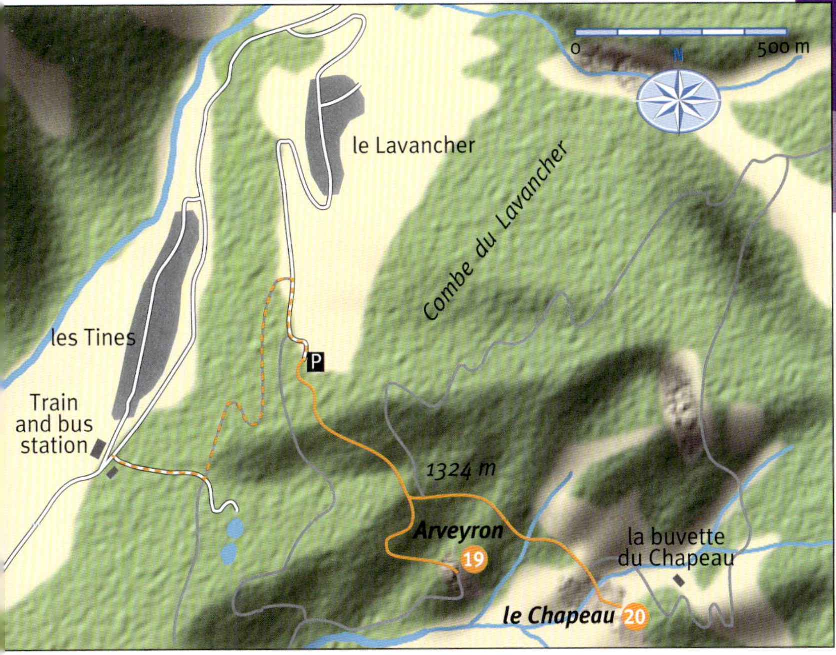

Surprise sur-prise. P2: 6a+

Main cliff

1 - **Voie Lactée**: **P1**: 6c, 31m. Boulder problem.

2 - **Barbouille**: 6a. Nice one.

3 - **Les 3 gollots**: the original line, lower down, has been modified: **P1**: 5a (20m equipped); **P2**: 6a.

4 - **Siffredi**: **P1**: 5c; **P2**:if the line of the bolts is followed direct, 6c+, 20m; traversing left: 6c.

5 - **Surprise pour un golgotte**: 6a, 20m.

6 - **Vol d'Icare**: **P1**: 6b+, 22m. The start is harder than it looks. **P2**: 7a, 20m. Superb.

7 - **Centrale**: one pitch, 5c+.

8 - **Surprise sur-prise**: **P1**: 4c; **P2**: 6a+.

9 - **Total detox**: **P1**: 6c, 20m. An uncomfortable crack. **P2**: 5c, 30m. Nice slab climbing (this pitch is also accessible from route 8).

10 - **?**: 6a.

11 - **Dernière cartouche**: 5c+, 30 m. The logical continuity of route 2 or 3.

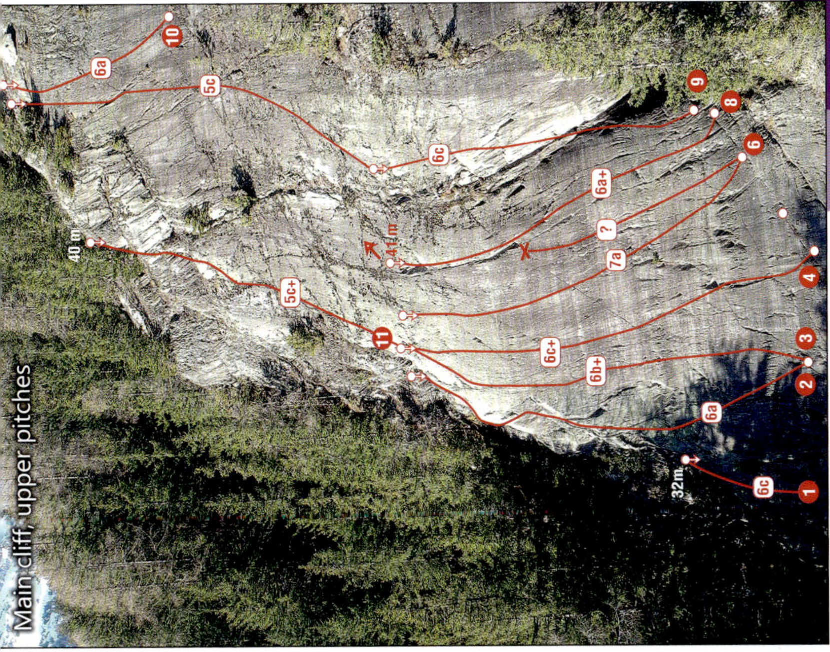
Main cliff, upper pitches
1
6c
32m
2
6a
3
6b+
4
6c+
11
5c+
40 m
7a
?
6a+
41 m
6
8
6c
9
10
6a
5c

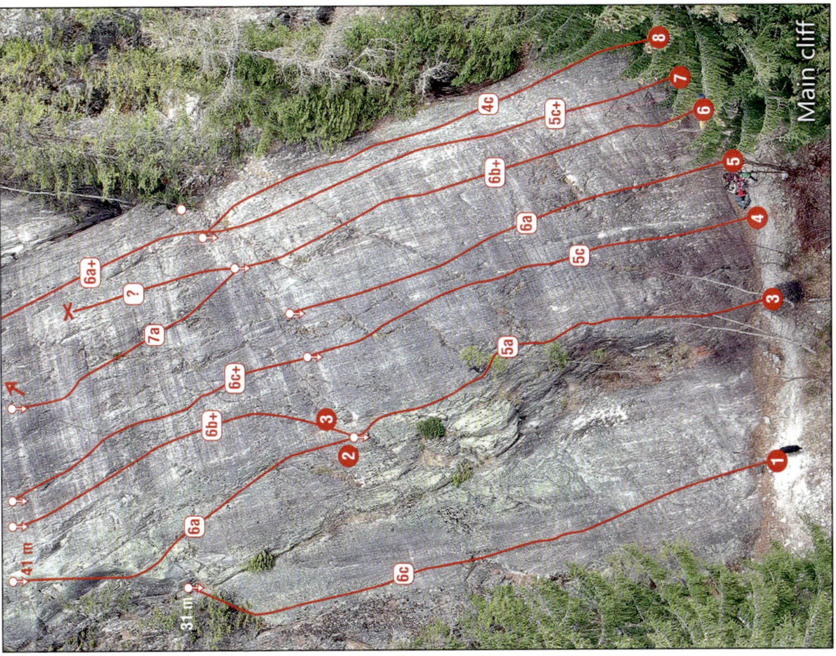
Main cliff
1
6c
31 m
2
6a
41 m
3
6b+
5a
4
5c
6c+
5
6a
7a
6
6b+
?
7
5c+
6a+
8
4c

Right hand section

Two nice routes today re-equipped.

Access : pass the cliff, than scramble left across the forest to reach the crag. Follow the cairns. (5 mins).

1 - **Pilier d'extrême droite**: start to the right of the pillar. D-. 100m. **P1**: 5b+, 30m, crack. **P2**: 6a, 40m. **P3**: 5b, 30m.

2 - **Direct du gauche**: start to the left of the pillar. 100m. TD. **P1**: 6b, (A0/5c), 30m, crux is at the end; **P2**: 6b, 25m, delicate climbing; **P3**: 6b, 25m, short difficult sections; **P4**: 5c, 25m.

3 - **?**: 6c, 30m. A beautiful crack. Ac cess: from the second belay o route 2 traverse 30m to the left tc reach a ledge. Start of the route 3.

Dalle de l'Arveyron
right hand section
5c
5b
6b
6c
6a
6b
6b
5b+
3
2
1

20

AREA 05 **LE CHAPEAU**

Le Chapeau

1600 m | W

25' - 40'

2 3

1 5 16 5 | 120 m

Very popular in the 1990s, Le Chapeau routes are today a bit neglected. As a result, moss and lichen cover the rocks. However, there are some lines clean and well protected to reconcile with this beautiful place.

Rock : granite slab, steep wall and cracks in Dark Cristal sector.

Climbing : 40 routes from 70 to 140m long. Welcome to the world of friction climbing! Delicacy and precise footwork are essential to avoid engaging reverse gear...! The friction is better in the morning. The "Oasis" area is equipped with cemented-in ring bolts; the other areas with 10 mm bolts + hangers.

Equipment : glue bolts sometimes spaced. 2x50m ropes (for abseil), 10 to 15 quickdraws depending of the route.

The site : the "Chapeau" offers great views over the Chamonix valley, the "Mer de Glace" and the "Aiguilles de Chamonix". You need a bit of a head for heights to get to the bottom of the routes, but non-climbers can always continue along the path to the pretty snack bar. Don't get caught out here in a thunderstorm.

Access : **by bus**: bus line 1 or 2, "Le Tines" bus stop. **By train**: "les Tines" station. **By car**: from Chamonix take the main road (RD 1506) towards Argentière. After 7 km just after the avalanche barrier, turn right, direction Le Lavancher. Go through the village to the end of the made-up road and continue another 500m on a very good track. Carpark.

Approach : **by train or by bus**: from the train or bus stop of Les Tines 40/45 mins. Follow the little road signed to le Lavancher which goes up into the forest. At Le Lavancher follow the direction of the "buvette du Chapeau" until you reach the carpark by the water tower. From Le Lavancher carpark, 30 to 40 mins depending on the sector. Follow the path to the "buvette du Chapeau". Access to the various sectors see over the page.

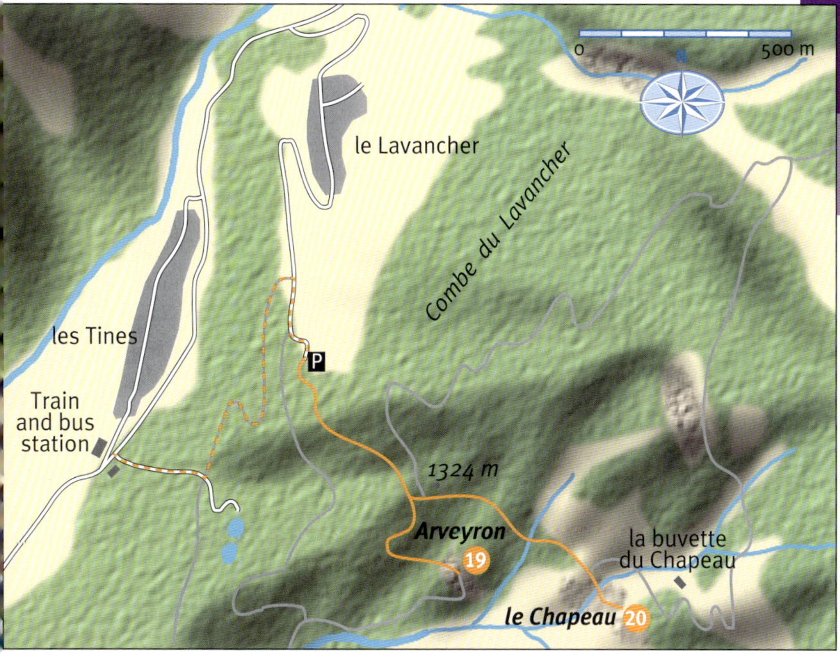
0
500 m
N
le Lavancher
Combe du Lavancher
les Tines
P
Train
and bus
station
1324 m
Arveyron
19
la buvette
du Chapeau
le Chapeau
20

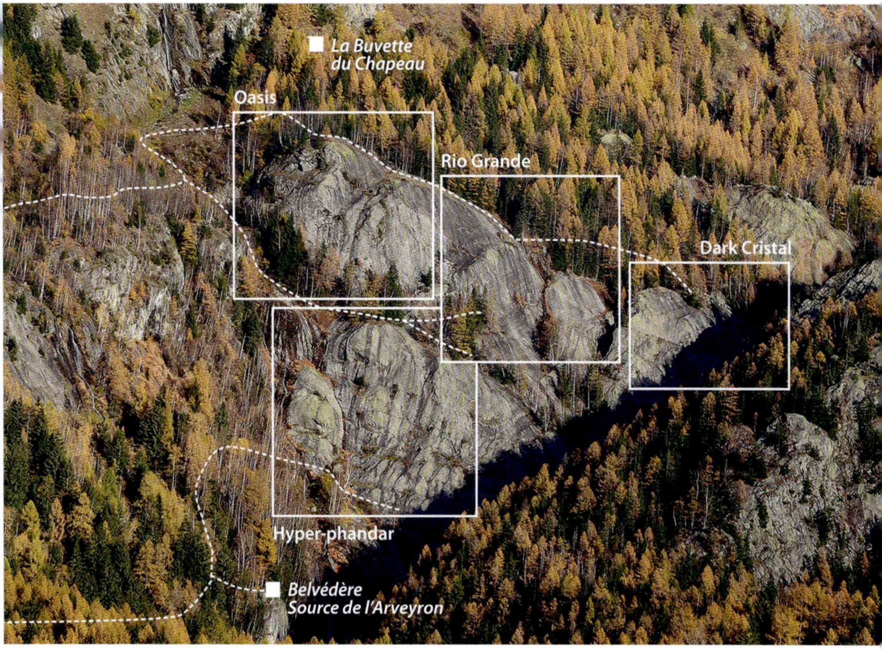
La Buvette
du Chapeau
Oasis
Rio Grande
Dark Cristal
Hyper-phandar
Belvédère
Source de l'Arveyron

Access to the different sections

1 - **OASIS**

20-25 mins. Take the path leading to the "Buvette du Chapeau". After crossing two wooden walkways and just before a left pin turn, descent a narrow path to the right (cairn) to reach the Oasis terrace.

2 - **HYPER-PHANDAR**

These are the slabs below Oasis terrace. Access with rappels. Belay A: traverse terrace to the end, the rappel chain is on the wall. Belay B: go down 30m, belay is to the right nearby a larch tree.

Belay A: routes 17 to 21.

Belay B: routes 21 and 22.

3 - **RIO GRANDE**

Access routes 9, 10, 11.

Continue down the same track then Hyper-Phandar belay B. Lower 20m is the start for route 10 and 11.

Access to routes 12 to 16.

Traverse Oasis terrace and continue along the black wall to its far end (start of "Le roi se meurt"); descend a steepish slab to reach the banks of the "Rio Grande". It is possible to fix a rappel.

4 - **DARK CRISTAL**

40-45 mins. Continue towards the Buvette du Chapeau. After passing the strean, we enter the forest. Leave the path to the right to go down a steep narrow path (cairn). You reach the top of Oasis sector. Carry on the descent to the left following cairns and pieces of yellow rope. At the top of the cliff, look for belay C nearby a larch tree on a ledge.

Oasis sector

1 - **A quatre pattes dans les Carpates**: **P1**: 4a; **P2**: 7a. Moss covers the rock.

2 - **L'enfer des Incarnés**: 6c, 50m; traverse from the ledge on Au grand Dam...

3 - **Au Grand Dam de ces Dames**: 100m, D. A classic. **P1**: 5a, start by a traverse to the left; **P2**: 5c; **P3**: 5b; **P4**: 5b. Descend on foot or rappel in route n° 5 "Zéro de conduite".

4 - **Arthur, c'est dur**: 70m. ABO. **P1**: 5a; **P2**: 7c ou 7a (ou A0); **P3**: 4c; **P4**: 6c; the second pitch has a very technical section, (well protected), 7c, which can be avoided by moving slightly left, then traversing back horizontally to the right, 7a. The last pitch is one of the gems of Le Chapeau... Moss covers the rock.

5 - **Zéro de conduite**: TD+. 80m. **P1**: 6b; **P2**: 6b; **P3**: 4a. Slab style.

6 - **Un îlot de loisir dans un oasis de plaisir**: TD+. 80m. The first route put up at Le Chapeau, (1983); one of the best classics at the moment. **P1**: 6a+; **P2**: 6a.

7 - **Tour de vice**: ED. 80m. **P1**: 6c+; **P2**: 6a.

8 - **La marmite de la Mère Royaume**: AD. 110m. **P1**: 4c; **P2**: 3b; **P3**: 3b; **P4**: 4a. Four pleasant, easy pitches. "...route put up in honour of one of the most famous citizens of Geneva, who, in December 1602, helped to repulse the evil Savoyard invaders, by pouring a pan full of vegetable soup on the head of one of their glorious warriors!" (Michel Piola, 1985, Vertical n° 2).

Hyper-Phandar sector

Routes 17 to 21: the routes are nice and well-equipped. Some mossy spots making climbing a bit tricky. Don't hesitate to give it a quick brushing when abseiling.

16 - **Purgatoire**: **P1:** 6b+; **P2:** 7a, 60m. Some protection needs replacement; overgrown.

17 - **Voie Piola 1**: **P1**: 6c+, 35m. A very nice pitch. **P2**: ?, 40m. Poor protection. Exit route n. 18.

18 - **Hyper-Phandar**: **P1**: 6b+, 30m; **P2**: 6c, 40m. Petzl bolts. Two nice pitches on slab.

19 - **Idéal**: **P1**: 6b+, 30m; **P2**: 40m. Slab climbing, bolt resin.

20 - **Voie Bellin**: **P1**: 6a+, 20m; **P2**: 6a. 45m. Anchors. Goes up via a depression. A bit mossy.

21 - **OMS**: 110m. A nice route re-equiped in 2019. Access by abseiling down in the route from belay station B. **P1**: 5C, 40m; **P2**: 5c, 30m; **P3**: 6a+, 30m. Fingery start.

22 - **Rimaye de luxe**: 110m. The most popular route in the area. Clean and well-protected. Access by abseiling down from belay station B. **P1**: 4c, 10m. 1 bolt on slab. **P2**: 5c+, 30m, beautiful and varied. **P3**: 5b, 30m. **P4**: 5b, 35m. Low angle slab.

Hyper-Phandar sector
A
45 m
40 m
B
7a
?
6c
6b
6a+
5b
5c
6a
30 m
30 m
5c
6b+
6c+
6b+
6a+
6b+
20
5b
30 m
17
18
19
16
40 m
5c+
5c
?
4c
21
22

Rio Grande sector

Routes 9, 10, 11, 12. 25m. Superb wall with natural red lines. Excellent protection on resin anchors.

13 - **Bain de Minuit**: **P1**: 3a. This pitch continues along the rocky crest and joins. **P2**: 6a. A delicate start. **P3**: 6a. **P4**: 6b. The most technical section is the crossing over Rio Grande. **P4'**: variant 6a+. **P5**: 3a.

14 - **?**. **P1**: 6b. **P2**: 6a. Some protection needs replacement, exposure.

15 - **Après moi le déluge**: same start as Route 16. **P1**: 7a+. Resin anchors. Starts after belay station R1 on route 16. **P2**: 7a+. Technical climbing on a superb slab with small finger holds.

16 - **Le roi se meurt**: **P1**: 6c. **P2**: 6a. Diagonal overgrown crack. **P3**: 5c. **P4**: 3c.

Rio Grande sector
3a
5c
3c
3b
8
6b
6a+
7a+
3b
6a
7a
6
5
4c
7
3
6a
6a
6c
16
15
8
25 m
6b
6a
Descente
Descent
14
3a
6a
5c
5c
5b
9
10
11
12
13

Dark Cristal sector

Located in the narrowest part of the Gorge de l'Arveyron, the place is rather impressive. Alain Payot put recently new routes on a beautiful vertical granite rock. Considering the difficult access and the serious level of the routes, the place is reserved for experienced climbers.

Access : see page 154. 3 rappels. It is also possible to fix on belay D a 60 meters static.

1 - **Dark Crystal**: **P1**: 7a+/7b; **P2**: 7c+/8a. **P1+P2**: 8a, 45m. Very technical.

2 - **Old one**: 6c+, 25m. Good warm up.

3 - **Surprise party**: 60m. **P1**: 7a+, don't stop at the belay of route 2. Boulder problem. **P2**: 7a.

4 - **Surprise de taille**: 120m. **P1**: 7b+ **P2**: 7a+, superb; **P3**: 6a+.

5 - **L'Oeil**: 120m. **P1**: 6b+; **P2**: 7a+ with 1 p.a. or ?; **P3**: 6c.

6 - **Last but not least**: 7a+.

7 - **Dedeleum 2**: 6b+.

8 - **Vas-y-Paulette**: 120m. **P1**: 7a; **P2**: 6b; **P3**: 6a+; **P4**: 5b.

9 - **L'heure de la soupe**: **P1**: 5b+; **P2**: 5a. Nice route, the easiest of the place.

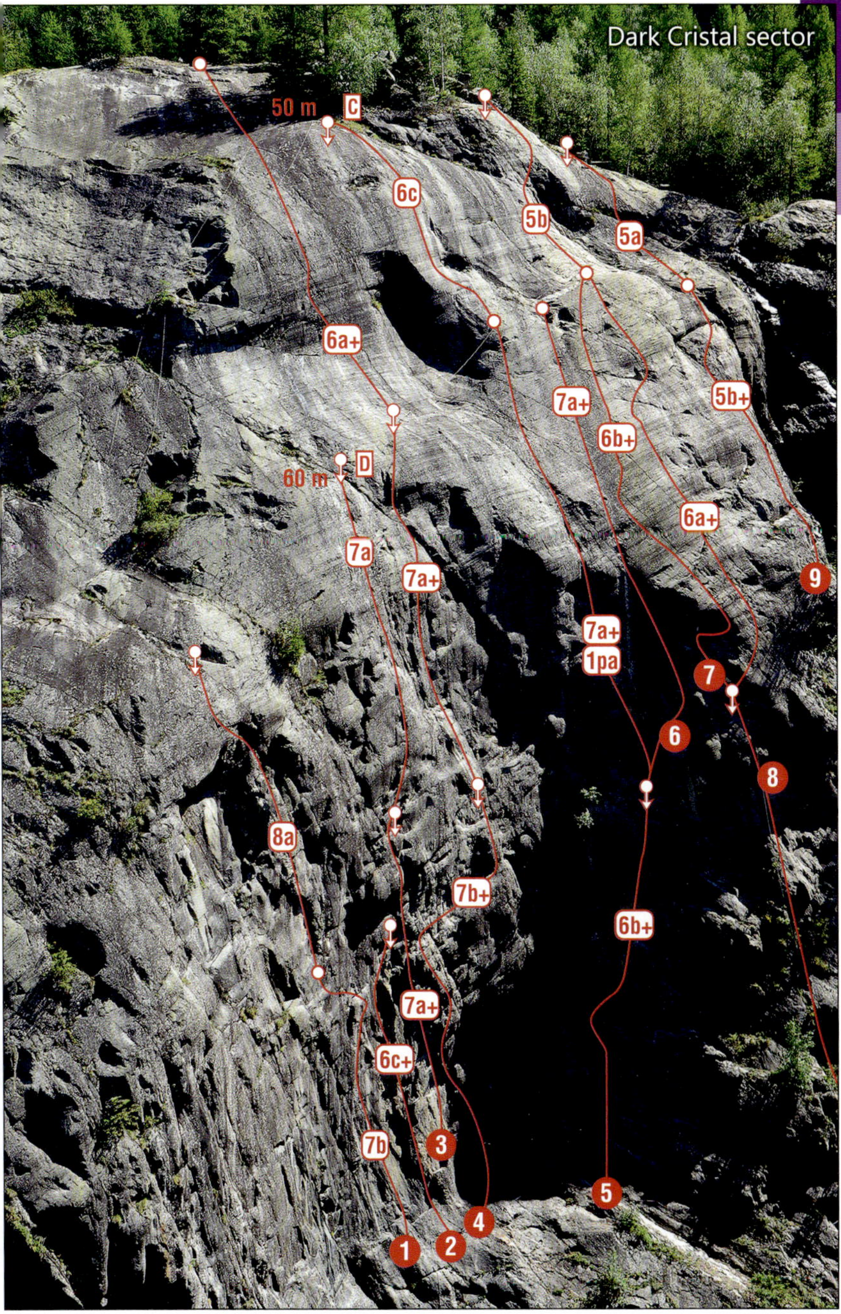
Dark Cristal sector
50 m
C
6c
5b
5a
6a+
7a+
5b+
6b+
D
60 m
7a
6a+
7a+
9
7a+
1pa
7
6
8
8a
7b+
6b+
7a+
6c+
7b
3
5
4
1
2

Area **06**

La Joux
Chauffria Monolith 1
Chauffria Monolith 2
Moraine d'Argentière
L'Aiguillette d'Argentière
Les Chéserys - Remuaz

La Joux

1250 m | SE

15′

3

7 | 11 | 16 | 5 | 12-70 m

For a long time popular with the local guides, this small crag has been given a new lease of life, thanks firstly, to Roland Ravanel, who put up the routes on the left hand section, and secondly to the extensive cleaning and equipping work, carried out by the guides of the U.C.P.A. centre in Argentière.

Rock : rough gneiss.

Climbing : 52 routes. The climbing here is very varied; slabs, diedres, chimneys, overhangs..., but also very technical, as the holds are often facing the wrong way. There is something here for climbers of all standards; several well equipped routes of 3 and 4, a good choice of routes between 5 and 6c, several "sevens" of merit, and two projects at 8.

The site : La Joux means "the forest" in Savoyard dialect. Facing south, with a small stream running below it and an unrestricted view over Mont-Blanc, this pleasant crag is growing in popularity. It is ideal for family outings.

Access : **by train**: la Joux station, request stop only. **By bus**: bus line 1, les

Grassonets bus stop, 5 mins by foot up to la Joux. **By car**: from Chamonix follow the RD 1506 for 5 km east towards Martigny. Just after the avalanche barrier turn left for la Joux. Carpark next to the train station.

Approach : (10 mins) walk up above the railway line to the the charming village of la Joux. Fork right on the path going north. After the large clearing the path leads into the forest and comes to a stream. Take the steep path to the left, still in a northerly direction (do not take the left turn halfway). Within a few minutes you get to the rocks which are easily visible on the left.

Bijoux de famille. 6c

Right hand section

All the routes are equipped and the names are written at the bottom.

1 - **Surfer le vague**: 7b, 15m, "à vue" major pitch for on sight climbing.

2 - **?**: 8a. Boulder problem

3 - **Bonjour les Martiens!**: 7b, 8m.

4 - **Volage**: 6b, 8m.

5 - **Joe le taxi:** 6c, 11m.

6 - **La beauté du péché**: 6a+, 11m.

7 - **On la Joux cool**: 5c (one move), 11m.

8 - **Variation de On la Joux cool**: 6a.

9 - **Cailloux, bijoux, La Joux**: 4a (chipped holds!), 12m.

10 - **La Jouvencelle**: 4b, 12m.

11 - **Grâce à Snell**: 5c. (2004, Piotr Packowski, Fabrice Monier) to the left of "Gruyère". Watch your back.

12 - **Gruyère**: 6a, 15m.

13 - **Décalcanéum**: 6c, 15m. Left without the crack.

14 - **Acajou**: 5c (corner), 15m.

15 - **Joyau**: 4b, 15m.

16 - **Les anciens du gaz**: 5b, 15m. An old route that has been re-equipped.

17 - **La voie de l'hôtesse de l'air**: 7a, 12m. Same start as 17.

18 - **La joufflue**: 4c, 15m.

7b
8a
7b
6b
6c
6a+
6a
5c
8
1
2
3
4
5
6
7
Le Gros Caillou

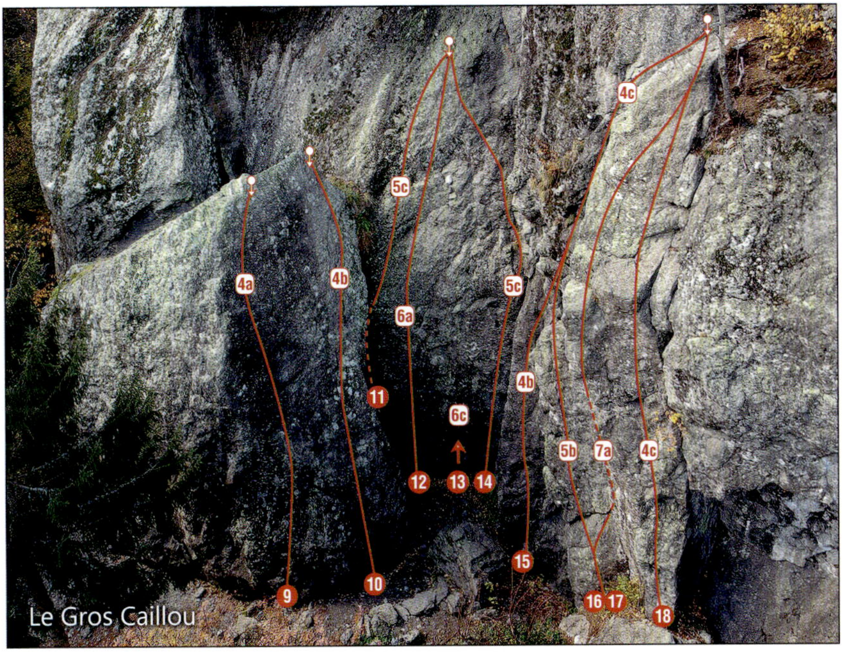
4c
5c
4a
4b
5c
6a
4b
11
6c
5b
7a
4c
12
13
14
15
9
10
16
17
18
Le Gros Caillou

Diamant sector

18 - **La joufflue**: 4c, 15m.

19 - **Attachez vos ceintures**: 6c, 15m. (Pulling up left after the first overhang is not considered as grounds for disqualification...!).

20 - **Bijoux de famille**: 6c, 15m.

21 - **Le diamant vert**: 4b, 10m, beware of the unstable boulder at the exit from the overhang.

22 - **Chulilla Pearl**: 6a, 10m.

23 - **Indiana Jane**: 5b, 10m, stay right after the overhang.

24 - **21 ans d'abnégation** (private joke)... 5c, 15m.

25 - Voie "**ENSA-Marco Troussier n°1**": 6b, 15m.

26 - **T.L.Y.**: 5c, 10m.

27 - **Torrent-ciel**: 5b, 10m.

28 - **Croule Britannia**: 5b, 15m.

29 - **Le voleur de lune**: (2004, Piotr Packowski, Fabrice Monier) 5c.

30 - **Les animaux du désert** (2004): 6a.

31 - **Bijou** (2004): 4b.

The last two routes have been equipped by Piotr Packowski and Fabrice Monier (top parts still to be cleaned and equipped).

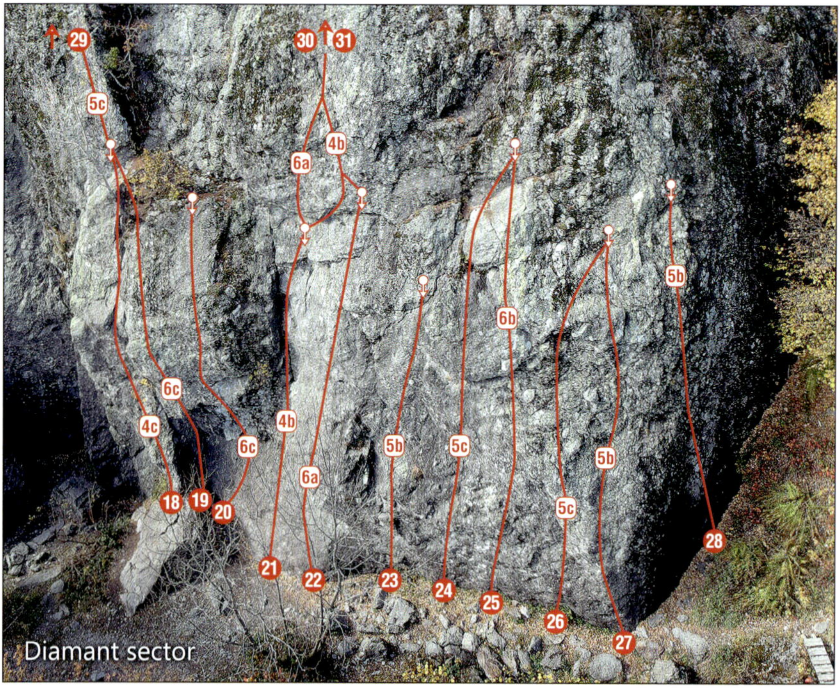

Le diamant vert, 4b

La Grande Muraille (The Great Wall)

This "paravalanche" is an artificial structure in a natural location, and is well suited to introducing beginners to climbing. It is situated on the other side of the stream running alongside the "Diamant vert" area. The routes are equipped and names are written at the bottom.

1 - **Parfum d'Orient**: 3b, 5m.
2 - **Chinoiserie**: 3c, 6m.
3 - **Le yin et le yang**: 4b, 7m.
4 - **Le baiser du dragon**: 5b, 8m.
5 - **Murmures**: 6a+, 6m.

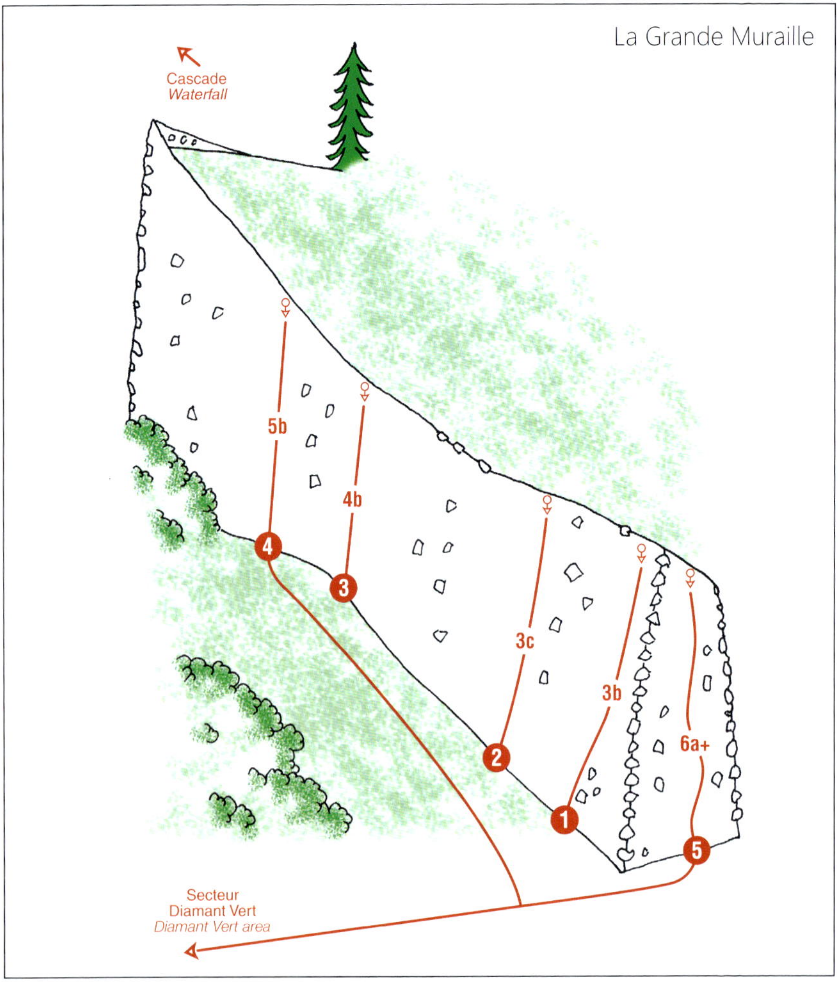

Left hand section

PLAQUE BELLIN

Today the moss cover the rock on the Plaque Bellin. However this place offers nice routes.

Equipment : 15 quick-draws. 70m single rope or 2x50m abseil ropes.

1 - **Le dièdre noir**: 50m. **P1**: 30m, 6a (5b mandatory), one medium side stopper to protect the crack on the first pitch. **P2**: 25m, 5b.

2 - **Dalle de Moenthieu**: 70m. **P1**: 10m, 6c (A0); 5c on the slab. Athletic start. **P2**: 30m, 5b.

3 - **Attack direkt**: 7m, 6c+, then Dalle de Moenthieu.

4 - **?**: 35m. **P1**: 6a+ for the first wall (5b mandatory); then slab climbing 5a. **P2**: 30m, 6a (5b mandatory).

5 - **La Titi**: 70m. Bolts. **P1**: 25m, 6a (5b mandatory), short hoverhang crack. **P2**: 35m, 5c+, slab. Descent: 2 abseils in the route.

6 - **?**: **P1**: 5b; **P2**: 5b.

Chauffria Monolith 1

1400 m SW - E

30'

3

0 0 4 12 15-40 m

This crag is once again gaining in popularity, thanks to the work carried out by some of the young local guides.

Rock : the rock is compact but well sculpted gneiss.

Climbing : 25 routes from 6 to 60 metres long. The climbing is generally quite athletic and a little exposed. The routes are equipped with cemented-in ring bolts or 10 mm expansion bolts with hangers. These are quite spaced out and most routes are committing.

Gear : 15 quickdraws if you climb P1+P2. Single 70m rope or double 50m ropes.

The site : situated in a forest, it is an ideal place for squirrel hunting, mushroom picking climbers. However the approach is on a steep, slippery track which is not suited to non-sporty friends and family who may wish to accompany you. The east face of the monolith and the surrounding crags take a while to dry.

Access : **by train**: La Joux station. **By bus**: Le Lavancher bus stop. **By car**: see page 164.

Approach : (20 mins) the path goes a little bit out of the way so as to avoid crossing private property. Cross the railway line and take the path heading to the north-west. After crossing a stream, climb up a steep path for 50 metres to join the "balcon sud" hiking trail. Turn left and walk in the Chamonix direction for 800 metres, crossing 2 footbridges. After the second one climb a very steep path to reach the crag. The path is marked with blue paint and several cairns.

The routes

EAST FACE AND PILLAR

1 - **Archipel des îles Thy**: 7a+, 35m. Demanded crack.

2 - **Tectonique des plaques à vent**: 7a, 35m. Tricky.

3 - **Pied de Mouton**: 7a, 35m. Athletic.

4 - **La Forêt de Brosse et Yande**: 6c+, 35m. Bouldery problem.

5 - **L'Aspi Râle Infernale**: 6a, 25m. End up in route 4 (to the right of the belay). 6a+, 35m.

6 - **Mémoire de Genoux**: **P1**: 6a, 25m, a good corner; **P2**, 6c, 15m, crack and overhang; **P1+P2**: 6c.

7 - **Pic Aya grimpus**: 6c+, 40 m. Start in route.

8 - **Pic Aya grimpus direct**: 7a.

SOUTH-WEST FACE

9 - **Murray's route**: 7a+,35m. Nice route. Commited.

10 - **Ralf**: 74, 35m. Yellow bolts.

11 - **Super Calou**: 7c, 35m. The line of the spot.

12 - **Tiens voilà du bourrin**: 7b, 35m. Very athletic.

13 - **La Bombe Humaine**: 7a, 35m. An hidden two fingers hold in the first overhang.

14 - **Crache ton venin**: 6b+, 35m. Loose rock section.

15 - **La petite dérobée**: 7b, go left after the sixth point.

NUNU SECTOR

A 15 meters high boulder located 50 meters to the right of the S-W face of the monolith. First points are quite fare.

1 - **Du mou pour minou**: 7a+.

2 - **Nid de poule**: 7a+

3 - **Résistance 2020**: 7b.

4 - **Calamity Julie**: 6b+.

South-east face
35 m
7a
7a
6c+
1
2
3
4

Pillar
35 m
35 m
6a+
6c
6a
6c+
7a
7a+
5
6
7
8
9

Sam Beaugey in Super Calou, 7c

South-west face

Chauffria Monolith 2

1420 m | E - SE

35'-45'

3 4

0 0 3 9 | 20-50 m

Higher up from the Chauffria 1 other towers of gneiss emerge from the forest. The most tapered of them all has been visited by new routers. Several endless pitches and an aerial finish makes for an atmospheric climb.
A dozen routes are open to date. It's a perfect site for those hot summer days.

Rock : the gneiss rock is compact with zones of fragile fractures.

Climbing : some quite steep slabs, followed by short athletic overhangs. As often with gneiss, it isn't easy to read the rock just by looking at it. The quality of the rock is variable, excellent alternates with less good within the same pitch. It is strongly advised to wear a helmet.
An outlying sector below the tower provides 4 interesting shorter pitches of a higher grade.

Equipment : cemented rings and 10mm bolts.

Gear : for the routes on the tower allow between 20 to 25 quickdraws, with several long ones to reduce rope friction. 100m single required to lower off. With shorter rope fractioned the descent on intermediate belay.

The site : magnificent balcony facing the mountain chain.

Access : (plan p. 164) idem for Chauffria Monolith 1.

Approach : see Chauffria Monolith 1. From the South-West side of the first monolith follow the path which leads North-West in the forest (cairns) 10 mins. 40 mins from La Joux carpark.

The routes

LA TOUR

50 meters of non stop climbing. It's also possible to climb most of the tower's routes in two pitches.

1 - **Intelligeance émotionnelle**: 7b, 30m. Tricky crux.

2 - **Green washing**: 7a+, 48m, 22 points. A long route with varied climbing style.

3 - **Kétamine express**: 7a+, 48m. Few quickdraws are already on place. «7a» is written at the bottom. Several loose rock section in the route.

4 - **Slow Rush**: 7b, 48m, 22 points. A beautiful route with increasing difficulty. **P1**: 6c.

5 - **Tour de Babel**: 6c+, 50m, 22 points. An athletic finish, put long sling to limit the friction of the rope. **P1**: 6b.

6 - **2ème dose**: 6c+, 48 m, 23 points. Fragile rock at the bottom, excellent in the second part of the route. **P1**: 6c+.

7 - **Ostracisme Révolu**: 6b?

8 - **Sérotonine**: 6c?

LOWER SECTOR

Situated bellow the tower. Go down the track underneath the start of route 5 to reach the place.

9 - **Click and collect**: 7c+/8a, 20m. Tricky movs.

10 - **Dernière vague**: 7b+, 20m. 2 boulders styles sections

11 - **Salto**: 7a+/7b, 30m. Good balance movements.

12 - **Aboulie**: 6b ?

The Crag Climbs in Chamonix Guide on your mobile
Scan me
whympr
Chamonix-Mont-Blanc
Mer de Glace
Aiguille du Midi
3842m - Sommet
Glacier du Tacul
La Vallée Blanche
Glacier du Géant

Argentière moraine

1300 m

15′

20 14 15 12 5 m

Romains Desgranges spotted these boulders amongst the beech trees in the moraine of the Argentiere glacier while flying over them in a helicopter. After considerable cleaning, "wallid wood" hosted a gathering of climbers during the world cup in July 2006.

Rock : granite blocks 2-5 metres high.

Climbing : crimps on the easiest problems, friction and small features for the rest. Problems are marked with arrows from yellow to black depending on difficulty (as in les Bossons).

Gear : bouldering mat, brush.

The site : 15 or so boulders in the shade of the beech trees. Fast drying. It's hard to miss the famous "Cremerie du Glacier" restaurant on the way, renowned for its tarts and cheese croute specialities. Good for families.

Access : take the main road RD 1506 from Chamonix, take the turning for the Grands Montets lift station at the entrance to Argentiere. **By train**: Argentière station stop, then 5 mins walk to the Grands Montets lift station. **By bus**: Argentière.

Approach : from the Grands Montets car park take the dirt track to the cremerie du glacier and the heliport (300 metres). From the cremerie buvette follow the mountain bike trail to the east, go over the stream (bridge) and go up the stream 100m on the right bank (cairns) then go up the moraine on the left to get to the site.

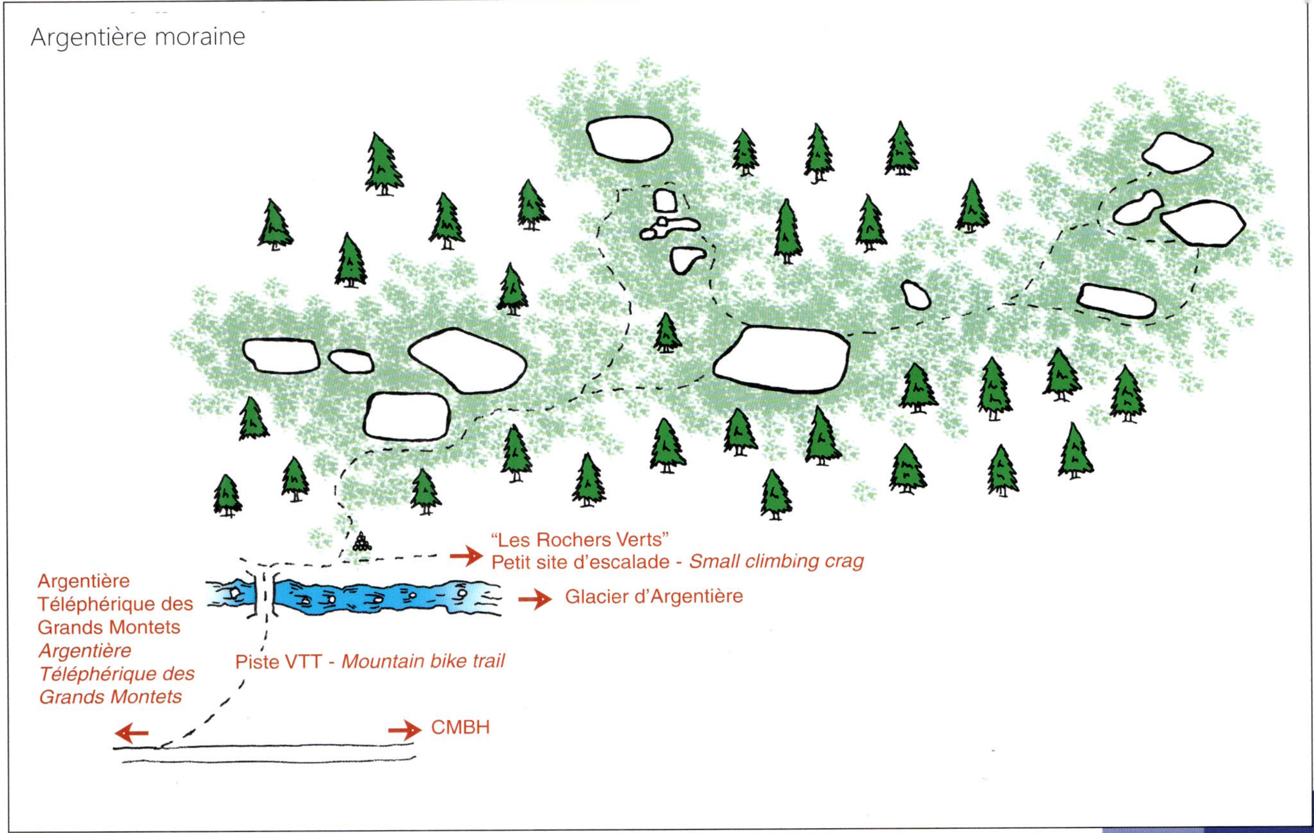
Argentière moraine
"Les Rochers Verts"
Petit site d'escalade - *Small climbing crag*
Glacier d'Argentière
Argentière
Téléphérique des
Grands Montets
Argentière
Téléphérique des
Grands Montets
Piste VTT - *Mountain bike trail*
CMBH

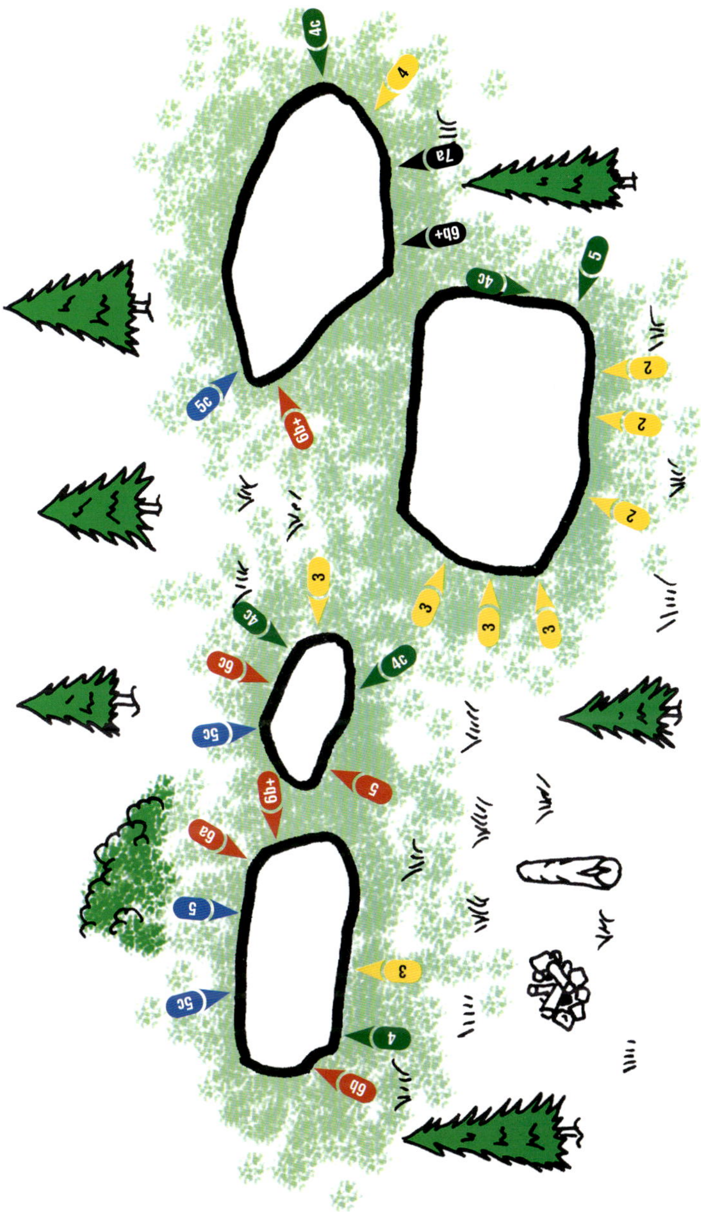
4c
4
7a
6b+
5
4c
2
2
2
5c
6b+
3
4c
3
3
3
6c
4c
5c
6b+
5
6a
5
3
5c
4
6b

Central sector

5c
7c
7a
7b+
7a
5c
3
3
4
6a+

L'Aiguillette d'Argentière

1900 m
SE
60'
3
8 6 4 0 20-150 m

Dominating the village of Argentière, this monolith has seen many an apprentice mountaineer stand upon its lofty summit, posing for posterity. Its first ascent is credited to a shepherd, at the end of the 19th century.

Rock : excellent gneiss, although getting a bit polished on the more popular routes.

Climbing : 17 routes. There is varied climbing on each of the faces and this is a great place to learn. Most of the routes are in the middle grades (4 or 5).

Fixed protection : cemented in ring bolts and 10 mm bolts. The crag has been re-equipped over the past few years by the U.C.P.A. and E.N.S.A. The most recently equipped routes are Biscante, Siesta, Bip-Bip, Pyrene, L'Epine d'Ours and L'Etagne, and the work was carried out by Emanuelle Schmutz, from E.N.S.A..

Equipment : 10 quickdraws and double 50m ropes.

The site : the crag lies opposite the Aiguille Verte and the Argentière glacier Despite the long approach, this crag is very popular in summer. The "Tour of Mont-Blanc" route, passes the foot of the Aiguillette.

Access : **by train**: Montroc station then take the path toward Tré-le-Champ (10 mins). **By car**: from Chamonix (RD 1506), go up the valley to Argentière, then follow the road up to the Col des Montets. 500 metres before the col, at the hamlet of Tré-le-Champ, park in a small car park on the left (10km).

Approach : 1 hour. Follow the Lac Blanc footpath until you get to some metal ladders at the foot of the Aiguillette.

0
500 m
N
Tré-
le-Champ
P
les Frasserands
Tour du Pays
du Mont Blanc
Tour du Mont Blanc
les Chéserys
26
25
Aiguillette
d'Argentière
Argentière

Opposite the Aiguillette

1 - **Civet de porcelaine**: 5b, 30m.

2 - **Plus belle la vue**: 170m. D. Luc Aubertin, François Burnier, Denis Poussin, Septembre, 25th, 2018. 5b obligatoire. **P1**: 5c, 35m. One harder move at the start, followed by a slab with quartz. **P2**: 4b, 25m. **P3**: 6a, 30m. Delicate section on slab. **P4**: 5b, 30m. Traversing left then climb two short steep sections. **P5**: 5b, 45m. Dihedral getting steeper. **P6**: 4a, 25m. A low angle slab. Descent: 5 abseils.

3 - **Déglingomaniaque**: 5c, 45m. Good climb.

4 - **La Fée des Druides**: 150m, D+, 5c (5b mandatory). Jean-Jacques Couton, Francis Ginet. Re-equipped in 2010. Four superb, well equipped pitches. 12 quick draws. 2x50m ropes. Start to the right of a corner. **P1**: 6a, 40m, nice wall on edges; **P2**: 5b, 45/50m, slabe and 2 littles overhangs. 45m to B2, 50 to B2' (comfortable); **P3**: 5a, 40m, slab climbing; **P4**: 5c, 35m, to the left than a crack finish. Descent: the same as route 2.

P1: La Fée des Druides

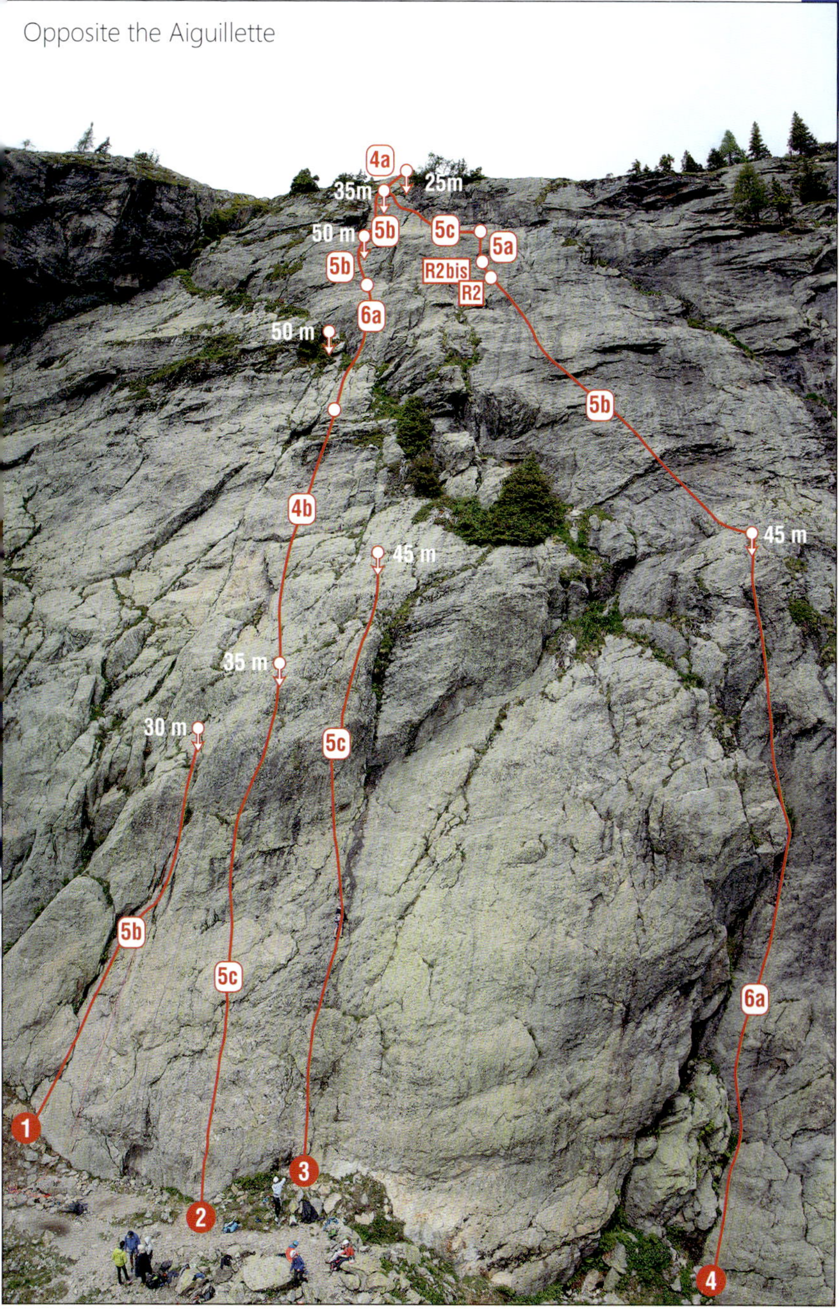
4a
25m
35m
5b
5c
5a
50 m
5b
R2bis
R2
6a
50 m
5b
4b
45 m
45 m
35 m
30 m
5c
5b
5c
6a
1
2
3
4

Aiguillette d'Argentiere above the path

1 - **Bip-Bip**: 5b, 20m.

2 - **Siesta**: 5a, 18m.

3 - **La cheminée**: 4c, 25m; quit the chimney after about ten metres for the slab on the right. From the summit of the pinnacle, a bold step leads back on to the aiguillette.

4 - **La voie normale**: 20m; this route follows the S.W. arete at first, then traverses right, before the overhang: 4b.

5 - **La Rébuffat-Terray**: 5c, 20m (4c for the right-hand variation).

6 - **L'arête NE**: 4c, 20m. Follow a slanting crack left to reach the NE arete (belay advised). Climb the NE arete then traverse right under the summit, 4b.

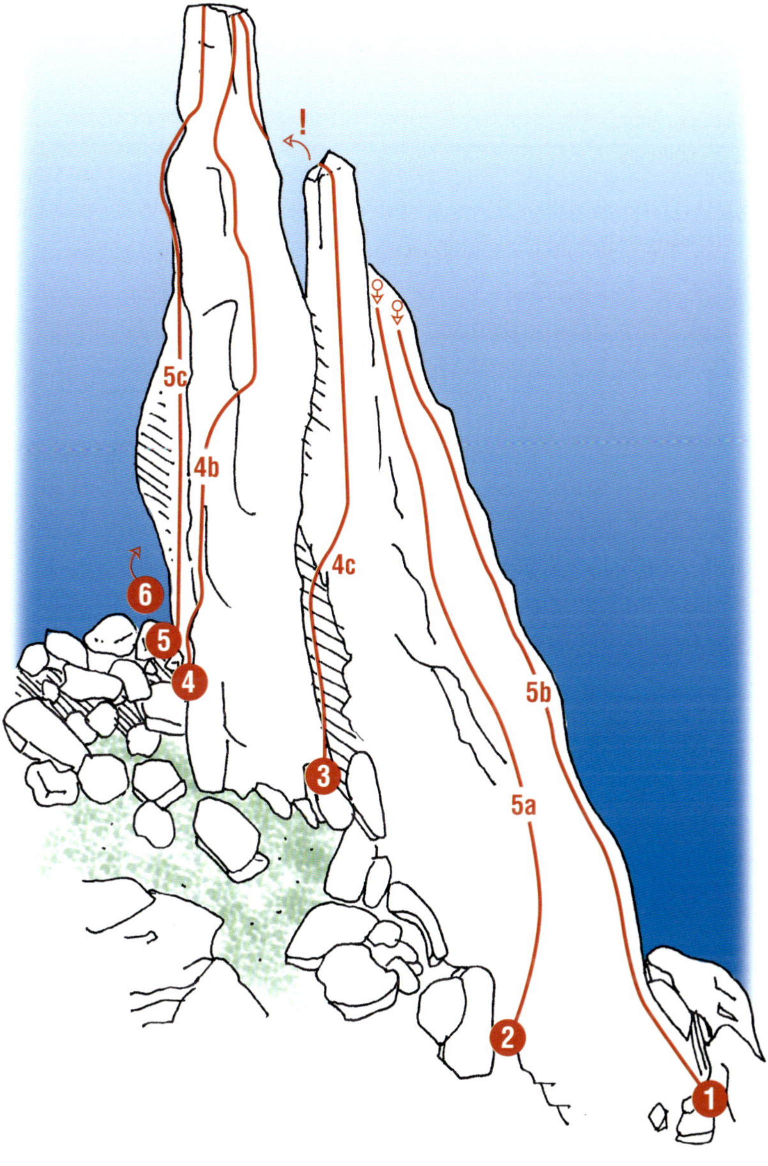

Aiguillette d'Argentière - Above the path

Aiguillette d'Argentiere Integral North-East Ridge

This four pitch route has been named "La Biscante" (Louis Lachenal's nick-name).

Access : reach it by traversing alongside the north face of the "Aiguillette" (cairns). A short 10 metres abseil or downclimb brings you to the start of P3. You can also reach this point directly on foot.

SOUTH-EAST FACE - Two routes have been equipped by Jean-Jaques Couton On the left, 6a+, on the right, 5c.

Access : as for "La Biscante". Cross the notch on the right-hand side of the Petite Aiguillette to reach the foot of the south-east face. There is a hard move at the start.

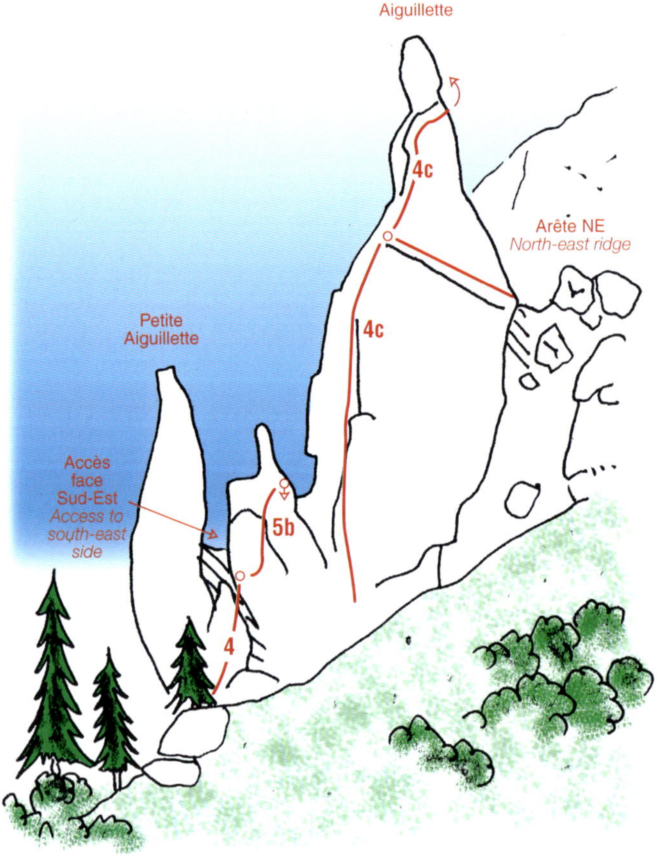

Petite Aiguillette and Gendarme South-West

Lower down is the "Petite Aiguillette", a smaller monolith, climbed for the first time by H. Beaujard and the guide, J. Simond, around 1902, by throwing a rope over the summit! On 1st September 1913, J. de Lépiney free-climbed it, using a devious route which spirals round the pinnacle. The Petite Aiguillette is rarely climbed these days.

- **L'Etagne**: SW face of the Petite Aiguillette, 20m, 6b.
- **Pyrene**: SW face of the SW Gendarme, 24m, 6a+.
- **L'Epine d'Ours**: SW face of the SW Gendarme, 30m, 6a+.

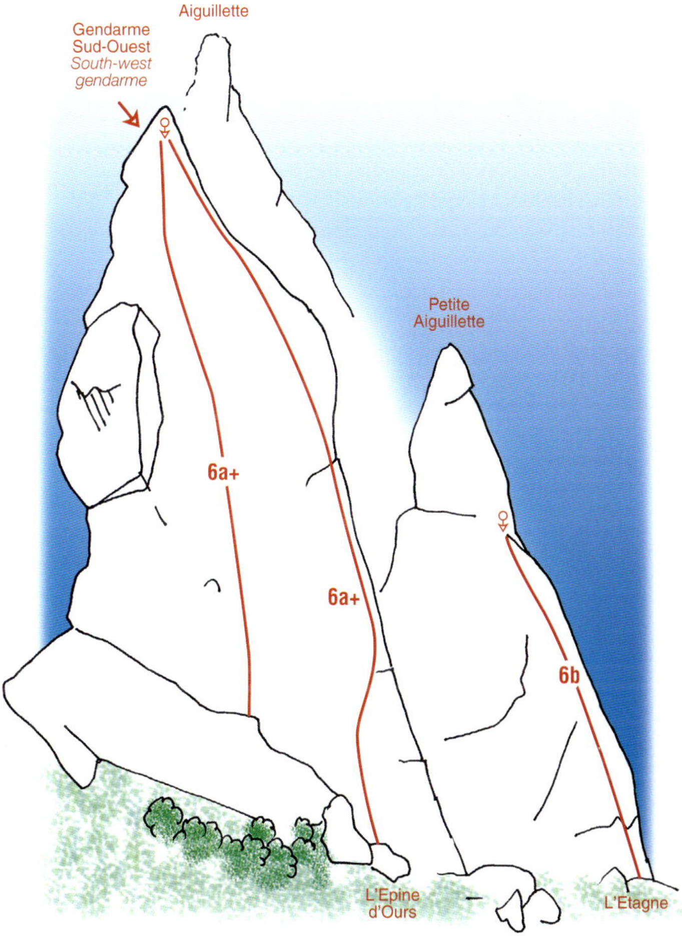

Les Chéserys - Remuaz

1750 m SE

55'

3 4

2 8 10 0 100-240 m

This south-facing crag forms the base of the Aiguilles Rouges. It stretches for almost two kilometres west from the col des Montets. The crag has been a favourite with climbers for over fifty years, for its wide range of routes. Several new routes have been opened up in the last few years. With the entire Mont-Blanc massif as a backdrop, the crag seems to be right in the heart of the mountains.

Climbing : mainly slabs with some beautiful cracks and dihedrals. Minimum level required rarely accedes fifth grade. A guide from Argentière Gilles Ravanel, and René Ravanel opens the first routes during spring 1970: la Rouge, la Jaune, la Bleue et la Blanche. Working at the time at the FIS chairlift, they meant to increase the need for the lift during summer time. The now dismantled lift would reduce access time to the crag to 15 mins only. Nine new and very pleasant lines have also been put up recently by a few individuals.

Equipment : cemented bolts, 10mm expansion bolts, some old pegs. The classic routes were re-equipped in the 80s by the UCPA, and more recently by the EMHM.

Gear : 50m abseil rope, 12-15 quick-draws, slings, set of stoppers for some routes.

The site : these crags are in the Aiguille Rouge nature reserve and you can expect close encounters with marmottes and ibex! The bottom of the routes is flat but watch out for falling rocks.

Access : see pages 186 and 187.

Approach : (55 mins) follow the Lac Blanc footpath for about 40 mins. Pick out the line of chimneys which split the crag vertically, forming the descent route. Reach the foot of these chimneys, where there is an adjacent slab, about 20 metres high. This is the start of "Voie Bleue". Going along the face to the left from here (westwards), there is the start of "La voie de l'EHM" (pegs), then that of "Voie du Psychiatre", and a good 100 metres further on, the magnificent initial slab of "Voie Blanche".

Lady sector: see page 206.

P2: La Blonde, 4b

Aubade sector

Four nice routes are now open on this part of the Cheserys.

Descent : on foot: from top of routes 1,2,4. Walk 100m up to lac Blanc trail. Go left to the next cross then left again to reach the bottom of the face. 30 mins. Abseil (2x50m) the route 1 or 2.

1 - **Une balade pour V.V.**: 250m, D, François & Victor Burnier, Denis Poussin, 2014. **P1**: 5b, 20m, crack then slab; **P2**: 5b, 25m, stepper slab; **P3**: 5c, 25m, one movement on a wall; **P4**: 4b, 20m; **P5**: 4a, 30m slab; **P6**: 4a, 25m, climb up to the right after B5; **P7**: 4a, 25m, climb ledges ledges up to the left; **P8**: 5c, 25m, nice wall; **P9** 4a, 30m, slab.

2 - **Le Blond for ever**: 250m, D+. 12 quick-draws, 2x50 m rope. François Burnier, Denis Poussin, 2013. **P1**: 5b, 25m, slabe; **P2**: 5c, 40m, steppes slave; **P3**: 6a, 40m, overhang and a wall; **P4**: 4a, 50m, B4 on the ledge at the bottom of the pillar; **P5**: 4a, 25m; **P6**: 4a, 25m; **P7**: 4a, 15m, traverse left; **P8**: 5b, 25m, nice pitch; **P9**: 4a, 30m, above the tree.

3 - **Sonate**: 110m, D+, François Burnier & Denis Poussin, 2013. **P1**: 5b, 35m, slabe; **P2**: 5c, 30m, short hoverhang; **P3**: 6a, 45m, steeper slabe.

4 - **Aubade**: 200m, D-, 4c compulsory. Equipped with "Fixe" bolt hangers. François Burnier, Denis Poussin, Robert Lehmann, September 2008 and 2010. The longest route on the Cheserys. A nice little journey. Descent - via abseil. Slab climbing with a few steeper bulges. Nine 30-35 metre pitches. Start on the large boulder at the side of the path (sign "reserve des aiguilles rouges"). Abseil ropes 2x50m.

Aubade sector
3b
4b
4a
5a
4c
5a
4
5b
5b
6a
5c
5b
3
4a
4b
4c
4a
5b
4a
50 m
4a
6a
5c
5b
2
5c
4a
4a
50 m
50 m
4a
4b
50 m
5c
5b
5b
1

"La Blanche" sector

5 - **Voie David et William Ravanel**: 110m, TD. **P1**: 5c; **P2**: 6a; **P3**: 5c. Interesting route, but gear is spaced out and getting old.

6 - **Moulinette**: top rope. 20m, 5c, very well equipped. Shared belay with 4.

7 - **Un Père Noël pour Lucy**: 110m, D+, 5c mandatory. Michel Piola, Jean-Pierre Seydoux, 6 and 10 december 2004. Five good pitches of increasing difficulty. Reassuringly equipped with bolts.

8 - **La Blanche**: 150m, D+, 5b mandatory. A Cheserys classic, with a magnificent slab at the start and the white spot move on P3. Consistant route. Five pitches.

Grimpeur local. ***Local climber***

9 - **Dalle de la Blanche directe**: 35m, 5c, slab of "la blanche" direct, superb variant at the start.

10 - **Dune**: 120m, TD-, 5c obligatory. Michel Piola, 26 and 27 septembre 2006. The most difficult route in this sector. Three long pitches of varied climbing (**P3**: 50m). Slabs and overhangs. Crosses R1: Dune is to the left.

11 - **Désert de Samba**: 120m, TD-, 5c obligatory. Michel Piola, 22nd and 23rd May 2007. A pleasant line you can enjoy without scaring yourself. Fixed bolts. Three pitches of approx 40m.

12 - **?**: 130m, TD, 6a mandatory. Fix golden bolts. Start on the left of the route 11 in a corner. Very nice route. **P1**: 5c, 40m. Crack and corner followed by a traverse to the left; **P2**: 6a, 35m. A slab, the crux is when you reach the belay; **P3**: 6b, 25m. Well protected pitch. A short overhang section; **P4**: 6a, 45m. Short boulder problem at the start. Rappel in the route 15 recommended.

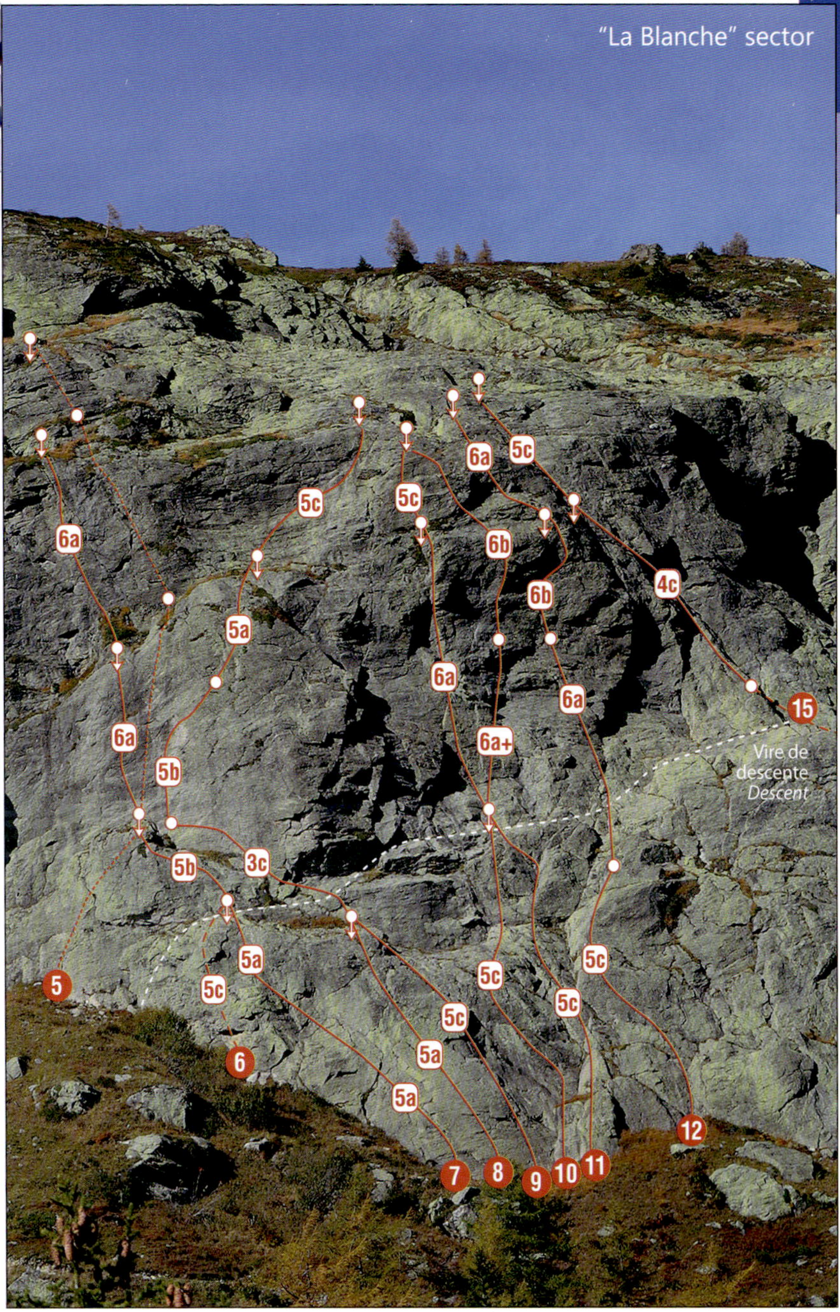
"La Blanche" sector
6a
6a
5b
5c
5a
5b
3c
5a
5c
5c
6a
6a+
5c
5a
5c
5a
6a
5c
6b
6b
6a
5c
5c
4c
Vire de descente
Descent
5
6
7
8
9
10
11
12
15

"La Bleue" sector

13 - **Voie du Psychiatre**: 150m, AD (well spaced on the easy sections). Six pitches with the easiest at the top. The route crosses the descent route at the top.

14 - **La gamate**: 30m, the fixed protection is not great, nice 5c slab.

15 - **L'EHM**: 150m, D+, 5b obligatory. Superb final pitch.

16 - **Sur le fil**: 30m, 5c. Alternative start to EHM.

17 - **La Bleue**: D+, 150m. Another Cheserys classic. Beautiful, varied climbing. The corner on the second pitch witnessed many a hopeful aspirant guide sweating their way up in big boots in the 70s!

18 - **Dalle de la Bleue directe**: 25m, 5c.

19 - **Belle...** D+. 150m. Unavoidable moves of 6a. Name at the bottom. **P1**: 4c, 20m, nice slab climbing; **P2**: 5c, 30m; **P3**: 4a, 30m, easy slab; **P4**: 6b+, (A0/6a), 25m, traverse to the right a steep wall; **P5**, 5b, 25m. Abseil route 13.

20 - **Douce renaissance**: 150m, D-, 5c (compulsory 5a). Consistant route on good rock. Jacqueline & André Grobéty, Anne-Lyse Jost, May 2011. Starts 25m to the right of "La Bleue". Silver "Kinobi" bolt hangers. **P1**: 30m. 5b. A delicate move on the pillar; **P2**: 35m. 5a. A wall with inverted moves; **P3**: 35m, start move 5c (compulsory 5a), then 4b; **P4**: 35m. 4b. Follow the ramp to the right towards the tree; **P5**: 5a. Descent with 4 abseils: the second abseil point is left of the route.

Descent : routes 5, 6, 7, 10 and 11: abseil the route. Other routes: via the central pillars reached by down climbing (watch out for rock fall) to a small ledge with anchors. Five abseils. The last two abseils can be avoided by traversing west, towards Mont Blanc, and following the sloping slabs approx a hundred metres reaching a small wall (3c) at the end. This is the fastest way down.

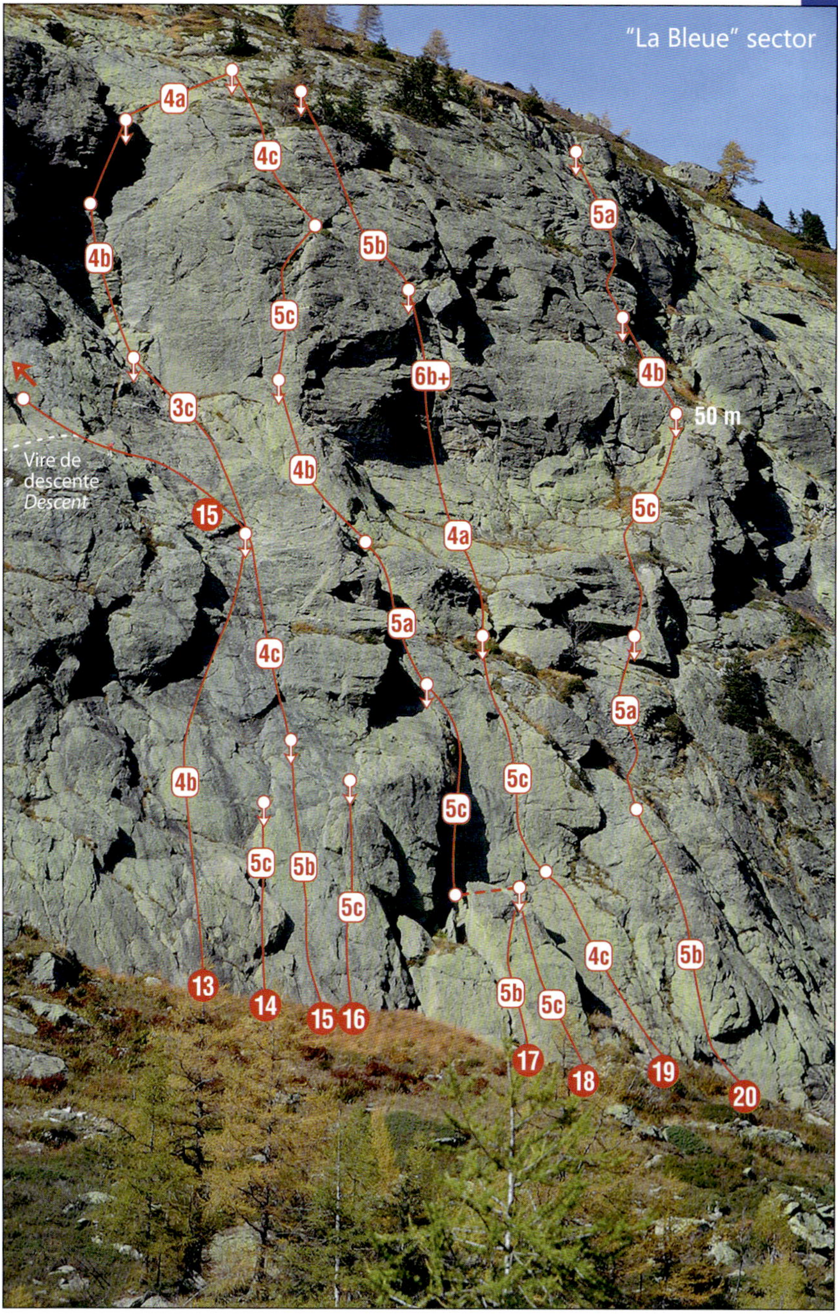
"La Bleue" sector
4a
4c
4b
5b
5c
5a
6b+
3c
4b
50 m
Vire de descente
Descent
15
4b
4a
5c
5a
4c
5a
5a
4b
5c
5c
5c
5b
5c
5c
4c
5b
5b
5c
13
14
15
16
17
18
19
20

"La Jaune" sector

100m on the right of the dirt area at the foot of la Bleue there are three nice, well- equipped lines. Descent - abseil the route (2x50m). 12 quick draws.

21 - **La Noire**: poor protection.

22 - **La Brune**: 130m, TD -, 5c. André Grobéty and Pierre-Alain Chevalley, October 2009. **P1**: 6a+, 45m, slab; **P2**: 25m, 6a (5c compulsory), go around the overhang to the right; **P3**: 5a; **P4**: 6a, exposed move; **P5**: 4a. Name of the route is written at the bottom. Descent - abseil the route. Descent of R2 only with a 60m abseil.

23 - **La Blonde**: 150m, AD+, 4b obligatoire. André et Jacqueline Grobéty, Anne-Lise Jost, septembre 2009. Nice route on very good rock. "Fixe" bolt hangers. Name written at the bottom. **P1**: 30m, 5a; **P2**: 30m, 4c; **P3**: 30m, 4c; **P4**: 35m, 4c; **P5**: 5b.

24 - **La Jaune**: 150m, AD. Cemented bolts. Opened by the Argentiere guides in 1969. Varied climbing; ideal route for first go at lead climbing. **P1**: 4b; **P2**: 4b; **P3**: 4a, inclined corner; **P4**: 3c; **P5**: 4c. 20 - 30m pitches. Descent - abseil the route.

"La Jaune" sector
4a
6a
5b
5a
60m
4c
4c
6a
3c
4c
4a
6a+
4c
4b
21
22
5a
4b
23
24

"La Rouge" sector

Located 10 mins from the main crag, away from the path to Lac Blanc, with some interesting routes. Abseil rope (2 x 50m). 12 quick draws.

Access : follow a small path towards the east that follows the rock face (5 mins). After going down a scree slope (the path gets a bit lost amongst the boulders), you will see the start of the Rouge route, and the foot of the rocky hump.

25 - **La Rouge**: 150m, AD+, cemented bolts. Good slab climbing. Slightly aerial, but bolts are well placed on the harder moves. **P1**: 5a, slab with a section on flakes; **P2**: easy slab; **P3**: 4c, steeper exit; **P4**: 4c; **P5**: 4c; **P6**: 4b; **P7**: 2. Descent - abseil the route.

26 - **La Rousse**: 150m, D, 5b mandatory. André and Jacqueline Grobéty, September 2009. "Fixe" bolt hangers. Start 10m to the right of la Rouge. Name written at the start. **P1**: 5a, slab; **P2**: 4b, slab; **P3**: 5b and 4a; **P4**: 6a (compulsory 5b), short overhang; **P5**: 5b. Descent - abseil the route.

27 - **Greg Bufat**: 150m, AD, 5a (4c mandatory). Access: at the foot of the previous routes, traverse 5 mins to the end of the ledge. Start on a pillar. Petzl bolt hangers. **P1**: 4a, to the right of the pillar; **P2**: 4c, short jump; **P3**: 4c, follow the white slab; **P4**: 4a, traverse the couloir. Follow on to the right, 3b; **P5**: 4a, slab. Descent - abseil the route.

28 - **Sortie Ravanel**: 80m. Same start as R3 Greg Muffat. Traverse the couloir then go up on the left, 4c; **P2**: 4c, a slightly aerial traverse on the left; **P3**: 5a, crack. Descent - abseil the route.

"La Rouge" sector

"Lady" sector

Two routes opened by the sadly missed Jean Louis Le Garrec and Laurent Collignon. The 280 meters climb on some great slabs provide for a very enjoyable vertical escapade.

Approach : 45 mins. From the Tré-le-Champs carpark follow the path to Les Chésery, Aiguillette d'Argentière. After the wooden walkway the path leads up through the forest, continue on a first zigzag then a second bigger one. The path becomes rocky as it takes you slightly down to meet a small stony stream bed. Turn right leaving the path by a small boulder (cairn). Follow the little path for 10m and turn left.

29 - **Lady**: 280m, D-. Laurent Collignon et Jean Louis Le Garrec 12th September 2019.
Follow the base of the wall for 100 meters, the name is indicated at the foot. The equipment is spaced further apart in the easier portions, be careful not to lose your way between the points. The rock is more compact after the R4. Direct alternative route in L8 on a steeper wall. Last belay on large platform, ideal for picnics.
Descent: 7 abseils (2X50m ropes). Belay stations 6, 7 and 8 are to the right of the route.

30 - **?**: 6b.

31 - **Penny Lane**: 280m, D-. 5b mandatory. August 3rd and September 29th, 2019. Laurent Collignon and Jean Louis Le Garrec.
Start on the beautiful pillar along the path. Slab climbing on good rock.
Descent: 6 abseils (2X50m). Belay stations 3, 4, 5 and 6 are to the left of the climbing line.

"Lady" sector
29
30
31

Area 07

Le Chenavier
Le Col des Montets - Argentière side
Le Col des Montets - Vallorcine side

Le Chenavier

1550 m — SW

35′

2

4 2 1 0 — 20 m

This small beginners crag is not well known. It is on the south side of the Posettes mountain, in the middle of a beautiful larch forest.

Rock : huge granite boulder.

Climbing : 10 routes equipped wit expansion bolts and cemented-in rinc bolts. At the bottom, a pile of large, eas boulders gives something to amus adults and children alike. Above, a "gen darme", about 20 metres high, has sev eral easy, equipped routes. A small cra on the left also offers several equippe routes, of two short pitches.

Access : see page 212.

Approach : (35 mins). From the car park on the right, before the Col des Montets follow the footpath leading to the Aiguil- lette des Posettes. Just before the track leading back down to Le Tour, take tc the bush on your left in the direction of the crag, which you can make out in the distance. Find your way to the bottom of the main tower (15 mins).

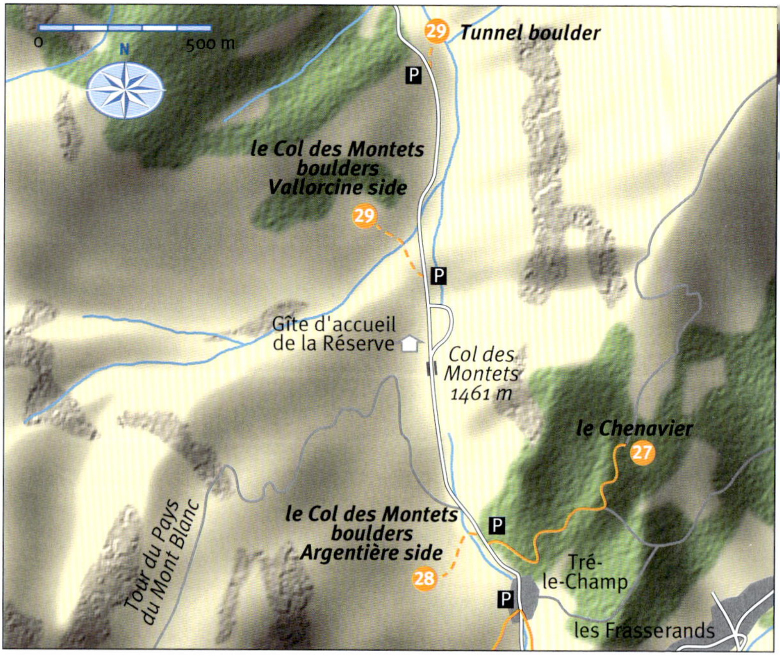

Le Chenavier

Left rock, east side

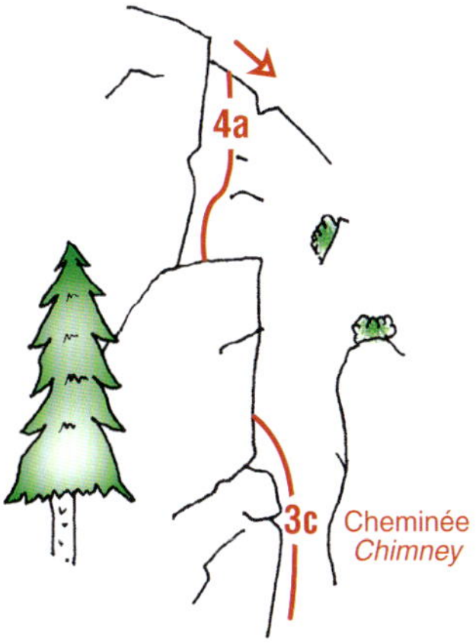

Left rock, south side

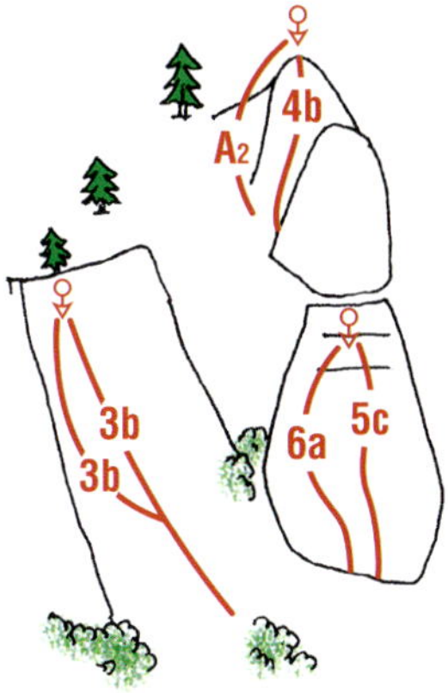

The Tower

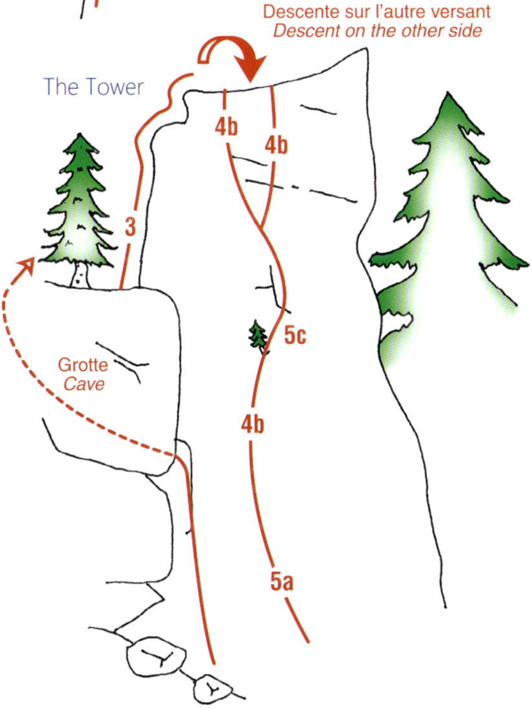

Le Col des Montets - Argentière side

1400 m

5′

12	16	26	7	3-5 m

About twenty boulders lend themselves to all manner of gymnastics. The seven classics are described here. Even though these boulders have been used by climbers for many years, it is always "rediscovered" by each new generation.

Rock : hard gneiss, which seems to wear well despite the passing of many feet.

Climbing : 80 boulder problems.

The site : the col is a windy place and the boulders dry quickly. The surroundings are bucolic, with a great view over the Aiguille Verte and the Argentière glacier. In summer, the crowds in the "square" are enormous (Transat area) here, Mr. and Mrs. Average-Gumby mix with the Chamonix jet-set. For spectators, note that the "rock-jocks" get going at around 7 p.m.

Access : map page 210. **By bus**: line V2 stop at col des Montets (bus services work during the summer). **By train**: Montroc train station. Take the foot path toward Tré-les-Champs then col des Montets, (20 mins). **By car**: from Chamonix, take the main road (RD 1506) past Argentière, towards Switzerland. About 300 metres before the col des Montets, there is a large car park on the right. The boulders are opposite.

Argentière side

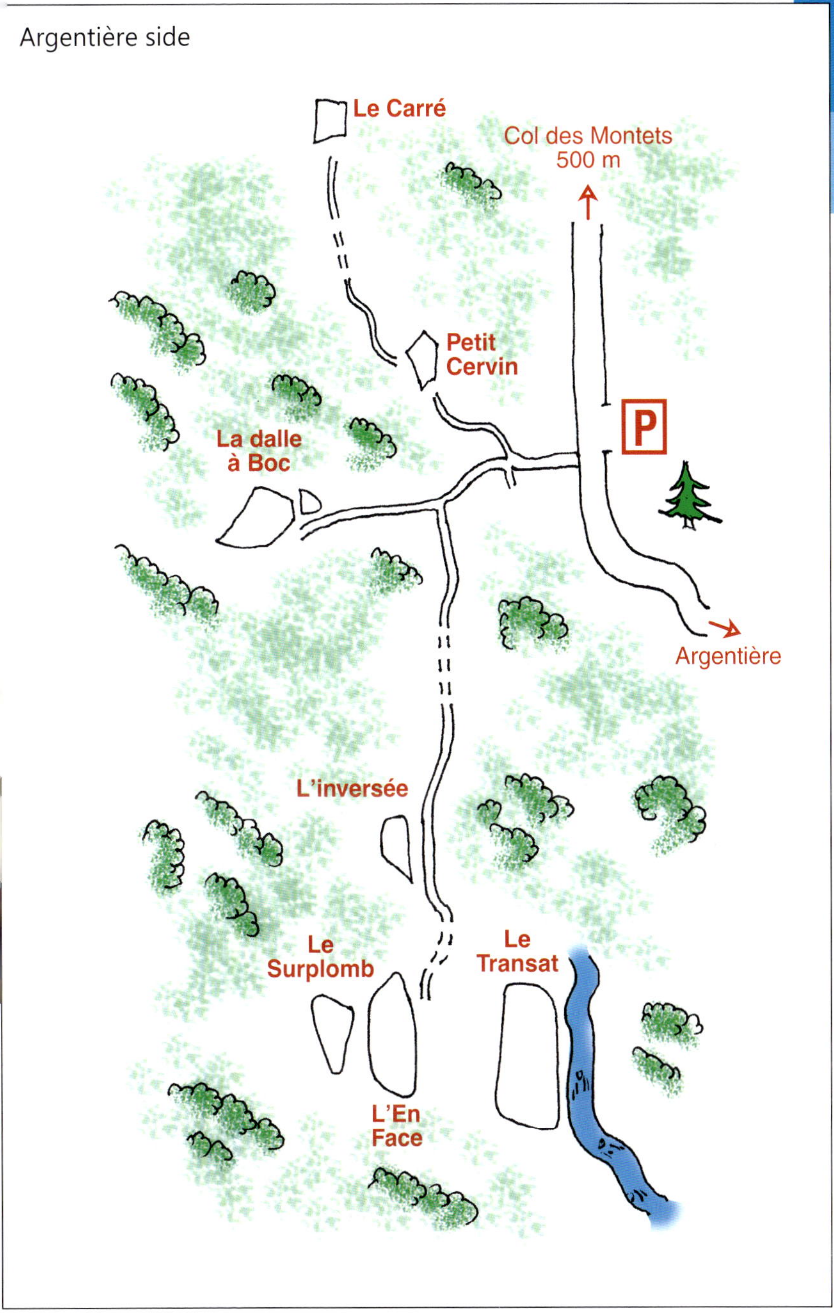

Le Petit Cervin

This "little Matterhorn" has seen some traffic!

- **Voie normale**: the north arete, 2c.

1 - **Face NE**: 3c.

2 - **L'arête de droite**: 4c, fairly committing finish.

3 - **La directe**: 5b/5c, fairly committing finish.

4 - **La fissure**: 4c, LA classic, fairly committing finish.

5 - **L'arête du Petit Cervin**: uses holds in opposition, 7a.

6 - **La salière**: famous little overhang, given this name (la salière = the salt pot), because of a small hole, reached with the fingertips, 6c.

7 - **Le tour**: one move de 5c/6a.

Le Carré

Situated to the north east of the "Pet Cervin", interesting and not too popular

1 - **Côté Route**: 4c.

2 - **Les manolles**: 4c.

3 - **Le Pilier**: 6c.

4 - **Le surplomb**: 6a.

5 - **L'arête**: 5b/5c.

6 - **La demi-lune**: 5c.

7 - **La Traversée**: A - A, one move de 6b

8 - **Zénitude**: 6c+.

9 - **Le tour du Carré**: 7c, 8a from righ to the left.

Le Petit Cervin

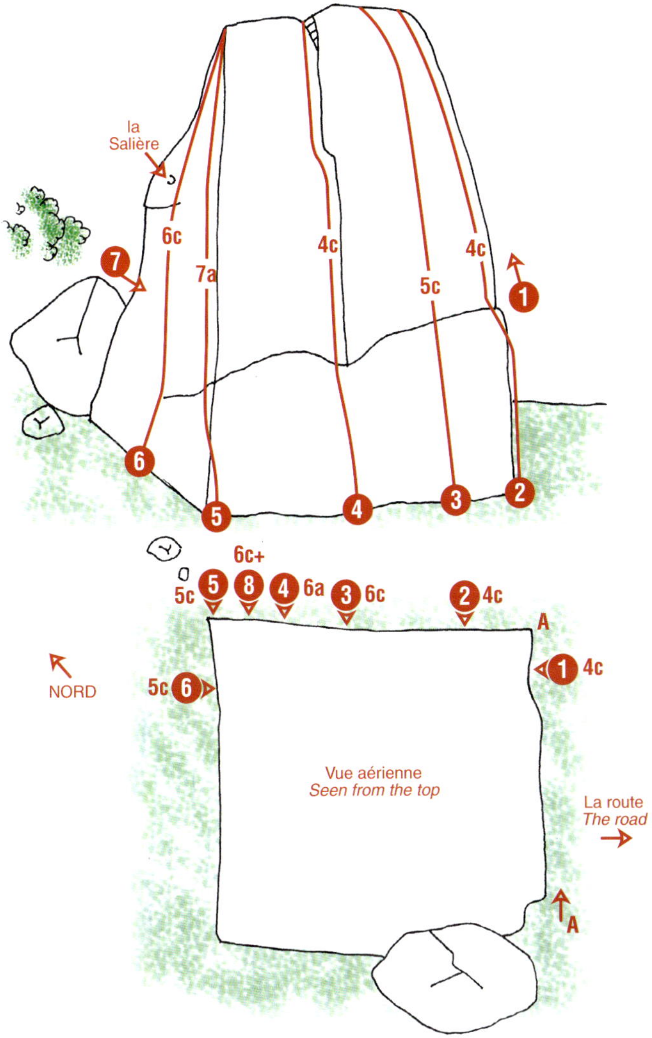

Le Carré

Le Petit Cervin
7
6c
7a
4c
5c
6
5
4
3

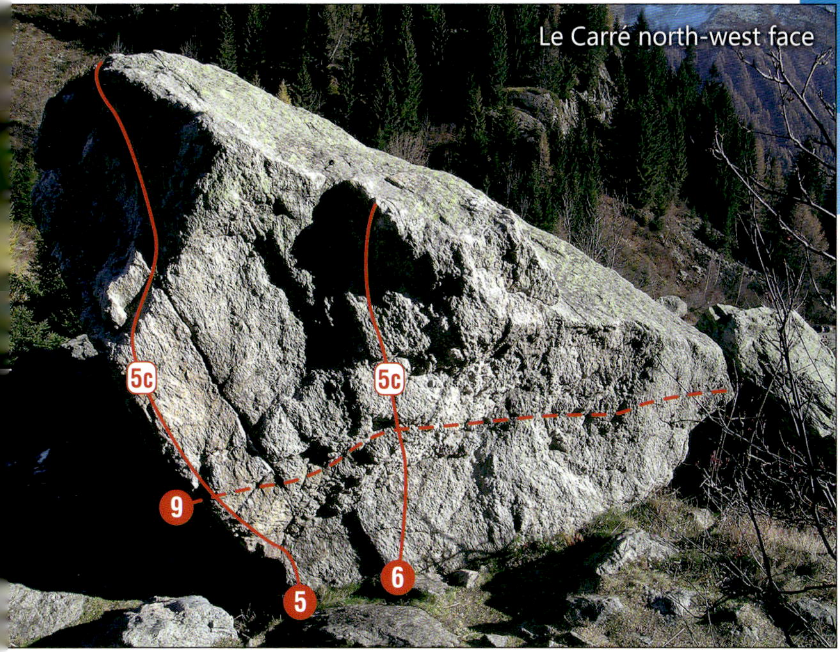
Le Carré north-west face
5c
5c
9
5
6

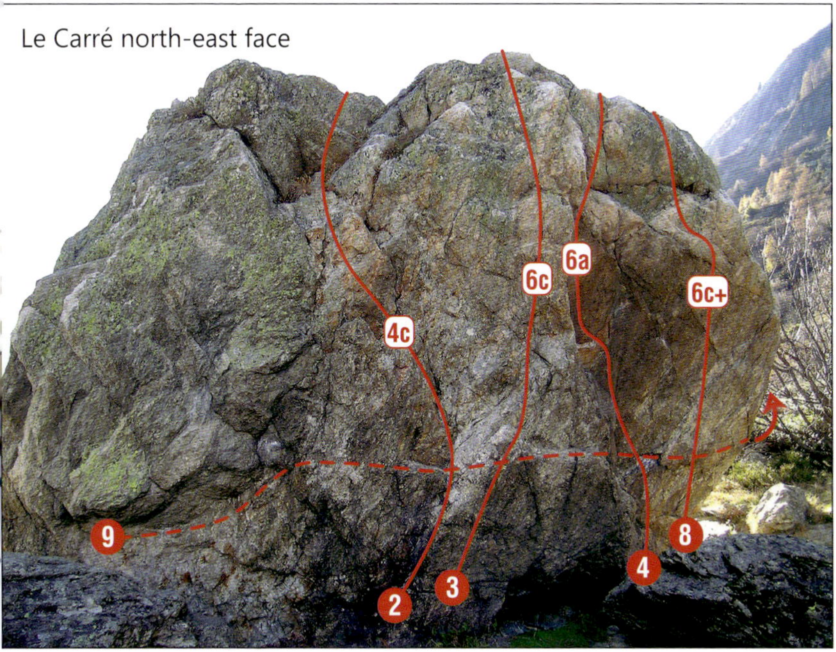
Le Carré north-east face
4c
6c
6a
6c+
9
2
3
4
8

La dalle à Boc

A 7m, easy angled slab, good for beginners.

1 - **Le coin**: 5c.

2 - **La dalle**: 3b.

3 - **La dalle directe**: 3c.

4 - **La voie normale**: 2b.

On the other side, there is an interesting traverse in grade 3b.

L'Inversée

A small boulder, barely 3m high, situat ed beside the path leading to the bigge classic boulders.

1 - **La facette**: 3c.

2 - **Les sucres**: 6b.

3 - **L'inversée**: 5c/6a.

4 - **L'inversée directe**: 6a+.

5 - **Voie normale...** 1c.

Transat et l'inversée south face

La Dalle à Boc
2b
3c
3b
5c
4
3
2
1

L'Inversée
6a+
3c
6a
6b
5
4
1
3
2

Le Transat

The most popular boulder at the Col des Montets. There is an old anchor point on its summit. The "Tour du Transat" consists of linking 6 on the south face, 9 on the west face, 12/13 on the north face and 2 and 4 on the east face: 7b for the whole.

NORTH FACE

1 - **Courte voie d'initiation**: easy descent on the right, 3b.

2 - **L'escalier**: 3c; can be done without hands... 6a+.

3 - **L'escalier**: direct finish": a bit committing, 4c.

4 - Slab 5b, committing finish.

5 - **La fissure de droite**: 4c, committing finish.

6 - **La fissure de gauche**: 4c; without using the left hand: 6a+.

7 - **Le bénitier**: 5b, committing finish.

8 - **Les p'tits trous**: 6b.

9 - **La réglette**: 6a; (5c for the very tall!).

10 - **L'aplat**: 5c; without using the left hand... 6c.

11 - **Le petit mur**: 6a.

12 - **La traversée du haut**: C ← B ← A, 5c.

13 - **La crispette**: traverse which leaves the "Bénitier" horizontally: E ← D, 6b.

14 - **Sois souple, aie des doigts**: F ↔ G, traverse about 1 m from the ground... for contortionist basketball players!... 7b+.

EAST FACE

1 - **Le rétablo du haut**: one move of 5c.

2 - **Le cochon pendu**: traverse on heel hooks: one difficult move to get round the corner, 6b+.

3 - **Bien au chaud**: traverse without using the arete, 7c+.

4 - **Le rétablo du bas**: finish to the "cochon pendu" traverse in reverse (forms part of the "tour du Transat"), 6a+.

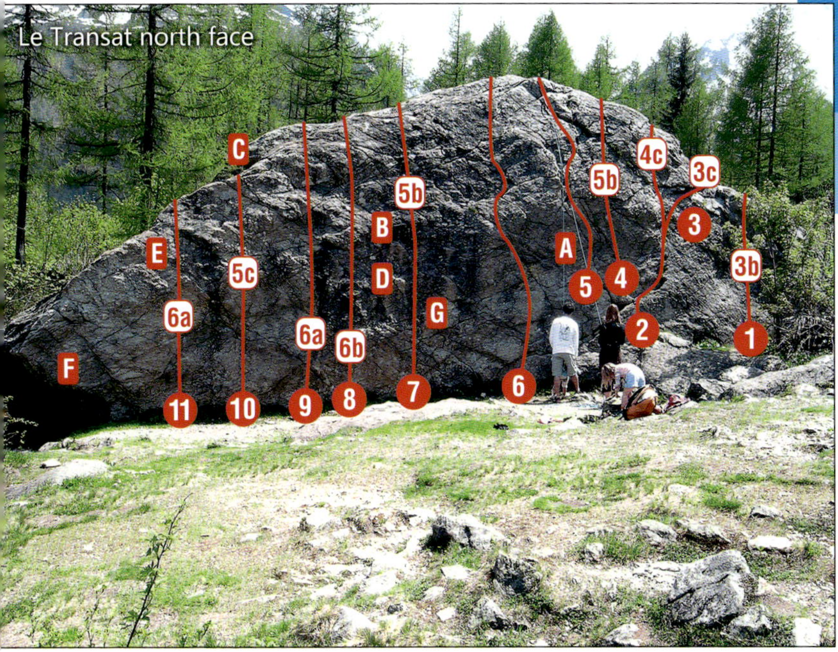

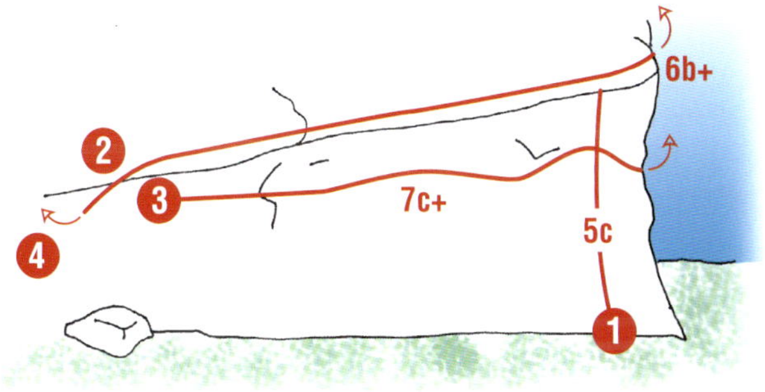

Le Transat east face

Le Transat, contd.

WEST FACE

1 - **L'écaille**: 3c, slightly committing finish.

2 - **La pincette**: start practically sitting down, both hands under the undercling, in a "squat" position. The flakes on the right are out of bounds. The key move is the pinch for the left hand, 7b+.

3 - **Le nez**: jam for the right hand, 6b. Starting sitting down is called "les doigts dans le nez", 7b+.

4 - **Le dièdre surplombant**: classic, 5c.

5 - **L'équilibriste**: 6c+; finishing to the right: 7a+.

6 - **Le grand pas**: 4c.

7 - **Du genou**: 4c.

8 - **La traversette**: 5b.

9 - **La traversée sous le nez**: A ← A, 7a+.

10 - **La traversée du haut**: B ← B, 7b+, a subtle heel hook.

11 - **Le Tour du Nez**: after "la pincette" (2), do "la traversée du haut", descend "le dièdre surplombant" to reach "la traversée sous le nez", then back to "la pincette", etc... 7c+.

12 - **La nausée**: link "le Tour du Nez" (stopping under "le nez"), with "les doigts dans le nez" (see 3), 8a.

13 - **Ras les pâquerettes**: traverse C ← C en below the good holds, 8a.

14 - **L'embrouille à Mômô**: go straight from the starting hold of "10", to the "letter box" of "9": the tall are at a slight advantage...

SOUTH FACE

1 - **Le surplomb**: 5c, quite committing.

2 - **La Desmaison de droite**: 6b, committing finish.

3 - **La Desmaison centrale**: 6b+, committing finish.

4 - **Au-dessus des bassines**: 6b, committing finish.

5 - **La grenouille**: 6c+, committing.

6 - **La traversée au-dessus de l'eau** ... B ← A, an absolute "must". Usually done from right to left. It's the last move that's hard...! 6a à 6c.

Le Transat west face
4c
5b
8
7a+
3c
B
B
7
4c
C
A
5c
6b
7b+
A
6c+
C
6
5
4
3
2
1

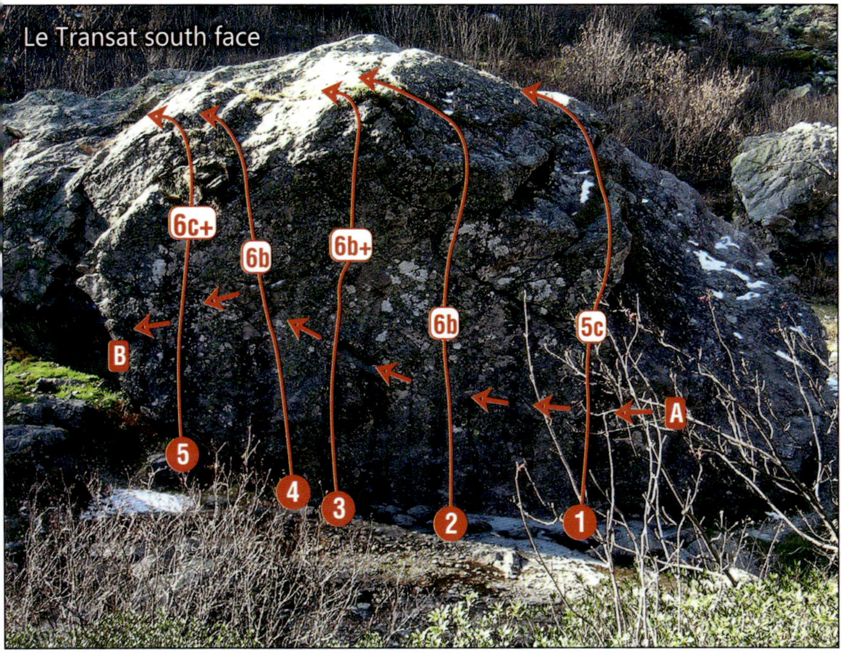
Le Transat south face
6c+
6b
6b+
B
6b
5c
A
5
4
3
2
1

L'En face

A "Montets" classic, about 5 metres high.

1 - **La traversée en face nord**: long reach welcome... 6a+.

2 - **Le petit pas con**: 5c/6a.

3 - **La grise**: 5c.

4 - **La croix**: wide stretch for the legs, and balance, 6c+.

5 - **Tourne ta main**: 7a+ : scandal! A chipped hold...

6 - **La dalle à Mora**: 6a+.

7 - **La grosse écaille**: 5b, classic.

8 - **La sortie expo**: 6a+.

9 - **Le Pilier**: 6a+.

10 - **Le surplomb d'angle**: 5c, "leg hook"

11 - **C'est pas si simple**: 6a.

12 - **Encore une gillouterie**: start as fo "La Croix", finish direct: 7b+.

13 - **Traversée**: A → A: 7a+.

Le Surplomb, face N

An overhanging boulder, 3.5m high. Good for sustained traversing, back and forth. On the south face, "la Zappette": 4c.

1 - **La barre fixe**: 5c; sfor the bold, can be finished facing out, back to the rock, by swinging your legs over your head (spotter recommended!) 6b?

2 - **Le surplomb à droite**: 6a.

3 - **Le surplomb au centre**: classic, 6a.

4 - **Le surplomb à gauche**: 6a+; without using the feet, hanging start, 7b... can be done by "dyno-ing" from the lower flakes to the summit arete with both hands!

5 - **La cul à cul**: traverse A ← A, start and finish sitting, 7b.

6 - **La Totale**: traverse A ← A ← X, 7b+.

7 - **Traversée du haut**: B ← B, 6b: the idea is to do as many return trips as you can... Possible without using the feet: 7c.

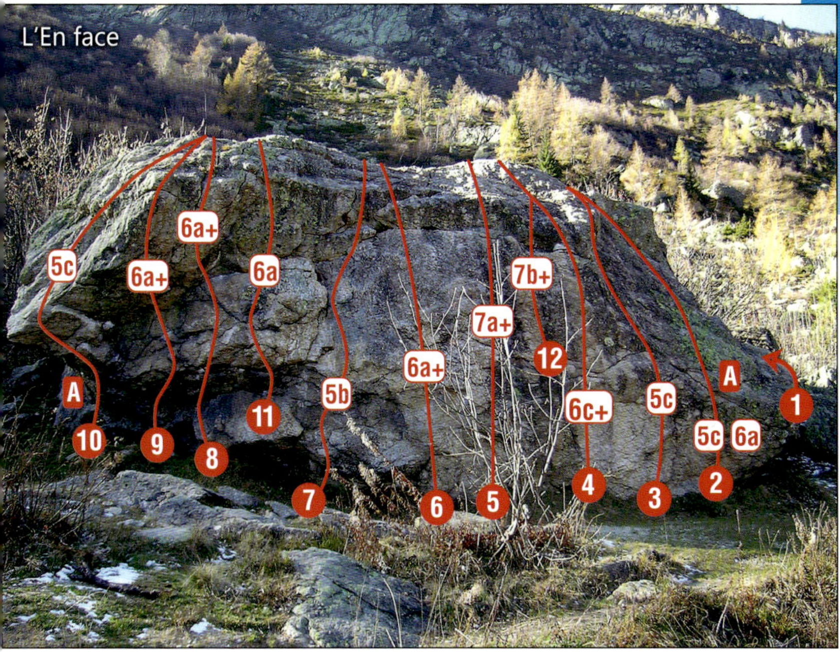
L'En face
5c
6a+
6a+
6a
5b
6a+
7a+
7b+
12
6c+
5c
A
1
A
10
9
8
11
7
6
5
4
3
5c
6a
2

6a+
B
A
6a
B
6a
5c
4
3
2
1
A
X
Le Surplomb

Le Col des Montets - Vallorcine side

1460 m

5'

15 | 10 | 18 | 8 | 4-10 m

40 boulder problems. There are many boulders on the other side of the Col des Montets, where the road descends to Vallorcine.

The rocks here are higher and more overhanging than those on the French side. The difficulty and continuity of the problems allow extreme and complicated variations and combinations of routes.
The highest boulder has an easy side where beginners can take their first steps on rock, or learn to abseil.
At the back of this book, you will find step-by-step photographs of the best traverses.

Access : see page 210. Pass over the Col des Montets in the direction of Vallorcine park 200m lower down on the right, on the old road.

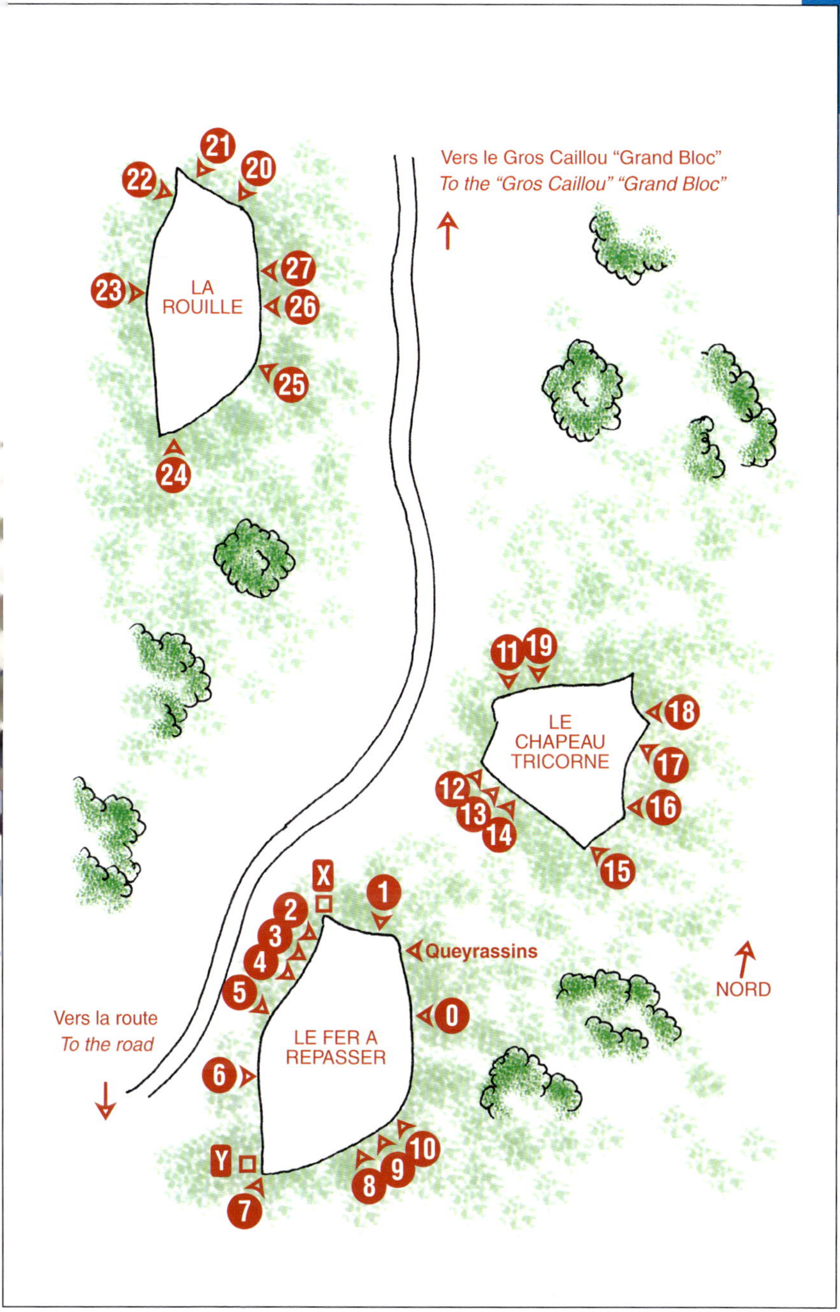
Vers le Gros Caillou "Grand Bloc"
To the "Gros Caillou" "Grand Bloc"
LA ROUILLE
21
22
20
27
23
26
25
24
11
19
LE CHAPEAU TRICORNE
18
17
12
13
16
14
15
X
1
2
3
Queyrassins
4
5
NORD
0
Vers la route
To the road
LE FER A REPASSER
6
10
Y
9
8
7

Le Fer à Repasser

0 - **Que c'est fin!...** 7a+.

0' - **La voie des Queyrassins**: 6b.

1 - **La voie normale**: 3c.

2 - **Le trottoir**: 5c, committing finish.

3 - **La cubelle**: 6a, committing finish.

4 - **L'écartelé**: 6b+, committing finish.

5 - **La fissure**: all depends on getting the sequence of the first moves right, 7b/c.

6 - **A grandes brassées**: 6a, pleasant.

7 - **L'arête**: 4c, committing finish.

8 - **La dalle à crispettes**: 6c+, committing finish.

9 - **Petit toit par la gauche**: 6c, committing.

10 - **La sucre**: 6b, committing.

X → Y - La traversée du Fer à Repasser (very low down!), 8b.

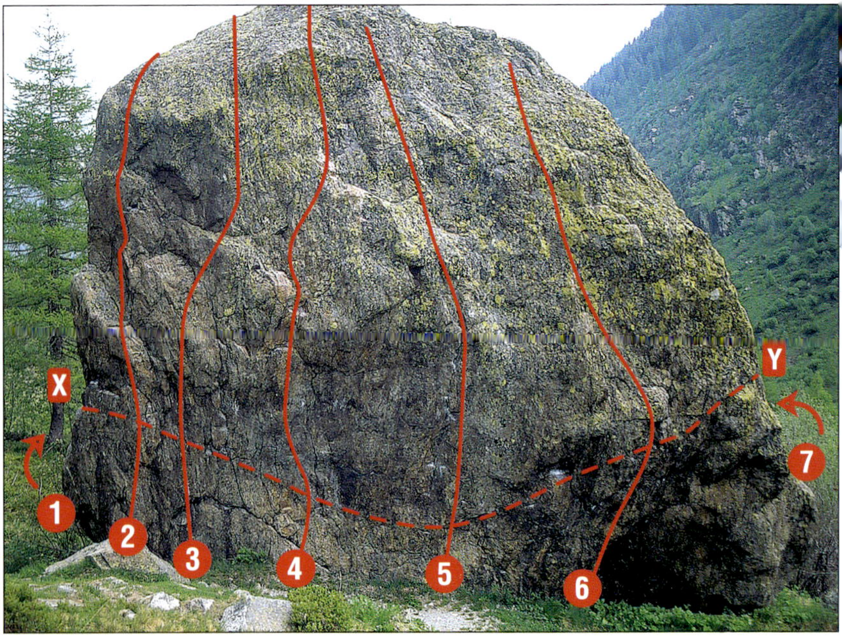

Le Fer à Repasser south-east face
6c+
6c
7a+
6b
8
9
10
0
0'

Le Tricorne

See page 227.

11 - **Voie normale**: 3b.

12 - **Pince-moi**: 5c.

13 - **Pince-mi**: 5c.

14 - **Le p'tit dièdre**: 5b/5c.

15 - **Les pieds dans la s'moule**: 5c.

15' - **Variante**: 6a.

16 - **La grande marche**: 5b.

17 - **Le surplomb, classique**: 5c.

18 - **L'agonie des limaces**: 5c.

19 - **A gauche de la V.N.**: 3c.

19' - 4a.

de 13 à 16 - **Traversée Ravanat**: 8c/c+?

La Rouille

See page 227.

20 - **La voie normale**: 3b.

21 - **Carlos**: 4b.

22 - **Mauvaise surprise**: 6a+.

22' - **Sitting start**: 6c+.

23 - **L'expo**: 6b+.

24 - **La fine arête**: 5b.

25 - **L'arrosoir**: 5b.

26 - **Dalida**: 4c.

27 - **Dalid haut**: 5b.

28 - **Le tour de la rouille**: great, 6c+ (hard between 22 and 23).

Chapeau tricorne south-west face

Chapeau tricorne east face

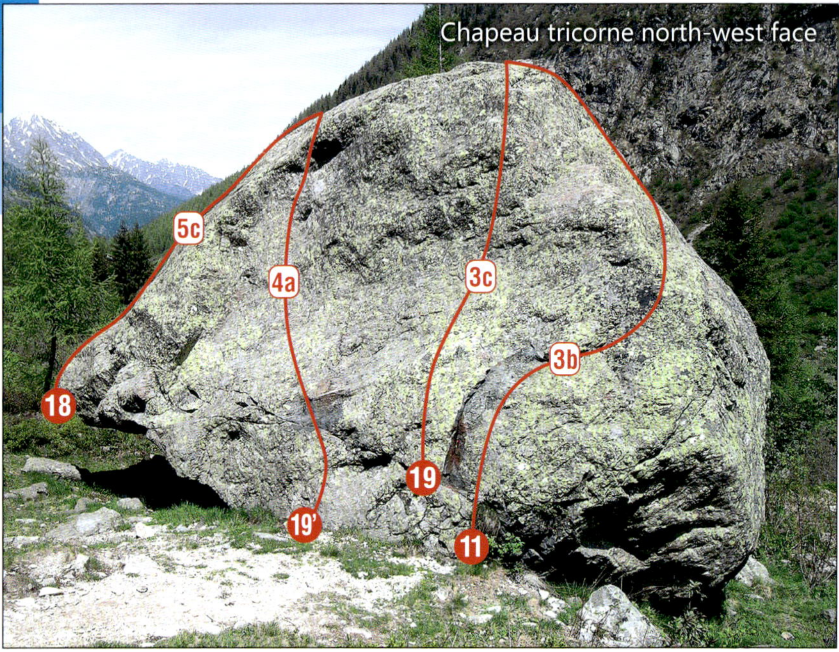
Chapeau tricorne north-west face
5c
4a
3c
3b
18
19'
19
11

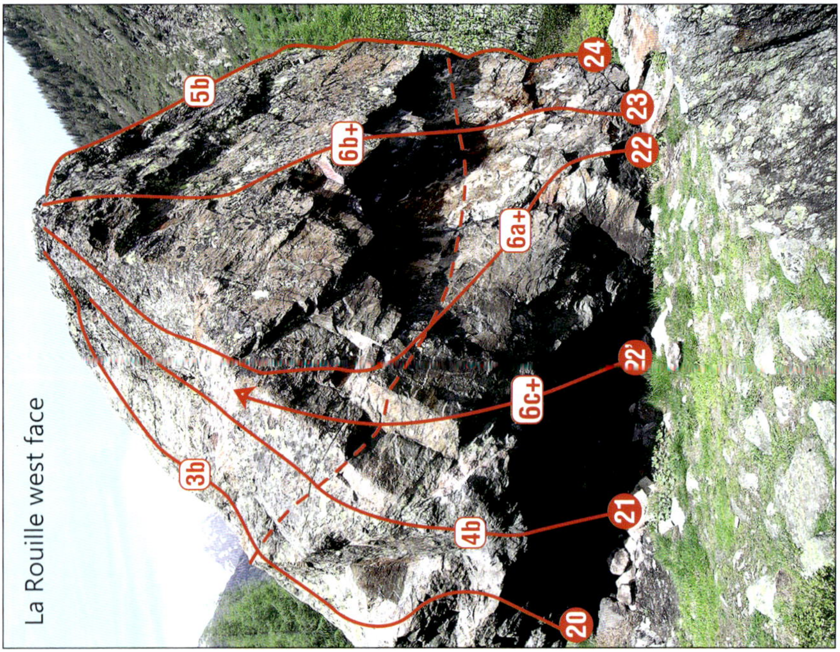
La Rouille west face
5b
6b+
6a+
6c+
3b
4b
24
23
22
22'
21
20

Le Grand Bloc

We describe here the south-west face of this boulder, a kind of "wailing wall". The east face is excellent for beginners; an anchor on the top allows safe top roping. The boulder is a good 10 metres high; its abrasive rock is very hard on the fingers. The routes on the south-west face are all difficult, and are top roped; the traverse called "Passe Muraille" is one of the best problems on the col.

1 - **L'arête**: 4c.

2 - **J'té dans la peau**: 7b+; as its name suggests, (jeté = dyno), a fiendish dyno to finish.

3 - **Tour de prise**: 7b.

4 - **Les cupules**: a beautiful classic, 7a+.

5 - **La randonnée des mutants**: 6b.

6 - **Le petit dièdre**: 6c+.

7 - **Les vieux clous**: old semi-artificial line, 6b.

8 - **La passe-muraille**: traverse A ↔ A, splendid, 7a+.

9 - **Basse-tension**: the lower traverse B ↔ B, 7c.

NOTE: on the north face, besides several committing problems which are not often climbed, there is a superb traverse, devised by Marco Troussier.

Tunnel Boulder

This large boulder close to the Vallorcine railway tunnel, is 500 metres before Buet village. It is visible from the road, and lies below it to the right. Its' south-west face is over 10 metres high and contains several great routes for beginners. Easily accessible anchor points make it easy to put in a top rope. There is parking along the main road but beware of busy traffic. Better parking can be found on the Vallorcine side of the Col des Montets, with a 200 metre walk along the road.

1 - 5m, 3a, slab + corners.

2 - 8m, 3b, corners + easy slab.

3 - 10m, 3c, overhang with athletic move, easy finish.

4 - 10m, 4c, idem.

5 - 12m, 6a, banked start, delicate holds to finish.

6 - 12m, 6a+, idem.

7 - 12m, 6b, energetic start, good crimps to finish.

From A to B: 6a traverse.

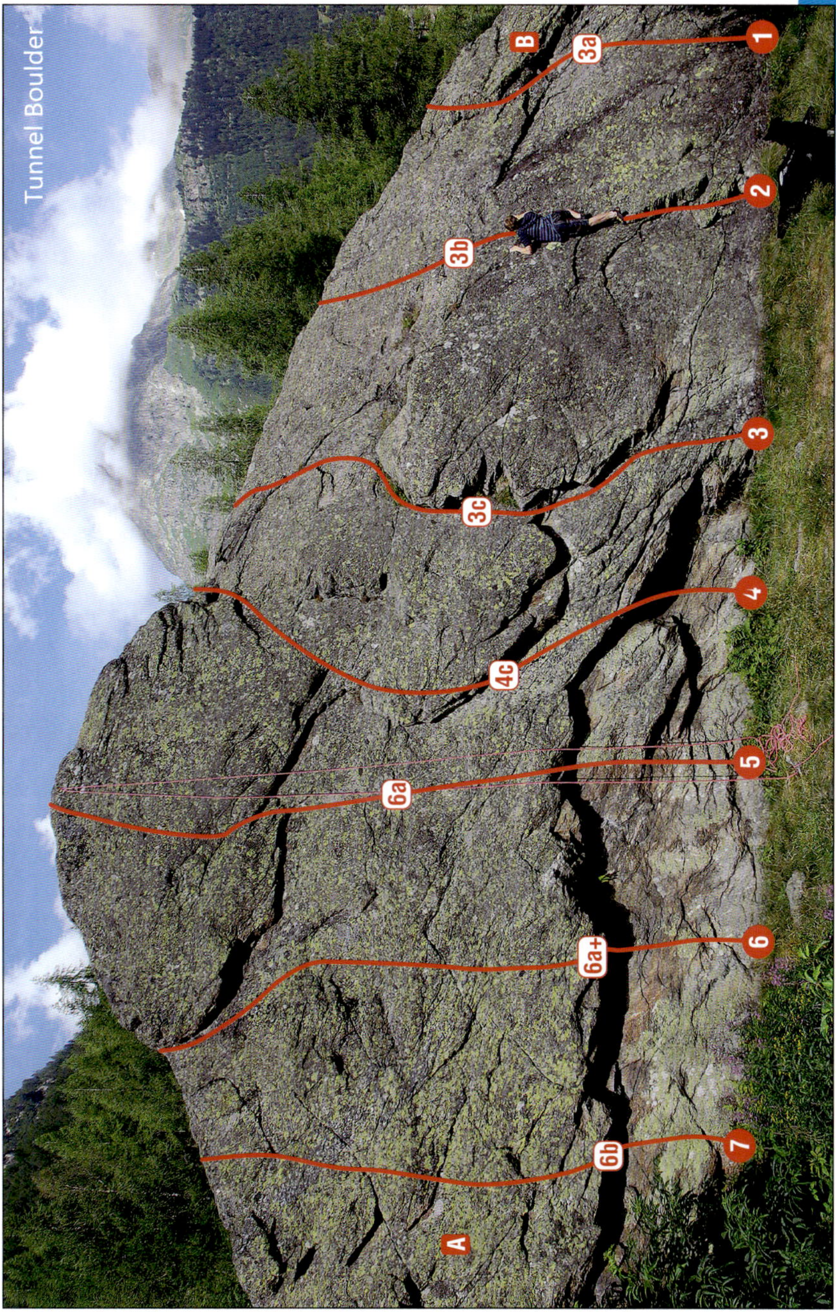
Tunnel Boulder
B
1
3a
2
3b
3
3c
4
4c
5
6a
6
6a+
7
6b
A

Area 08

Vallorcine rocher du Saix
Vallon de Bérard - Tête des Mesures (N-W)

Vallorcine rocher du Saix

1300 m | NE

15'

3 4

13	9	6	1	10-100 m

This excellent crag, with its ease of access, great rock, and varied climbing in the easier grades, is ideal for learning how to climb. A victim of its own success, however, the crag nowadays becomes overcrowded in the summer months, especially at the start of the week.

Rock : granite

Escalade : 25 routes. Vallorcine is perhaps the best granite crag in the whole region, especially for climbers at around 4b/4c and 5c/6a, who will find here a variety of climbing typical of granite; friction slabs, laybacks, corners... (the only kind of climbing not represented is a good "Chamonix" chimney...) The crag is about 100 metres high, and offers about 20 routes. Fixed protection is, on the whole, excellent, although a few routes are poorly equipped or have little fixed protection. WARNING: never use the chain at the top of the crag for belaying, it is simply a hand rail. A very convenient descent route has been equipped (metal ladders) on the left hand side of the face. Abseil descents are to be avoided, as they lead to pointless crowding on the belays (however, there is a line of abseil descent on the left; 2x50m).

The site : the crag overlooks the wooded slopes and meadows of the Vallorcine valley. The base is accessible to non-climbers.

Access : **by train**: Vallorcine train station. **By car**: from Chamonix (15km) take RD 1506 towards Switzerland. Car-park at Vallorcine train Station.

Approach : (10 mins), from the train station, cross the railway, then turn right. Reach a field and continue for 50m to take a path to the left that leads to the crag.

0
N
500 m
Vallorcine
Train station
le Morzay
30 Site d'escalade
les Montets
le Couteray
Cascade de Bérard
le Buet
la Poya
Buet Train station
Tour du Pays du Mont Blanc
31 l'Île aux Razmokets

Right-hand section

PILLAR

1 - **Retour aux ours**: cracks and slabs. 85m. **P1**: 30m, 4b; **P2**: 4b, 20m; **P3**: 4a, 25m, a nice Dülfer; **P4**: 4c, 20m.

2 - **Pilier de Vallorcine**: a typical Vallorcine climbing style. 85m. **P1**: 4b, 20m, cracks and slabs; **P2**: 4c, 25m; **P3**: 4c, 20m; **P4**: 4c, 20m.

3 - **La bourse ou la vie:** 55m. **P1**: 5a, 25m; **P2**: 4c, 20m. Then take route n. 2.

4 - **La cage aux vols**: 7a, 25m. Boulder problem.

CORNERS

5 - **Torre Dülfer**: 90m. **P1**: 3c, 35m untill the terrace; **P2**: 4b, 25m; **P3**. 5b; **P4**: 4c.

6 - **Variation of route 5.**

7- **Dibsy**: 5b, 12m.

8 - **Courage, dülfons!** 100m. **P1**: 5a, 20m; **P2**: 4c, 20m; **P3**: 3c, 20m. Climb the corner; **P4**: 5b, 25m; **P5**: 4c, 20m.

GRAND SLAB

The routes described below start from the "terrasse médiane", and are on a magnificent granite slab, with several narrow vertical cracks running up. The grades may seem a little severe, but will be understood after getting used to the crag. Cemented-in bolts and rings, take 15 quickdraws.

9 - **Point d'Interrogation**: 6b, 25m. Inox bolts. **P2:** 4c.

10 - **Traces de Grizzli**: **P1**: 6a+, 35m. Slabs and beautiful cracks. **P2** take route 11.

11 - **L'écume des ours**: **P1**: 6b+/c. Inox bolts, 30m, balance with very small holds. **P2**: 30m, 5c.

13 - **Dièdre couché**: 5a, 20m.

14 - **Variation route n. 13**: 5c, 20m, technical.

Rocher du Saix
Descente
Descent
20 m
25 m

Left-hand section

LARCH TREE SECTOR

The large number of routes and their proximity brings confusion. It gives a large choice of combination.

12 - **Le plantigrade magnésophage**: 100m, 4 pitches. Be careful! Fixed protection has been removed on P3 crack. Take small sized "Friends" or chocks. Also called "left-hand pillar" ("pilier de gauche").

15 - **Le dièdre de la dernière flèche**: 50m, 2 pitches: the first has a little fixed gear. Nice finishing move. **P1**: 6b, 35m. Technical slab. **P2**: 4b, 20m. Slab.

16 -**Crocs mignons et vieilles dentelles**: 100m, 5 pitches, equipped. **P1**: 5c; **P2**: 5c, 20m; **P3**: 4c, 20m, climb left of the rings (spits); **P4**: 4c, 20m (corner); **P5**: 4c, 20m.

17 - **La vache qui rit**: 50m. **P1**: 6b, 30m, thin crack.

18 - **Oursonne... le glas!** 40m, 5 pitches, equipped. Very varied climbing.. **P1**: 6a, 20m. Steep slab. **P2**: 4a, 20m.

19 - **Lune de miel**: 40m. **P1**: 5b, 20m, cracks; **P2**: 5b, 20m, nice slab.

20 - **La guerre du feu**: 6a+, 15m. A nice crack.

SHORT CLIMB SECTOR

Very busy in summer.

21 - **Batman**: 5a, 20m, 6 quickdraws. A short athletic movement.

22 - **Superman**: 4c, 20m, 6 quickdraws

23 - **Spiderman**: 4b, 20m, 6 quickdraws. Slab.

24 - **Riri**: 4c, 20m, 7 quickdraws. Slab.

25 - **Garfiled**: 4c, 28m, 12 quickdraws.

26 - **Pluto**: 5a, 30m, 12 quickdraws.

27 - **Dingo**: 3c, 23m, 11 quickdraws Slab.

28 - **Les Daltons**: 4a, 23m, 11 quickdraws.

29 - **Rantamplan**: 4b, 20m, 12 quickdraws.

30 - **Les escargots**: 3c, 20m, 12 quickdraws. Slab.

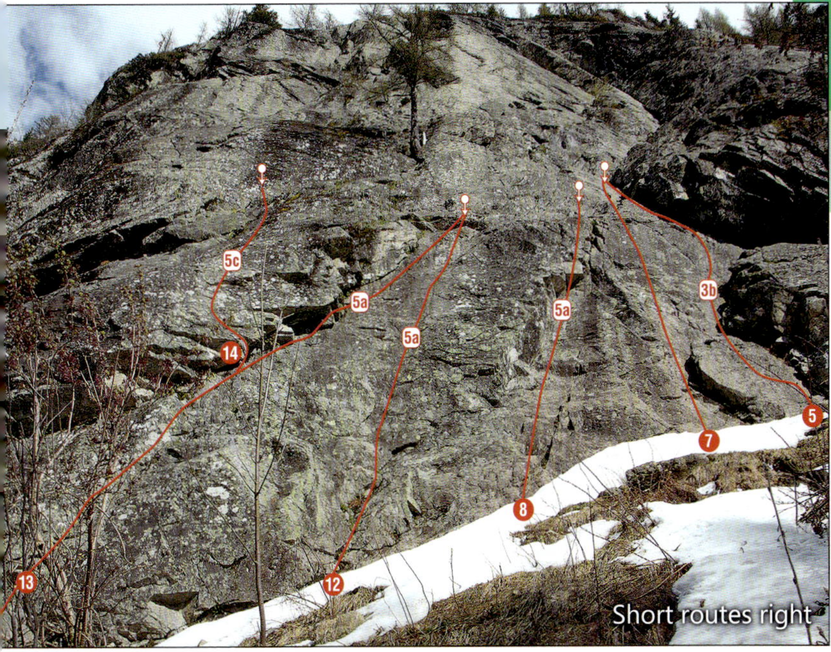
5c
5a
5a
5a
3b
14
5
7
8
13
12
Short routes right

Short routes central
5c
14
5c
5a
5a
4c
13
22
21
16

Vallon de Bérard - Tête des Mesures (N-W)

1586 m | NW

45'

3

0 0 2 0 | 320 m

Nice climbing in a rural setting. 320m slab. Exposed to the North-west, a pleasant to climb early afternoon onwards.You are likely to see resurgences after heavy rain, slow to dry due to overgrowing vegetation, especially on the upper wall.

Rock : compact gneiss.

Climbing : mostly slabs.

Access : **by train**: "Le Buet" train station. **By car**: from Chamonix (13km). Take RD 1506 towards Switzerland. One kilometre after the "Col des montets", just before the Buet hamlet, park on the right in front of the path leading to the "Crèmerie de la cascade de Bérard".

Approach : go to the "Crèmerie de la cascade de Bérard" (10 mins), and continue on the path leading up to the Pierre à Bérard mountain hut. When the path goes across the stream (15 mins), keep to the right bank (on the left when going up) and follow a small and vague path to the base of the crag.

Gear : 13 quickdraws, 100m abseil.

The routes

1 - **Ile aux Razmokets**. TD-. 320m. Sylvain Ravanel, Rodrigue Passy, 2001 classic route in the fifth grade, with even difficulty. Bolted, 13 quickdraws, 50m half ropes. At the base of the face, follow a narrow couloir to reach a ledge and start of route. **P1**: 5a, 30m. Traversing up to the left towards a horn looking knob. Obvious line, well-protected. After belay station R8 follow the narrow trail up the ledge to reach a steeper wall section. Access by abseiling down the route. Rope length just makes the belay stations at : R12 à R10, R6 à R4 (make a knot at the end of your ropes). Beware: at R2, abseil line straight down, and belay station in a chimney.

2 - **Ombre et lumière**. TD. 220m. Stéphane Durand, Corinne Meheut, Emmanuel Ratouis. Summer 2014. Beautiful route on slab, along the left side of the face. Some " nastier" sections. Bolted, 13 quickdraws, 50m half-ropes. Once at the base of the face, look for an isolated bolt. **P1**: 5c+, 45m. Slab with dubious flakes. **P2**: 6a+, 30m. Nice bulge, somewhat athletic. **P3**: 6a+, 30m. Slab, with a series hand-foot mantles. **P4**: 6a, 20m. Some delicate harder sections. **P5**: 6a+, 25m. Still delicate with a final boulder move. **P6**: 6a, 25m. **P7**: 5b, 25m, slab followed by a steeper section on big holds. **P8**: 4a. Descent by abseiling down the route.

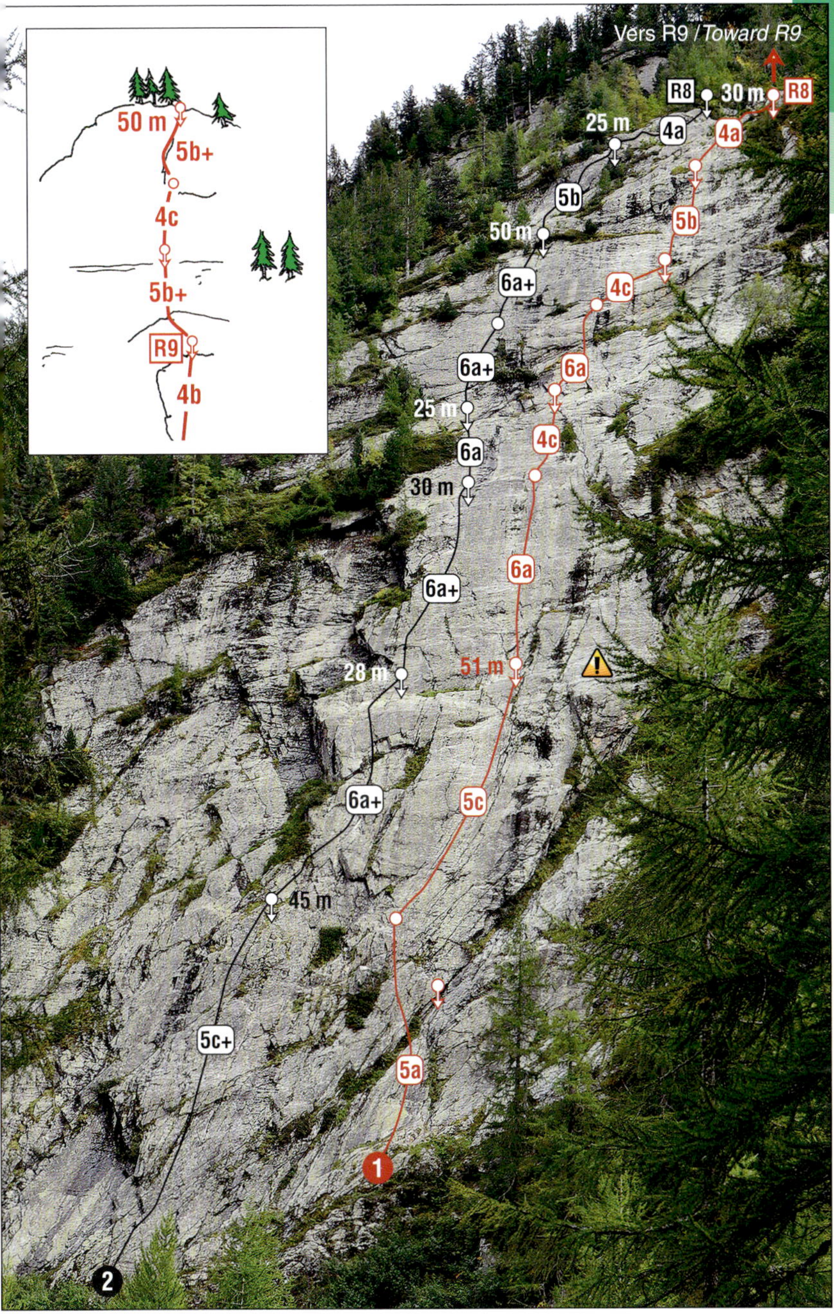
50 m
5b+
4c
5b+
R9
4b
Vers R9 / Toward R9
R8
30 m
R8
25 m
4a
4a
5b
5b
50 m
6a+
4c
6a+
6a
25 m
6a
4c
30 m
6a
6a+
28 m
51 m
6a+
5c
45 m
5c+
5a
1
2

Area 09

Le Passet -The Wall
Le Passet - Lower crag
Mur du Loup
Le Passet - Upper crag

Le Passet - The Wall

1500 m SE

60′

3

0 1 2 1 300 m

Four interesting 300m routes have been put up over the last few years, following an initiative by Alain Payot. The greatness of this wall makes it a crag for experienced climbers only.

Rock : compact gneiss. The rock is generally good, but there are some loose sections (weak flakes).

Climbing : generally slab climbing. Difficulties are mostly in the upper part of the wall. Be careful to avoid causing stonefall while on ledges or abseiling. The face does not get the sun for very long in the afternoon, so bring a woolly.

The site : the small valley leading up to the Col du Passet is a very peaceful vale surrounded with high cliffs where silent climbers are only barely disturbed by the gushing stream.

Access : **by train**: Châtelard (Switzerland). **By car**: from Chamonix RD 1506, take the main road towards Switzerland. Cross the Col des Montets, and 200m before the border, turn left to reach the hamlet of Barberine. Park here (18km).

Approach : (1 hour). From Barberine follow the road to the north-west, then the path to Col du Passet (starting just before the cablecar station). When you get as close to the crag as possible (between the lower and upper tiers) climb up the scree slope on the left on a clearly marked track (cairn).

Equipment : 10mm expansion bolts.

Passet The Wall
32
Passet Upper Crag
35
Passet Lower Crag "Mur du Loup"
33
34
Barberine
36
Giétroz
37
Pylône
37
Train station
Châtelard Frontière
SUISSE
FRANCE
Barberine
P
P
N
0
500 m

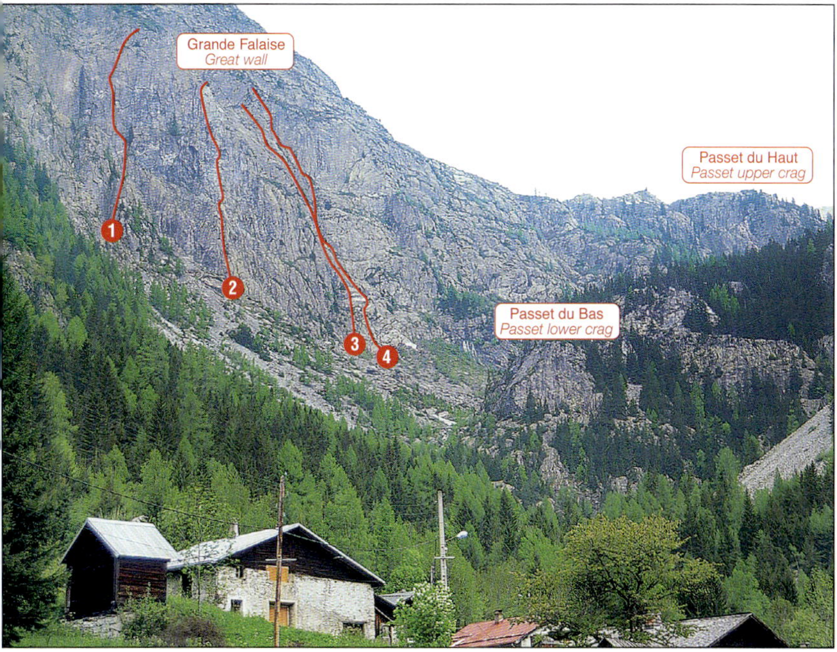
Grande Falaise
Great wall
Passet du Haut
Passet upper crag
Passet du Bas
Passet lower crag
1
2
3
4

The routes

From left to right.

1 - **Pourvu que ça dure!** ED+. 250m, 9 pitches, Double 50m ropes and 13 quickdraws required. First Ascent: F. Ancey, Y. Ancrenaz, S. Aubert, B. Mouillier, A. Payot. June 1999. Several difficult pitches which are interesting to "work". The hard sections can be bypassed by pulling on the bolts. De **P1** à **P4**: 5b/5c; **P5**: 7?, A0 ou 6a; **P6**: 6a; **P7**: 7?, A0/6a, sustained on hidden holds; **P8**: 6c; **P9**: 6b. Abseil descent.

2 - **Tout ça pour ça!** TD. 300m. Difficulties increase with height. Unavoidable moves of 5c. 8 pitches. Requires 13 quickdraws and double 50m ropes (small stoppers may be useful). First Ascent: F. Ancey, C. Cretin, A. Payot, F. Toucoulou. 01/07/96 and 21/05/97. **P1**: 5a; **P2**: 5a; **P3**: 5a; **P4**: 5c (slightly longer than 50m); **P5**: 6a, fissure; **P6**: 6a; **P7**: 6a. Climb back towards the crest of the buttress; **P8**: 6c+, 6c Do not climb this pitch (collapsed). Abseil descents following the route.

3 - **Ça se discute**: ED-. 300 m. Unavoidable moves of 6a. 10 pitches. Requires 13 quickdraws and double 50m ropes. Abseil descent. First Ascent: A. Payot, F. Toucoulou. July 2000. The last 4 pitches are worthwhile; a vertical wall climbed on edges and flat holds. It is not a good idea to attempt this route if there are other parties on it (risk of stonefall). **P1** to **P4**: 5b/5c, warm up; **P5** to **P7**: 6a+, a series of steep sections and ledges; **P8**, **P9**: 6c/6c+, a smooth, vertical wall.

4 - **Mille et une pattes**: D+. 350m 12 pitches. Unavoidable moves of 5c. Requires 12 quickdraws and double 50 m ropes. First ascent A. Payot, J. Landry, F. Toucoulou. September 1999. Good, sustained climbing in the 5b/5c grade. **P1** to **P4**: 5b. Climb a slab, then an easy angled corner followed by a succession of short, steep sections to reach the waterworn channel which runs right down the face **P5** à **P8**: 5b/5c. Climb up the right-hand side of the large slab **P8** to **P12**: 5b/5c: Friction climbing to reach a fore-summit. Descent 5 abseils. Use belay stations at the end of pitches 12, 11 and 10 and then follow the belay stations on the neighbouring route "ça se discute". The knot may jam on the 4th abseil if you're not careful.

Passet - The Wall
1
2
3
4

Tout ça pour ça

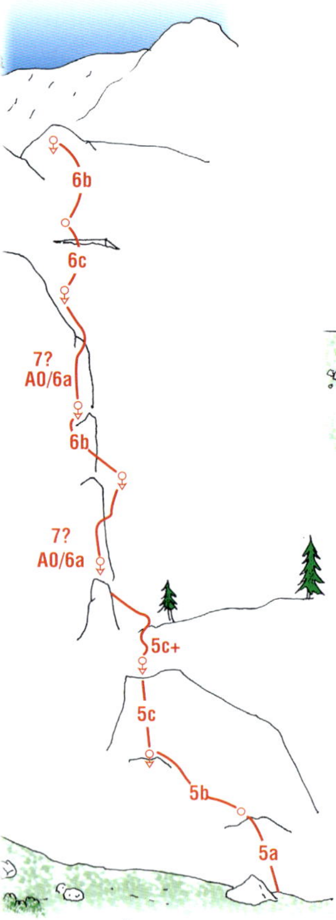

Pourvu que ça dure!

Ça se discute

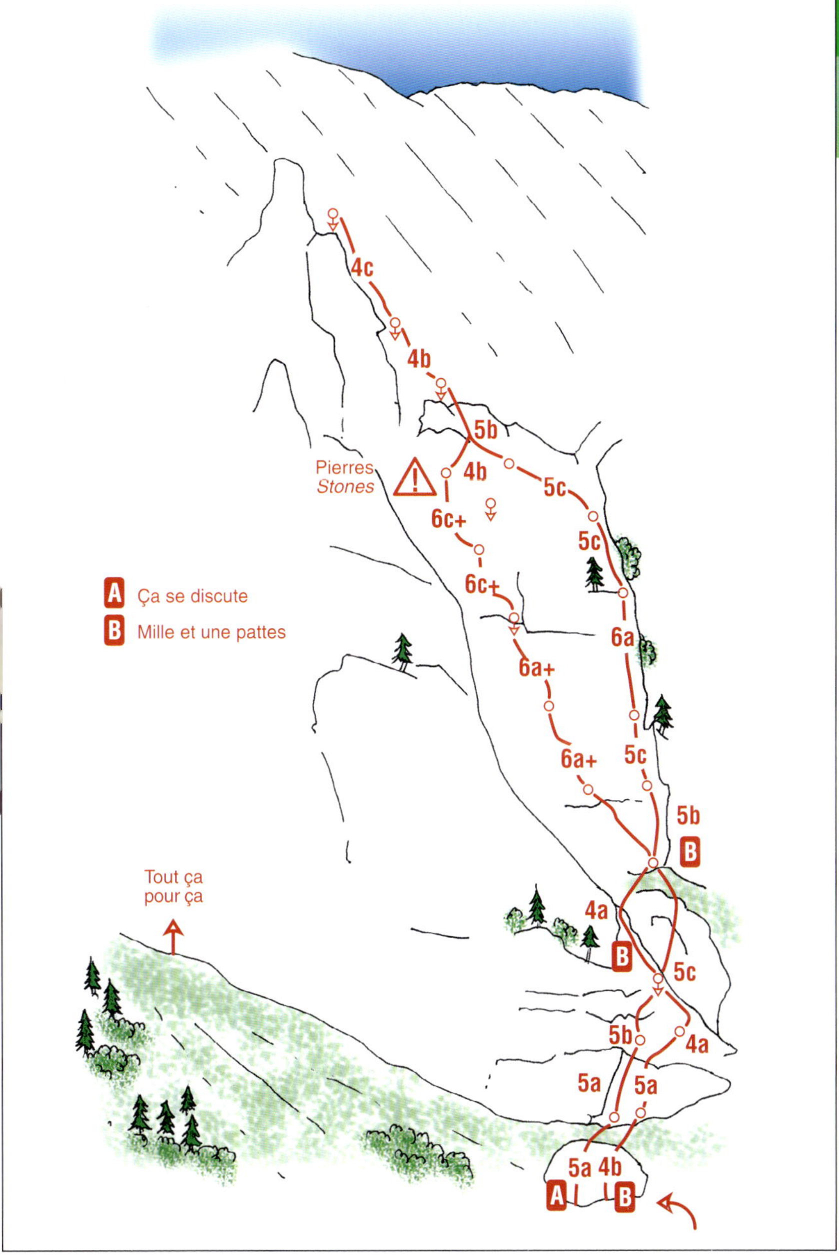

Le Passet - Lower crag

1300 m S

40'

3

4 5 8 2 15-70 m

Rock : granite.

Climbing : 15 routes 25m to 50m high. Beautiful slab climbing. Well equipped routes with cemented-in 10mm bolts. A lot of work is being carried out here by Michel Piola.

Gear : 12 quickdraws, 2x50m abseil rope or 80m sibgle rope.

The site and access : see pages 248 and 249.

Approach : 30 mins. Go up the road to the north-west, then follow the path (which begins just before the cablecar station), towards the Col du Passet. After the Barberine waterfall (1322m), the path follows the left side of a small valley. Continue to follow it until you are at the same height as the cliff, which can easily be seen on the other side of the river. Cross the river to reach the base of the crag.

West face

Granulous slabs, rather spaced up equipment.

1 - **La traversée du dragon**: 6c, 55m superb slab.

2 - **La mousson**: **P1**: 6a; **P2**: 6a, 50m.

3 - **Digue dingue donc**: **P1**: 6a, cemented bolts; **P2:** 6a+, 50m.

4 - **La village englouti**: **P1**: 6b+, cemented bolts petzl; **P2**: 6a+ to the left 6c to the right (old protection), 55m.

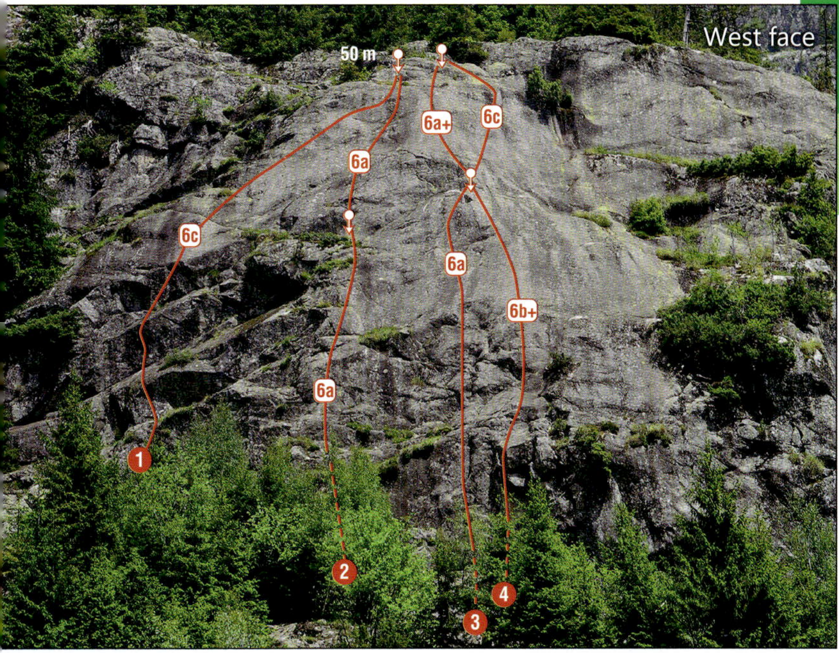

Mur du Loup, "Les loups sont entrés dans Paris", 6c+

"Le village englouti", 6b+

South face

A 70m high rock face, becoming steepe
in the top 20 metres.

1 - **Le cheval de Troie**: 7b, 10m.

2 - **Le cheval à bascule**: 7a+, 10m.

3 - **Emotion à Emosson**: 6c, 40m. A gem of a slab, calling for a gooc amount of intuition.

4 - **Les tendres souhaits**: 6a, 35m.

5 - **Bonne nuit les petits**: **P1**: 6a, 35m **P2**: 6c+, one movement above the B1. Then traverse to the right.

6 - **La cigale et la fourmi**: **P1**: 5c; **P2** 6a+.

7 - **Poèmes et comptines**: **P1**: 5a, 30m **P2**: 7a, 20m, slab plus small overhang.

8 - **Pimprenelle**: 5a, 25m.

9 - **La poudre de Perlin Pimpin**: **P1** 5b; **P2**: 6c good with continuous movement, develops in a traverse to the left.

10 - **Câlin nounourse**: 4a, 30m.

11 - **Pin et Chocolat**: **P1**: 4a, 30m; **P2**: 6b, 25 m.

12 - **Sur un petit nuage...** **P1**: 4c; **P2**: 5a Great pitch on the crest of the pillar.

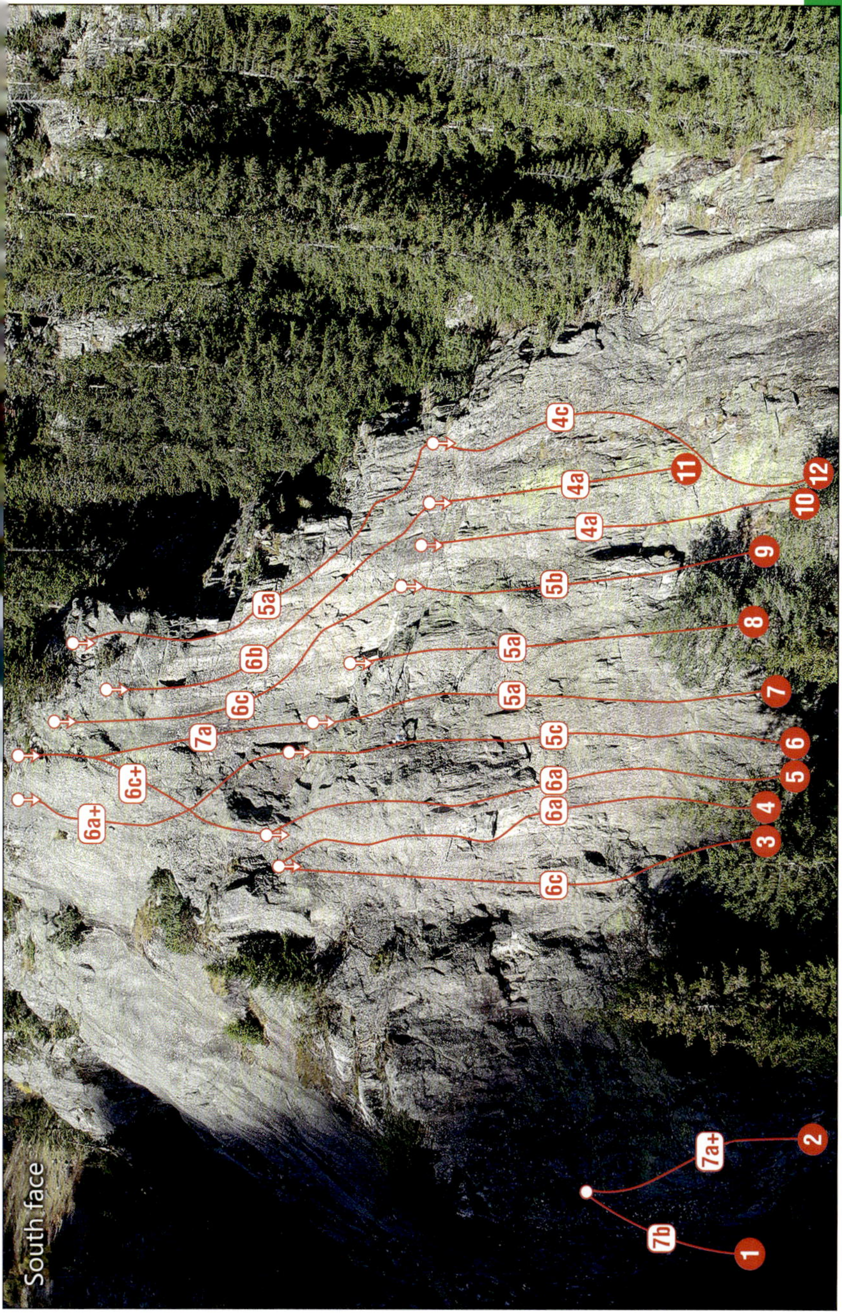
South face
1
7b
2
7a+
3
6c
4
6a
5
6a
6
5c
7
5a
8
5a
9
5b
10
4a
11
4a
12
4c
6a+
6c+
7a
6c
6b
5a

Mur du Loup

1300 m SW

45′

3

0 1 9 5 30 m

Rock : granite.

Gear : 70m single rope. 12 quick draws.

The site : an ideal place to escape the summer heat: in a shady, wooded setting.

Access : see page 248.

Approach : from "Passet - Lower crag" go down few meters and traverse east 100m.

The routes

A steep granite cliff. Fifteen nice and demanding routes. Good on sight challenges.

1 - **A l'ouest rien de nouveau**: 6a, 9 points. Good warm up.

2 - **Le nouveau monde**: 6c, crescendo difficulties.

3 - **Rocky mountain**: 6c, impressive overhang. 10 points.

4 - **Un air de Tenessee**: 7a, 10 points. Several overhangs.

5 - **Mystère**: 7b, 11 points. Hard move at the end.

6 - **Les Loup sont entrés dans Paris**: 6c+, 10 points. superb route.

7 - **Loup Garou**: 6c, 10 points, top.

8 - **Camaïeu**: 7a, 9 points, two technical walls.

9 - **Couleur Pastel**: 6c, 9 points, attractive diedre.

10 - **?**: 6c.

11 - **?**: 6b. Good line, varied climbing style.

12 - **Sous la loupe**: 5c, 10 points. pre-warming route.

13 - **Rémus et Romulus**: 7a, 9 points. Technical climb.

14 - **Le petit Chaperon Rouge**: 6c.

15 - **P'tit loup**: 6b+, an uncomfortable start than easier.

Mur du Loup

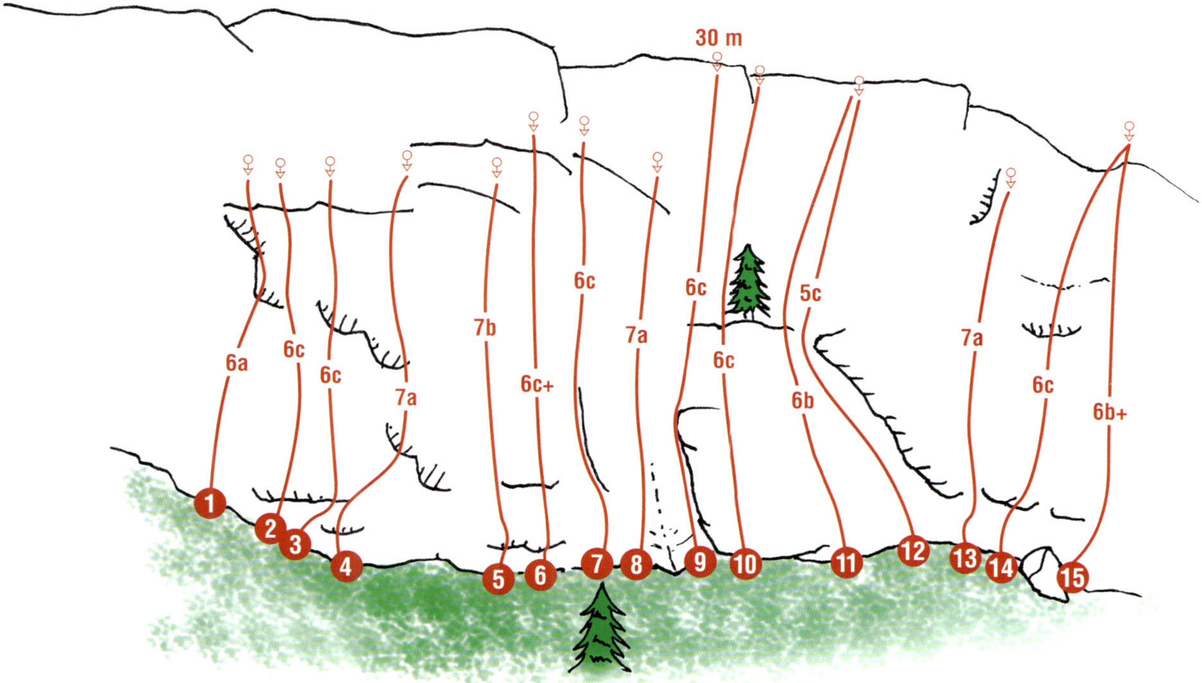
30 m
1 6a
2 6c
3 6c
4 7a
5 7b
6 6c+
7 6c
8 7a
9 6c
10 6c
11 6b
12 5c
13 7a
14 6c
15 6b+

Le Passet - Upper crag

1500 m S

70'

3

0 1 7 0 70 m

Rock : granite.

Climbing : 80m high. 8 routes. Discovered by Olivier Ratheaux during the summer of 1986, this small crag offers two to three pitch routes. The fixed protection is adequate, but some routes are a little committing. The starts of the routes are marked with arrows. From the top, you can either abseil down or walk down by a traverse to the west to join the path leading down from the col.

Gear : 12 quickdraws, 2x50m ropes or a single 60m rope.

The site and access : see pages 248 and 249.

Approach : 45 mins. As for Passet du Bas, but follow on the path. Cross the river and reach the base of the crag at the point where the path runs closest to it.

The site : you're in Switzerland!

The route

1 - **Variante de départ de Sue-Ellen** 6c.

2 - **Sue-Ellen**: magnificent route, wit a fairly technical crack high up. **P1** 6a+; **P2**: 6a; **P3**: 6b.

3 - **Dallas**: **P1**: 6c+, vertical wall o edges; **P2**: 6c+.

4 - **J.R.**: 70m. **P1**: 5c; **P2**: 6a+, a har move to get over an overhang; **P3** 5c. Brilliant route.

5 - **La Saga des Blanchards variation** 6b.

6 - **La Saga des Blanchards**: 70m 2 pitches, equipped. **P1**: 6a+; **P2** 6a+.

7 - **Clayton**: 40m. **P1**: 6a+. A stee wall; **P2**: 6a+.

8 - **Bobby**: 65m, 2 pitches, equipped **P1**: 5c/4c; **P2**: 5b/3/4c.

9 - **Pam**: 5c, 35m, 1 pitch, starts from the first belay of "Bobby".

Le Passet - Upper crag

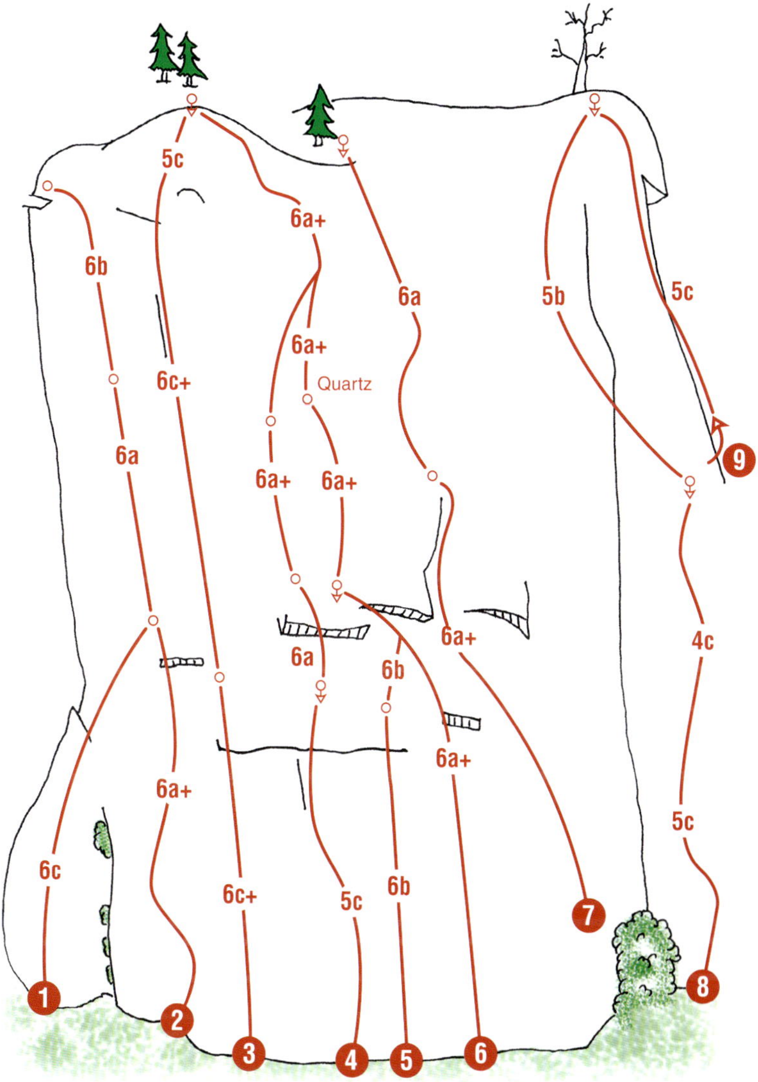

Area 10

Barberine
Châtelard - Giétroz

Barberine

The site gets its name from one of the hamlets of Vallorcine, even though it is located in the Valaisan canton. At the end of the 70's only the lower slab of this wall was equipped for climbing. It was Marc Volorio, a pioneer climber in the area, who opened the «Balade au bout des Combes» and «Vipère au Pied» the first two routes to cover this 300 m high, rocky bastion. Since then seven more routes have been added, all quite exceptional, offering climbers a rich and challenging climbing experience on this magnificent rock. About 15 years ago two new climbing "playgounds" were created; "la Zone" and "Downstairs" This was essentially the work of a couple with a passion for these rocks, Hilary Sharp and Jon de Montjoye, climber - new routers. Of the thirty odd routes opened at "la Zone", many would merit three stars in the a Michelin guide of climbing.

Rock : granit, solid and sculptured.

Climbing : about a hundred pitches for 30 routes between 15 to 250m high. Friction climbing on sloping slabs for the "la Dalle du Bas" sector. Verticle climbing with possible overhangs to negotiate in the longer routes, as in the "la Zone" and "Downstairs" zones.
A demanding style which requires concentration and gestural creativity.

Equipment : cemented rings and/or 10 or 12 mm bolts. The spacing of points varies depending on the routes with little or no risk of dangerous falls.

Access : from Chamonix (RD 1506), go in the direction of Switzerland and over the pass, "le col des Montets". Straight on through Vallorcine and 200m before the border, turn left, direction Barberine. Park by roadside (do not park in the small village square). **By train**: get off at the Châtelard- frontière train station.

Approach : 10 to 40 mins depending on the sector.
From Barberine : from the village square a path heading north leaves the village near the chalet named "Marie-Joseph". Once over the bridge which marks the border, go on for 100m and follow the little path on the left to the base of the crag (lower slab sector).
From the station at Châtelard - frontière : go back towards the customs post and take the road on the right indicated "Barberine"; follow this past the prefab buildings, go through the forest to get to the foot of the rocks on the right.

Passet
The Wall
32
Passet
Upper
Crag
35
Passet
Lower Crag
"Mur du Loup"
33
34
Barberine
36
Giétroz
37
37
Pylône
Train
station
Châtelard
Frontière
SUISSE
FRANCE
Barberine
P
P
N
0
500 m

A
B
C
D
A - Lower slabs
B - The long routes
C - La Zone
D - Downstairs

Lower slabs (100 m)

1200 m | SW

10'

3

1 9 5 1 30-100 m

A historical climbing crag in the valley, it is foot friction heaven, with very few hand holds.

Approach : 10 mins. Follow a narrow path, on the right, to the north-west (behind the house called "la Marie-Joseph"); it crosses a field and then a river (border), and then crosses a large field on the right. You get to two benches. Now walk up towards the crag through a scree slope in the forest.

Climbing : smooth low angle slab, great to build foot friction confidence

Descent : from the ledge, follow the cable to the right (exposed).

The routes

Only a few routes have names.

(1, 2, 3) - Three short routes to enjoy friction climbing. (4, 5) - Comfortable ledge at the start.

(6, 7, 8, 9) - More fine lines above a narrow ledge. To be avoided on crowded days.

10 - **The slab classic route**: Concentration still required.

11 - **P1**: 5c. Belay from the small ledge **P2**: 5c/6a.

12 - Starts on route 11 belay station. An outstanding pitch.

13 - Short top rope pitch.

14 - **Le Magicien d'Oz:** (see page 277): **P1**: 5c; **P2**: 6a. First two pitches equipped with resin anchors on clean rock.

15 - **Old bolts**: **P1**: 4b. Short pitch. **P2**: 5c. Technical. **P3**: 5b. Short friction section. Same exit as route 15, 16, 18.

16 - **The route with the famous 6a+ overhang section**: **P1**: 5c. Traverses up and left from the start. **P2**: 6a+. Feet placement is essential... **P3**: 5b.

17 - **Fantôme de l'Opéra**: A pebble stone with a friend drawn on it at the start. See guidebook page 268.

18 - Starts at the top of the ledge, after the tree. **P1**: 5b; **P2**: 5c. Another beautiful route.

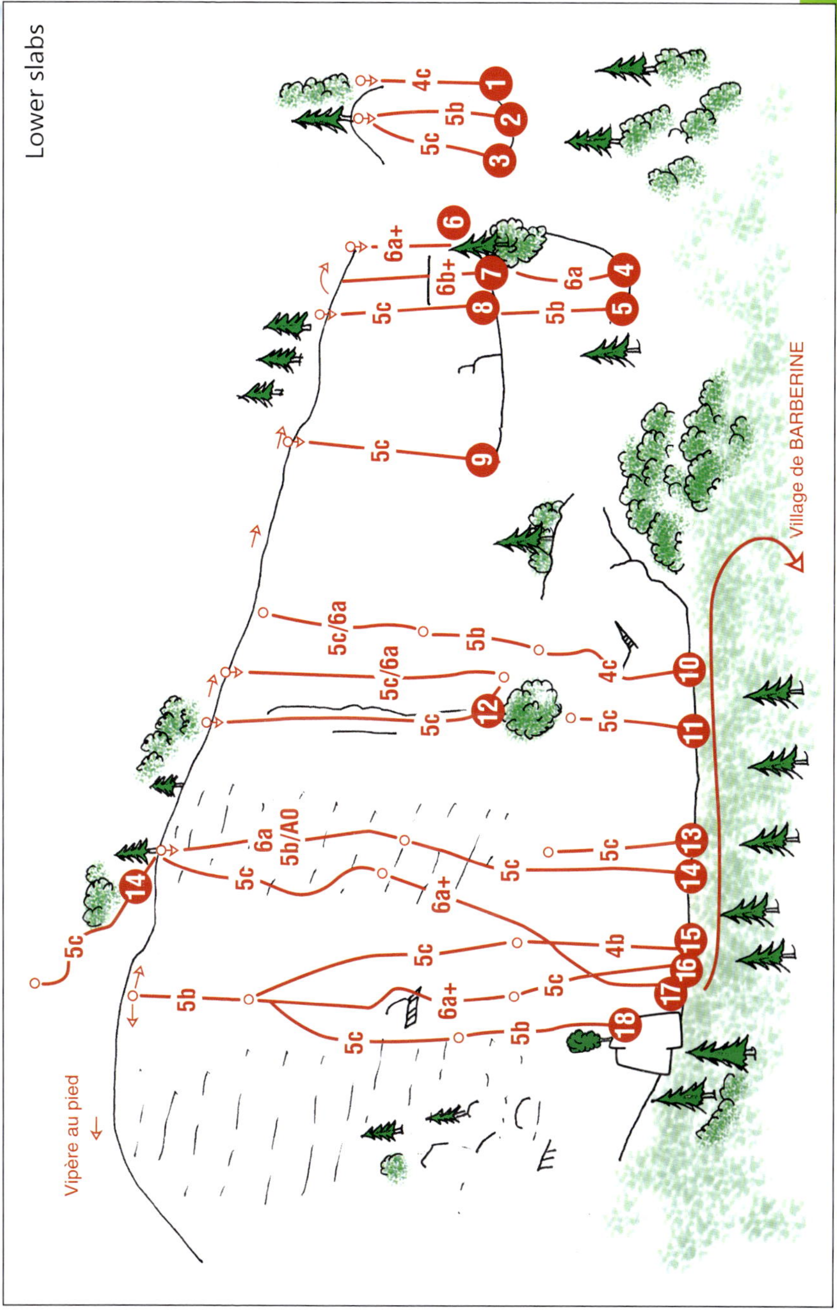
Lower slabs
Village de BARBERINE
Vipère au pied

The long routes

1300 m | SW

15'-30'

3

0 0 6 5 250 m

There are eleven beautiful 250m lines on a wide wall crossed by spacious ledges. The rock is solid and the routes can easily be seen as they form white streaks due to lichen brushing. Climbing always offers roughly the same outline: a few slab pitches, generally quite tricky, followed by steep walls, even overhangs in places. Although the equipment is perfect, the rock structure itself calls for precise and complex climbing, with a rather slow progression. For this reason, grades may seem a little severe at the first visit...

Access : 15 to 30 mins. Need to reach the upper ridge of the lower slab, excepted for "Sylvie Phobie", "Barbourine" and "Tour de Chauffe".

Descent : abseiling down is possible in "Sylvie Phobie" and "Barbourine". For the other routes, on the right hand-side, it is better to walk down to avoid any inevitable stonefall (the lower routes are crowded in summer). At the finish, walk up and join the tracks running along the top to the right hand-side. Be especially careful along a great black wall, which is the Afrique area of Giétroz (very important: do not cause any loose stones to fall!). Follow the path to the entrance of a gorge (hand-rail). Walk down this gorge, past a high cliff then take to the right as soon as the path starts climbing again. You will get to the footbridge and to Barberine in 20 mins. It is also possible to go down by "la Zone" via ferrrata. For that, take right hand a path before to go down the steep narrow gorge.

«Trad» climbing : Michel Piola opened a traditional climbing route in this sector. The route is partially equipped, with mainly protection at belay stations plus an isolated resin anchor here and there on slabs. The leader has to place protection, with nuts and cams. A common way of climbing in the high alpine nearby ranges, rarely found in the valley crags.
An interesting climbing exercise that requires experience in order to maintain safety at a good level. Additionally, trad equipment is out of many climber's budget: a set of ten pieces of requirement can easily reach 700€. The route "Fantôme de l'opéra" is for climbers who have already climbed trad routes before. The Saix crag in Vallorcine or the Roc à l'Os sector in Les Houches also offer routes adapted for trad climbing and training. Hiring a mountain guide is highly recommended to learn the basics of trad climbing.

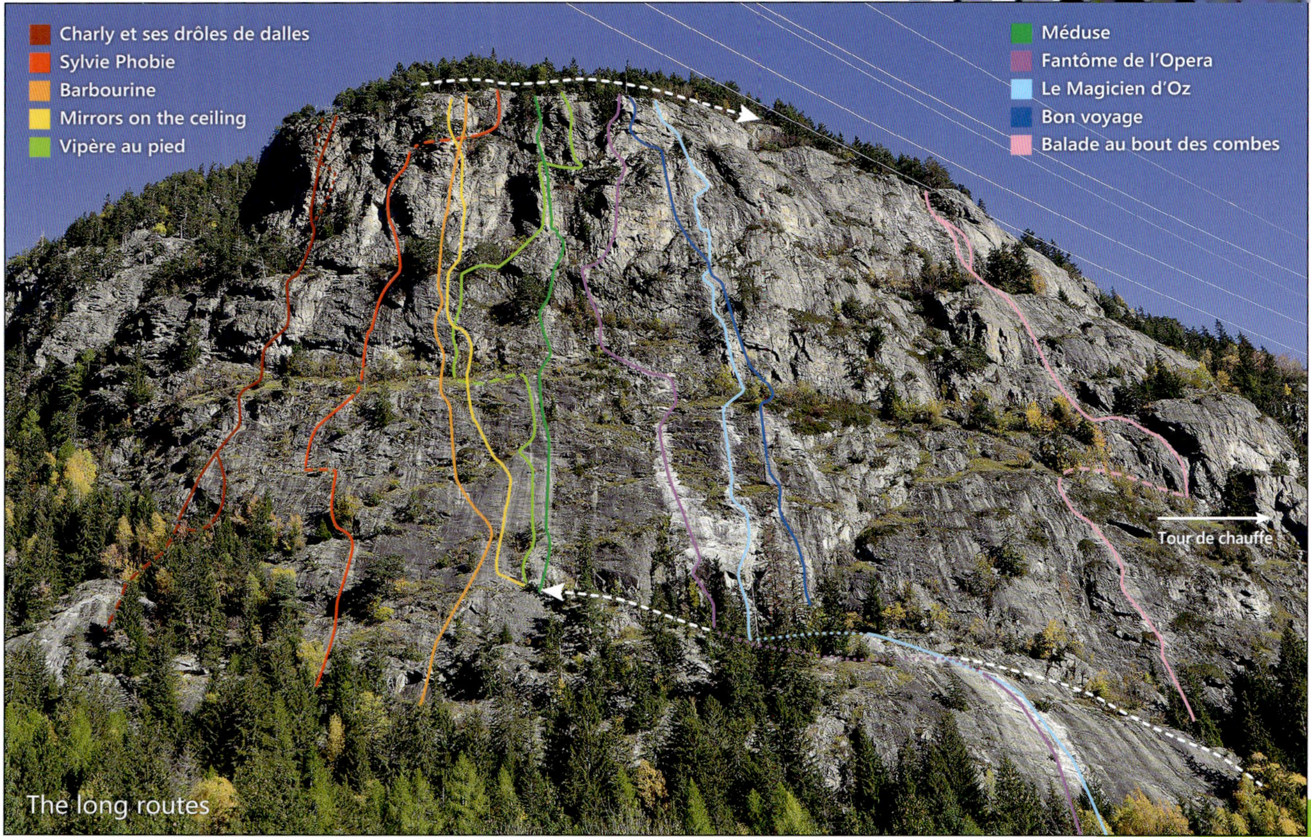

Charly et ses drôles de dalles
Sylvie Phobie
Barbourine
Mirrors on the ceiling
Vipère au pied
Méduse
Fantôme de l'Opera
Le Magicien d'Oz
Bon voyage
Balade au bout des combes
Tour de chauffe
The long routes

Charly et ses drôles de dalles

ED. 250m. Nicolas Annerau, Johann Vienney, spring 2013. 6c mandatory. 13 quick draws plus belay. 3 significant ledges on the route, some exposed sections. Rock needs some cleaning (lichen and moss).

Approach : follow the pink marks on the left bank of Barberine creek.

P1: 6c+, 25m. Pumpy overhang followed by a delicate exit. Possibility to bypass the pitch on the left.

P2: 5a, 40m. Slab, first ledge.

P3: 7a. Boulder movement.

P'3: Variant in 6b+, 50m. Steep slab, overhang, slab.

P4: 6c, 15 m. Second ledge.

P5: 6a+/A0 or 7(?), 40m. Dangerous start, dirty rock.

P6: 6b, 20m.

P7: 6b. Start on finger crimps (caution!).

P8: 7b. Beautiful rock. Sustained and technical reg rock.

P8': left; gets harder as you reach a technical bulge under the belay.

P9: 6c. Going left, a very nice slab with lichen...

P9': going right 6a. Down climb traversing right, to reach the upper section of the plateau. Abseiling: directly then to R9.

Sylvie Phobie

TD+. Nice route; varied and sustained. 250m. Unavoidable moves of 6a. 9 pitches. Requires 12 quickdraws and double 50m ropes. First ascent: Fabrice Oms, Rodrigue Passy, Sylvain Ravanel. 1993. Dries slowly after heavy rain.

Approach : (20 mins) - as for the lower slabs. Just after the bridge, follow a path leftwards to reach a scree slope. Climb up this to get to the foot of the route (cairns + a few red paint marks).

P1 to **P3**: 5a to 5c slab climbing to reach a ledge.

P4: 6b (5c variation on the left - only for wimps!).

P5: 3b. Short pitch to a ledge.

P6: 6c+/ A1; a steep and strenuous start followed by a long slabby section with a 6c+ finish. The hardest moves are at the top.

P7: 5c, rising traverse.

P8: 6b+, short overhang.

P9: 6a.

P10: traverse to the right to join last pitch (one point).

P10: 5c.

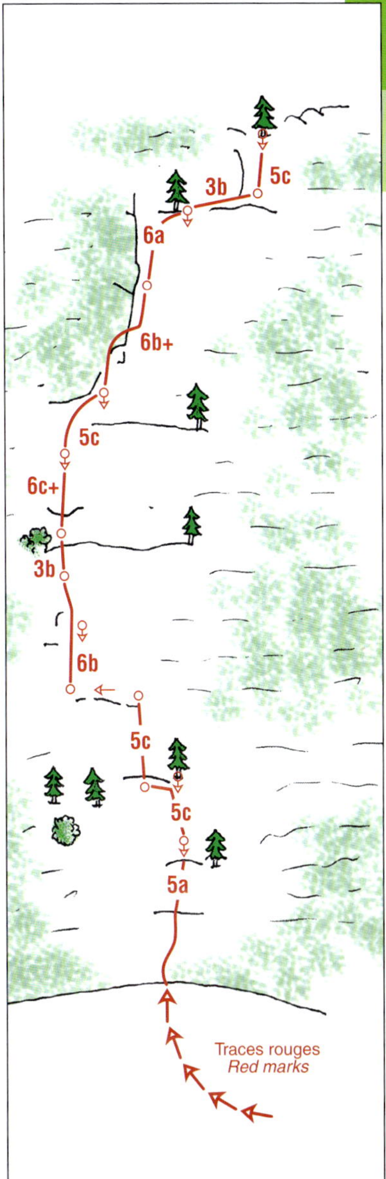

Sylvie Phobie

Barbourine

ED. 250m. South-west. Unavoidable 6b. Sylvain Ravanel and Christophe Fadda, June 2004. Superb line. First part on slab then 4 pitches up a steep wall. 13 quick-draws. 50m rope or abseil.

Approach : same as for "Sylvie Phobie". The start is a few metres to the right. Name written at bottom.

P1: 6a+. Slab. Small warming up over-hang.

P2: 6a. Slab.

P3: 6a. Delicate slab.

P4: 6a. Slab. Belay on ledge.

P5: 6c+ (unavoidable 6b). Start 20m further to the left on "Fixe" hangers 5m to the left of "Vipère au pied", blue mark.

P6: 6b, flakes.

P7: 6c (unavoidable 6a). Slab then over-hang.

P8: 6b. Getting to the second bolt is tricky. Possibility of finishing through "Vipère"".

Return : abseil down the route or walk down (see above).

Mirrors on the ceiling

ED. 250m, South-west. Unavoidable 6c. "Fixe" grey hangers. Jon de Montjoye (2005). 17 quickdraws (12 if you use the alternative belay). 50m rope. Tennis shoes for the walk down.

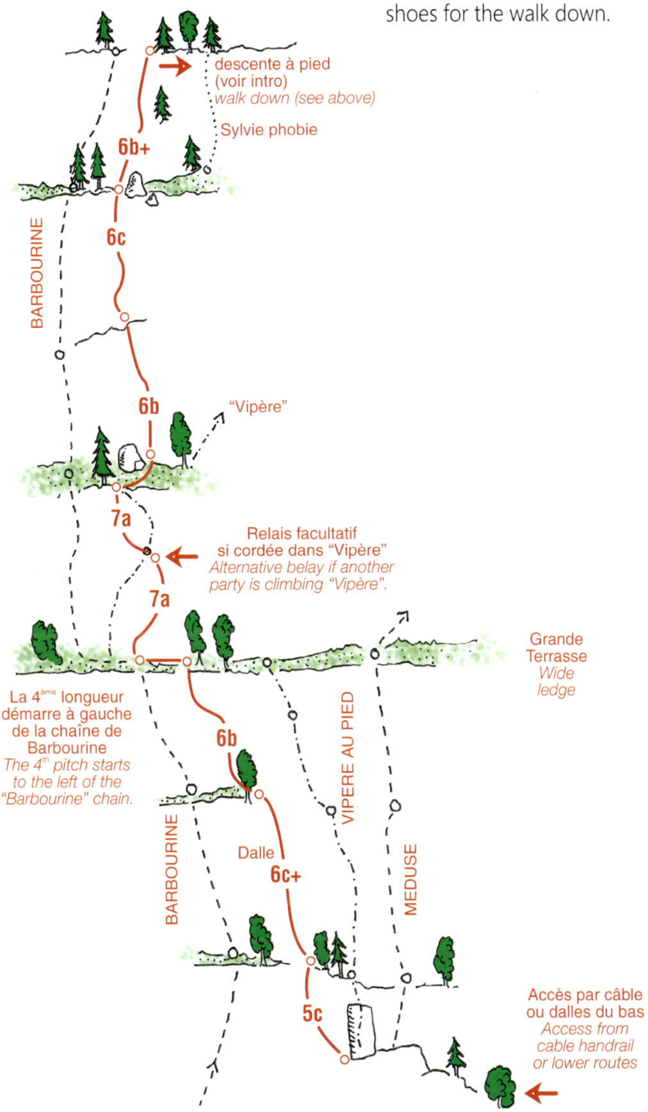

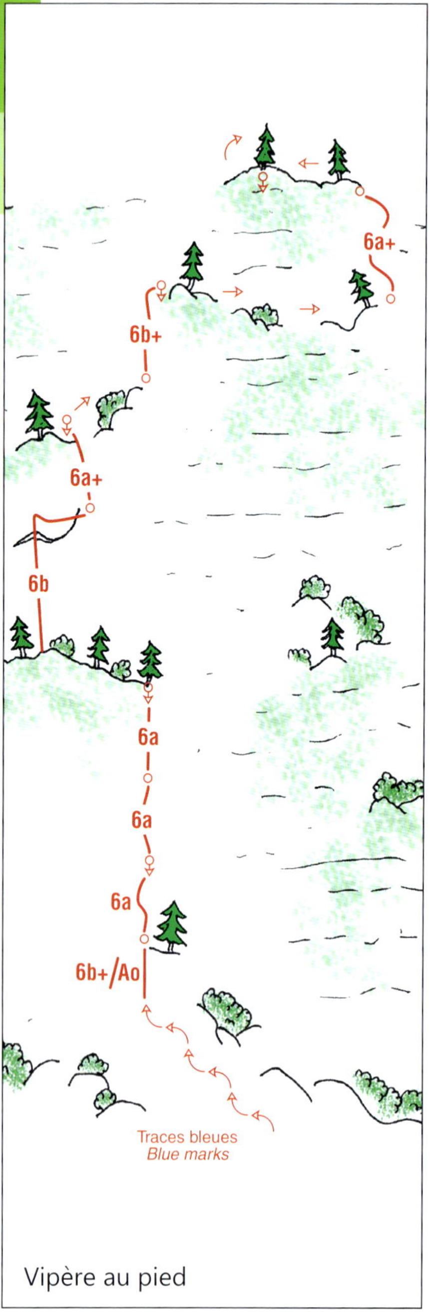

Vipère au pied

Marc Volorio, 1980. TD+. 250m. Unavoidable moves of 6a. 9 pitches. Requires 12 quickdraws and double 50m ropes. Superb, varied climbing. Sustained at 6a/6b. Quite exposed in places.

Approach : 30 mins. From the lower slabs, climb a steep path on the right, with a cable handrail (roping up advisable) to reach the top of these routes. You can also climb one of the lower routes.

P1: 6b+/A0, a new start (the original one fell down).

P2: 6a, traverse the slab; easily or with difficulty depending on the day...

P3: 6a, slab.

P4: 6a. Another tricky slab move. Keep concentrating....

P5, **P6**: 6b, 6a+. Two brilliant vertical pitches, quite athletic. "Vipère" is the middle route (gold-coloured hangers, blue blob).

P7: 40m linking pitch (ledge).

P8: 6b+. A slab, overhang and corner. Superb, sustained climbing. Traverse right from the ledge.

P9: 6a+.

Meduse

ED-. 250m. South-west. Jon de Montoye (2004). 13 quickdraws, 50m rope, tennis shoes foe the walk down. Grey hangers. A very beautiful route, mostly keeping to the right of "Vipère au pied". Magnificent slab in the first section followed by a nice pillar. The finish is up a corner and steep wall, to the left of the last pitch of "Vipère".

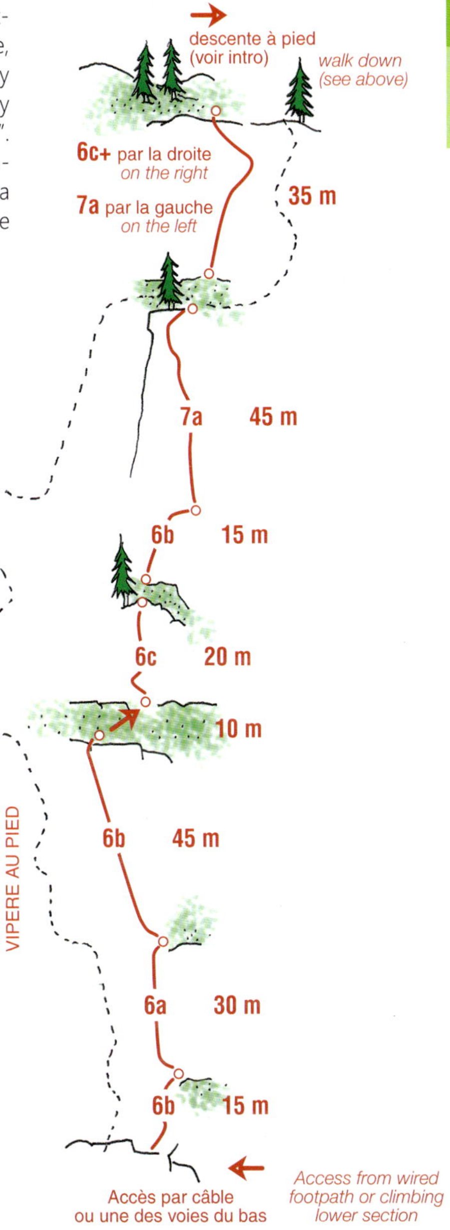

Fantôme de l'opéra

TD+. 250m. Unavoidable 6a. Michel Piola. 2015, 2016. Partially equipped. Bring a set of 4 small friends and nuts. On left hand side of lower slab. A pebble stone with a friend* drawn on it at the start of climb.

Approach : see page 266.

P1: 6a+. Climb up the cracks, then to the right onto clean rock. Harder to protect towards the end of the pitch (a possible exit going right by Magicien d'Oz). **P2**: 5c, easy to protect. **P3**: 5c, follows the protected pitch of Magicien d'Oz. Reach the other side of ledge, P4 starts just right of a large rocky flake touching ground. **P4**: 6a+. Some bolts in place. **P5**: 5b. Set up belay on a tree to the right. **P6**: 5c. Traverse to the left, fairly athletic at the start. One bolt at the end of pitch. **P7**: 6a. Overhang on good holds, easy to protect. Exit on a wall with cracks. **P8**: 6a+. Partly equipped. Climb up a dark rock wall going left. Some small athletic overhangs. **P9**: Short section traversing right to get to belay station. **P10**: 6a+. Climb towards an overhanging dihedral (1 bolt). Followed by a nice exposed pillar (a few bolts in place). **P11**: 6a. Continue up the fractured pillar to the right of the tree. **P12**: 6a+. Climb up the left side of pillar. Outstanding and sustained. **P13**: 5c. Start on a vertical wall, then go right to avoid overhang.

*name given to the first generation of mechanical protection nuts.

1. Le Magicien d'Oz

TD+. 230m. Unavoidable moves of 6a. Michel Piola. 13 quickdraws. 50m rope.

Approach : see page 266.

P1: 6a, 35m, slab.

P2: 5c, 35m. From P2 climb 20m on the edge.

P3: 6a+, 25m, nice wall.

P4: 6a+, 30m, technical movements.

P5: 6a+, 35m crack and slab.

P6: 6a, 35m, good holes.

P7: 6a+, 30m.

2. Bon Voyage

ED. 230m. Unavoidable 6b, Jon de Montjoy and Hilary Sharp, 2003. The name is written at the bottom.

Approach : climb a steep path right of the lower slabs, follow the cable toward the first ledge.

Return : on foot.

P1: 6b+, 40m. A demanding pitch.

P2: 5c, 35m, slab.

P3: 6a, 25m. A steep wall withe good pockets.

P4: 6a+, 25m.

P5: 6b, 50m. A long technical slab.

P6: 4b, 20m.

P7: 7a, 25m. A smooth and round crack than a technical overhanging wall.

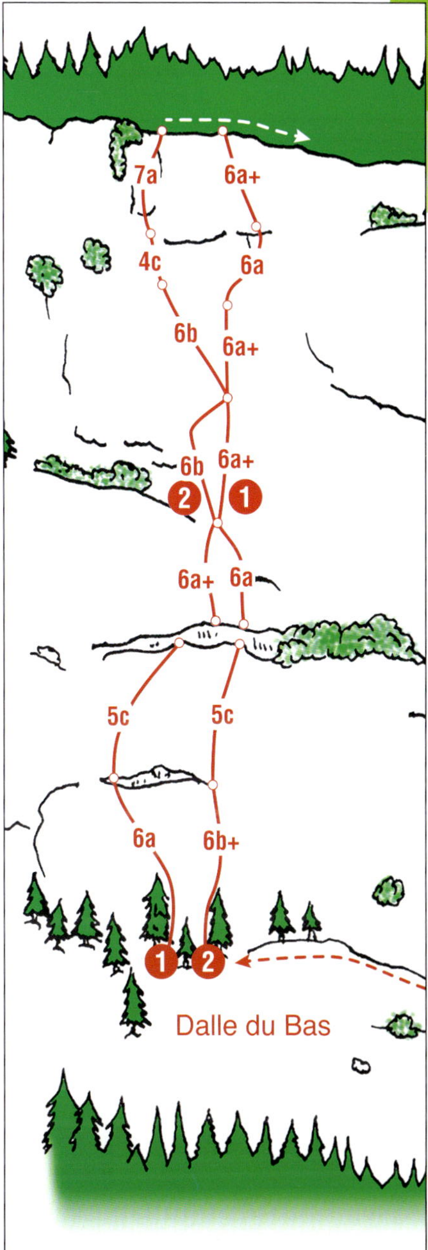

Le Magicien d'Oz & Bon voyage

Balade au bout des combes

Marc Volorio. TD+. 250m. Varied climbing on excellent rock. Unavoidable moves of 6a. 9 pitches. 12 quickdraw and double 50m ropes.

Approach : 20 mins. Same as for the lower slabs, then follow a steep path on the right to reach a black wall where you can see the first bolts.

P1 to **P3**: 6a+/ 6b+/5c.
Brilliant slab climbing.

P4: 2. Long, rightwards traverse (in-situ handrail).

P5: 6c. Steep, fingery wall.

P6: 6a. Short overhang at the end of pitch.

P7: 6a. Slab.

P8: left, 6b+; right, 6c.

P9: 6c.

Genesis, 6b+

Tour de Chauffe

ED. 250m. South West. Unavoidable moves 6a+. 12 quick-draws. 70m single rope or abseil 2x50m ropes. First ascent: Maxime Barbet, Jonathan Charlet, Zian Charlet, et Jean-Marc Della Volpe. 2007 june. An alternative to the walk to reach "Downstairs" or "La Zone" areas.

Approach : 20 mins. From the lower slabs, follow the path to the right through the woods; traverse a scree slope for 30m, then again under the trees. Go straight up to the base of the face. The first pitch stays wet for a few days after rain.

P1: 5c+, 30m. A black pillar, then an athletic overhang.

P2: 6a, 25m. Climb a slab toward the first ledge, then a nice wall.

P3: 2, 30m. Traverse the ledge to the right.

P4: 6a+, 30m. Superb finger crack pitch Access to "Downstairs" ledge.

P5: 6c, 25m (6a+ mandatory). Traverse the ledge to the last route to the right. Small crack at the start.

P6: 5c, 20m. A short mossy wall up to the terrace.

P7: 2. 15m up to the bottom of the wall (1 bolt).

P8 : 6b+, 30m. (6a mandatory). A sustained slab climbing pitch.

P9 : 3, 20m. A short junction pitch up to the "Zone".

P10: 6b+, 30m. Climb Génésis route.

P11: 6b, 30m. Slab and edges. 2 abseils down to the "Zone" ledge.

P12: not completed.

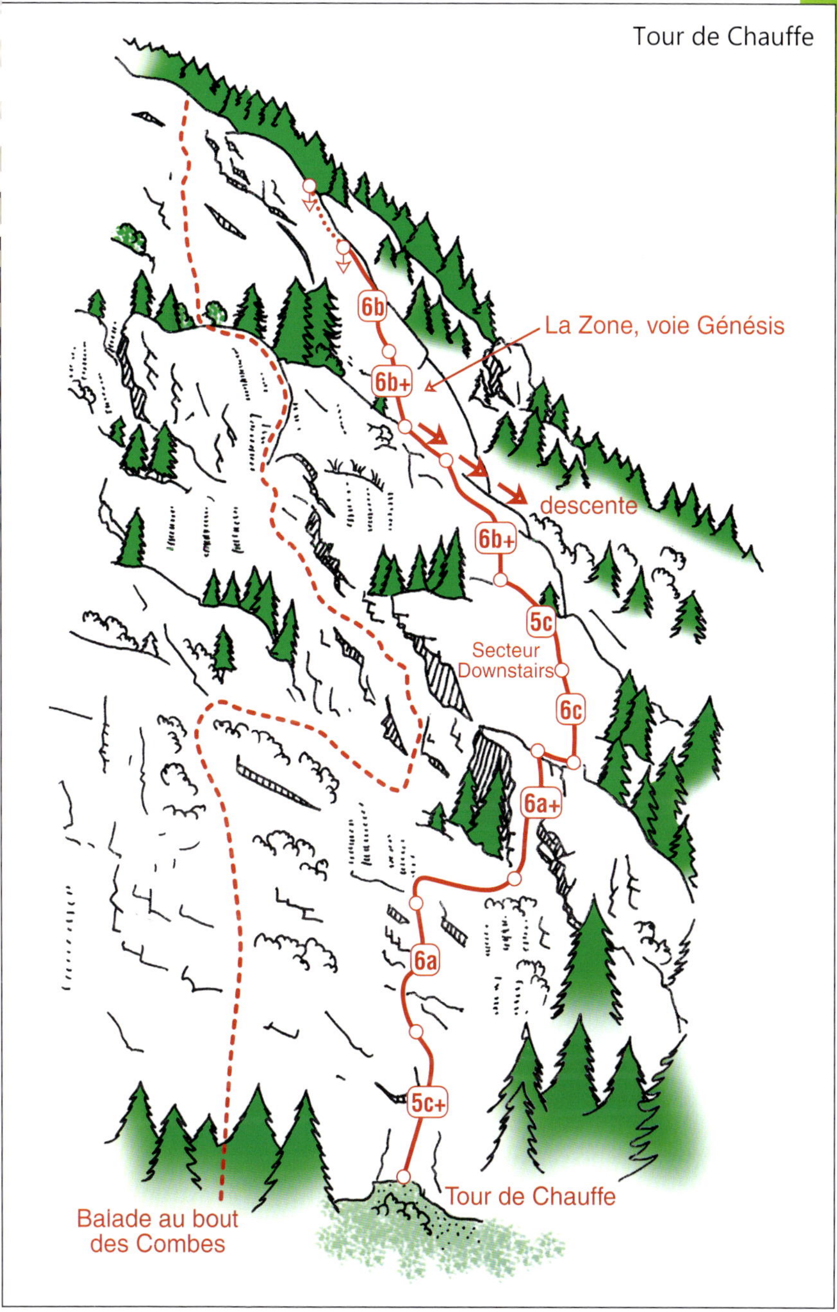
Tour de Chauffe
6b
La Zone, voie Génésis
6b+
descente
6b+
5c
Secteur
Downstairs
6c
6a+
6a
5c+
Tour de Chauffe
Baiade au bout
des Combes

La Zone

1300 m	S
40′	
	3
0 · 0 · 18 · 12	35 m

The "Zone" is an area 200 metres up the face, accessible via a steep path with two short passages of via ferrata. There is a comfortable ledge - sunny, even in late autumn. The routes are a good length.

Climbing : 18 pitches of 30 - 35m, 6b/c sustained; 12 of 7b/c. Crimps of a variety of angles and small foot holds make the climbing here highly technical and demanding. The walls are vertical with a few overhangs to spice things up a bit. Some of the routes have their names written at the base.

Gear : 70m rope, 15 quickdraws to be safe. Most belays equipped with carabiners.

Access : 30-40 mins. From the small village square in Barberine, follow the path to the left of the chalet "Marie Joseph". Go over the bridge and continue 100m, then follow the left hand path past two benches. Climb straight up through the forest via a rock path leading to the base of the slabs. Follow the path to the right, still climbing through the forest, crossing a boulder field then back into the forest. Arriving at a ledge, climb the steep scree marked with cairns (look for the electric pylon). Two laddered sections followed by a few zig-zags lead to the foot of the right hand side of the "Zone".

Moonshine, 6b+

The routes

1 - **California dreamin'**: 6c+, 30m. Determination and nerves of steel required on the final slab.

2 - **Les Doigts dans le nez**: 6c+, 30m. Same.

3 - **Des jours comme ça**: 6c+. Beautiful moves.

4 - **Bullet the Blue Sky**: 6c+. Delicat finish.

5 - **Mise en bouche**: 6b, 30m.

6 - **Fin de saison**: 6c, 35m. A committing route.

7 - **L'inversée**: 6c, 30m. Save some energy for the finish.

8 - **Apéritif**: 6c, 25m.

9 - **La voie Martin**: 6b+, 20m. Physical.

10 - Project.

11 - **Menhir**: 7c, 15m. Boulder problem.

12 - **Voie de la Souche**: 7a+.

13 - **Génocide**: 6b+, 7a. Slab climbing for P1, small finger cracks for P2. **P1 + P2** = 7a+. 80m rope required, or split the descent.

14 - **Génératrice**: 7b. Steep wall, fingery.

15 - **Génésis**: 6b+. Corner, then small overhangs with holds. Don't ease up.

16 - **Sam's route**: 7a, 35m. Overhang followed by steep wall. Superb!

17 - **Play it again Sam**: 7a+, 35m. Steep wall with small crimps. Technical.

18 - **Les doigts de Passage**: 7b. Edges on steep wall.

19 - **Touchstone**: 7a+, 30m. Power-endurence on edges.

20 - **Talisman**: 7a+. Hard to read...

21 - **La Zone**: 6b+, 35m. The classic. Superb.

22 - **Ça Roule la boule**: 6c+, 35m. Overhang to negotiate.

23 - **Monshine**: 6b+, 32m. Nice movements with resting points between. Superb.

24 - **Lune de miel**: 7a, 35m. Magnificent. Two uncertain moves.

25 - **Saloprises**: 7c+, 35m. Tenuous crimps.

26 - **Ma bête noire**: 7b+, 35m. Boulder problem at the start.

27 - **Le voleur**: 6b, 35m. Beautiful route, athletic with good holds.

28 - **Balade au bout des Combes (2)**: 6c, 35m. Slab. No rush.

29 - **Balade au bout des Combes (1)**: 6b+, 35m. Overhang, hidden hold, exposed finish.

30 - **Rando**: 6b+, 35m, fixed gold bolts, small moves on slab to finish..

La Zone left

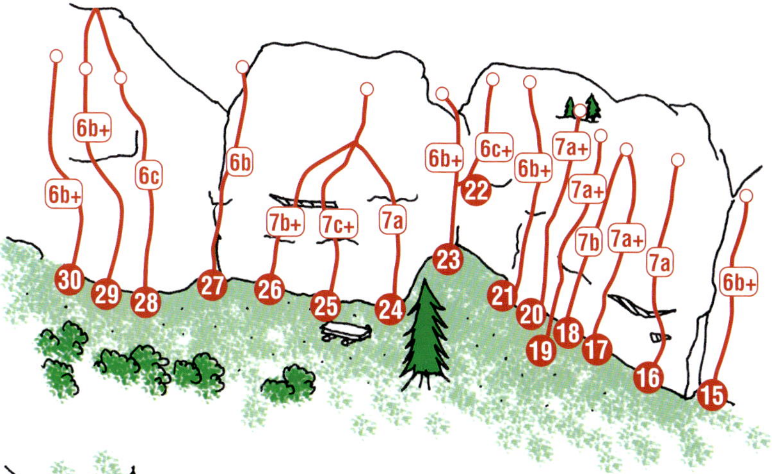

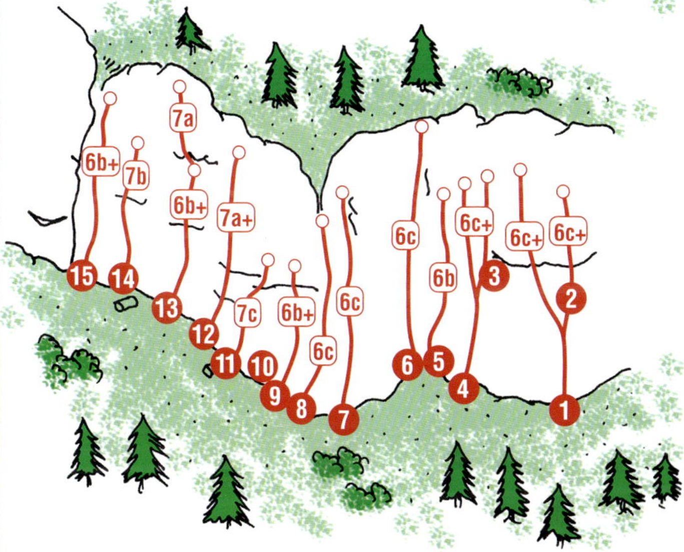

La Zone right

Downstairs

1250 m — S

30′

3

0 0 4 4 — 25-32 m

Located under the Zone, sheltered from the wind and south facing, Downstairs is a good spot for winter or north wind days. The first three pitches of "Tour de Chauffe" are perfect for warming up before starting on the other routes.

Climbing : it has everything - steep walls, overhangs, cracks and slab.

Gear : 15 quick draws. 70m rope.

Approach : see for the Zone (page 282). Half way along the scree - at the level of the electric pylon - go left to reach the crag you can see.

The routes

1 - **Hors saison**: 7a+, 32m. Sustained. A nice journey over a steep wall.

2 - **Hors de question**: 7b+, 30m.

3 - **Hors-piste**: 6c, 32m. A nice traverse section.

4 - **Head-banger**: 6c, 32m. Sustained, dülfer and inversed moves.

5 - **Marc route**: 7b, 20m.

6 - **Bienvenue en Suisse**: 8a+, 25m. A Xavier Vimal route.

7 - **B 52**: 6c+, 30m. Sustained. Excellent.

8 - **Tour de chauffe**: (P5), 6c, 25m, inox bolt hangers. Starts with a crack. Nice line. The route joins the Zone in four pitches.

Downstairs

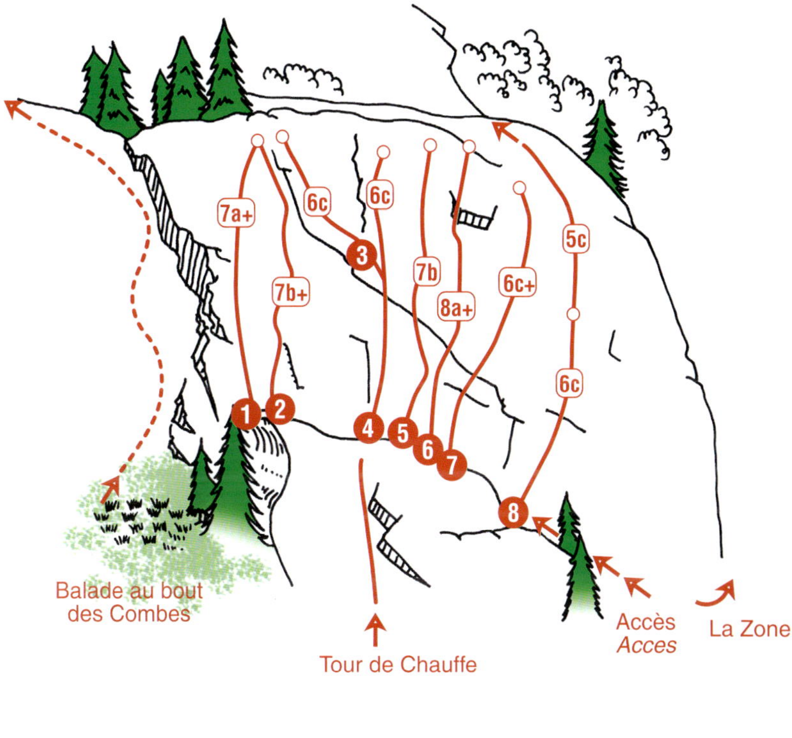
7a+
7b+
6c
3
6c
7b
8a+
6c+
5c
6c
1
2
4
5
6
7
8
Balade au bout des Combes
Tour de Chauffe
Accès
Acces
La Zone

Châtelard - Giétroz

At first known only to a few connoisseurs, Giétroz is becoming more and more popular. The rock is a compact, sculpted granite. The walls are steep and sometimes overhanging and the climbing is technical. Knowing how to use a hold and being able to "read" the rock, are just as important here as strength.

Rock : sculpted granite and gneiss.

Climbing : with 60% of the pitches being at least 6c or above, Giétroz is only for experienced climbers. The equipment is good if sometimes a little spaced on the older routes.

The site : access to the routes are reserved for experienced climbers and hikers (steep path). With its southerly exposure, it's preferable to come and climb in the mornings in summer, or to choose a shady sector like the Gorge.

Access : **by train**: to Châtelard - frontière. For A,B,C and D sectors you take the path to Giétroz which starts on the right hand side of the border post (30 to 45 mins depending on the sector).
By car: from Chamonix (24km), follow the RD 1506 direction Martigny. Sectors E and F : park at the Châtelard, just after the customs post. For the A,B,C and D sectors go to the Giétroz hamlet. To get there drive up the steep, narrow road on the left at the end of the village 800m the other side of the border.
You must park at the entrance to the village of Giétroz.

Approach : Sector A, B, C and D : from the carpark at Giétroz go through the village on the upper road. Continue west on a flat path for about 1 km. When you reach a small farmhouse continue to the meadow (bench and cross). Continue westwards and take the steep footpath which brings you to the various sectors.
Sector E : see page 298.
Sector F : see page 302.

Passet The Wall
32
Passet Upper Crag
35
Passet Lower Crag "Mur du Loup"
33 34
Barberine
36
Giétroz
37
Train station
37
Pylône
Châtelard Frontière
SUISSE
FRANCE
Barberine
P
P
N
0
500 m

A - Sanguine
B - Grande Face
C - Gorge
D - Afrique
E - Châtelard
F - Pylône
A
B
C
D
E
F

Sanguine sector

1350 m S

30'

2 3

0 0 9 5 25-80 m

Some major climbing lines, including Sanguine.

Approach :

- Routes 10, 11, 12: from the field (with the cross) hike up going North and towards a small crag.
- Routes 1 to 9 : continue west across and to the end of the field, then walk down a steep trail for about fifty meters and traverse right at the small rocky wall. Keep going left to reach the ledge to access route.

The routes

1 - **Le mépris**: (committing start): 7a.

2 - **Le mépris**: 7a, 30m. Good fun.

3 - **Who's next**: 7a, 30m.

4 - **Sanguine**: 7b, 30m. Superb.

5 - **?**: 6c.

6 - **Moskito**. 6c, 20m. A good warm up for the place.

7 - **Dégustation de lichen**. (part 2): 6b, 6c+.

8 - **Gay pied**: **P1**: 6b+, 35m; **P2**: 6c, 25m. Committing.

9 - **Courage blanc**: **P1**: 6c+ ; **P2**: 7b.

10 - **Silicose**: 6c, 30m.

11 - **Diagonale du fou**: 6b, 30m.

12 - **Magnum force**: 8a, short, 10m long route with a very tricky boulder move.

Sanguine sector

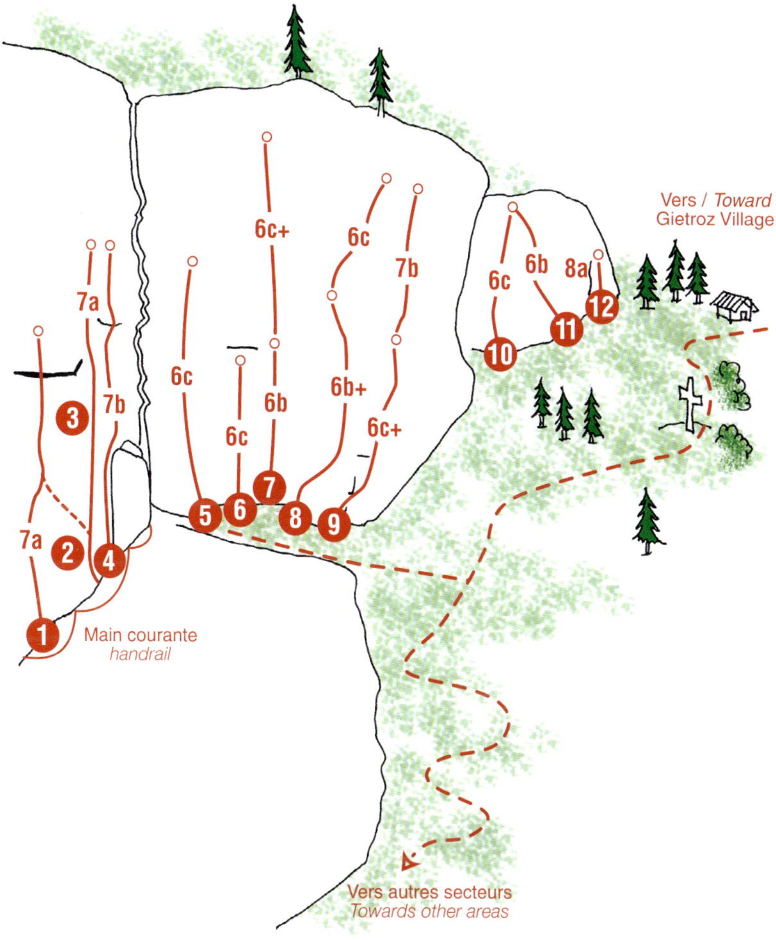

La Grande Face

1350 m S

35′

3

0 0 6 10 25-120 m

There are 20 routes, from 1 to 6 pitches long (up to 120m), on this wall, which offer some excellent climbing. Descent is by abseil (a 60m rope is sufficient). This sector has seen fewer climbers in the recent years; overgrowing vegetation and moss at the start of route 4 and 5.

Access : follow the path which leads to the foot of the face and then continue along the base to reach the start of the routes.

The routes

1 - **Serial hiker**: 6b+.

2 - **Le Jardinier**: 8a.

3 - **Mon Jardin Secret**: **P1**: 7a; **P2**: 7b; **P3**: 6c; **P4**: 6c; **P5**: 7a; **P6**: 6b. Brilliant line.

4 - **Goofy**: **P1**: 6b+; **P2**: 6b+ (committing); **P3**: 7a+; **P4**: 6c+. Not to be missed, typical Giétroz.

5 - **Gwendoline**: **P1**: 5c; **P2**. 6c+.

6 - **Petite lune**: **P1**: 6b+; **P2**: 6c; **P3**: 7b+. Superb.

7 - **Summer Daze**: 7c, 7b.

8 - **Fesse d'huître**: **P1**: 6b+; **P2**: 6c; **P3**: 6a+ (committing) ; **P4**: 6c.

9 - **Harpie**: 6c.

10 - **Ganesh**: 6c+.

11 - **Game over**: 6c+.

12 - **Poisson d'avril**: 6c+.

13 - **Rage et désespoir**: **P1**: 6c; **P2**: 6b; **P3**: 6b; **P4**: 7a+.

14 - **Pharaon ailé**: 6a; 7c (fantastic pitch).

15 - **Magie blanche**: 6b, 7a.

16 - **Pour le meilleur et pour le rire**: 7a+. Same start as "No time to waist", then to the left, on the overhang, join second belay of route 13.

17 - **La hulotte**: 7a+.

18 - **Bouge de là**: 7b.

19 - **Causes perdues**: 6c.

20 - **No time to waist**: **P1**. 6c; **P2**: 7a.

21 - **Dégustation de Lichen**: 6a, 6a (Part 1).

La Grande Face

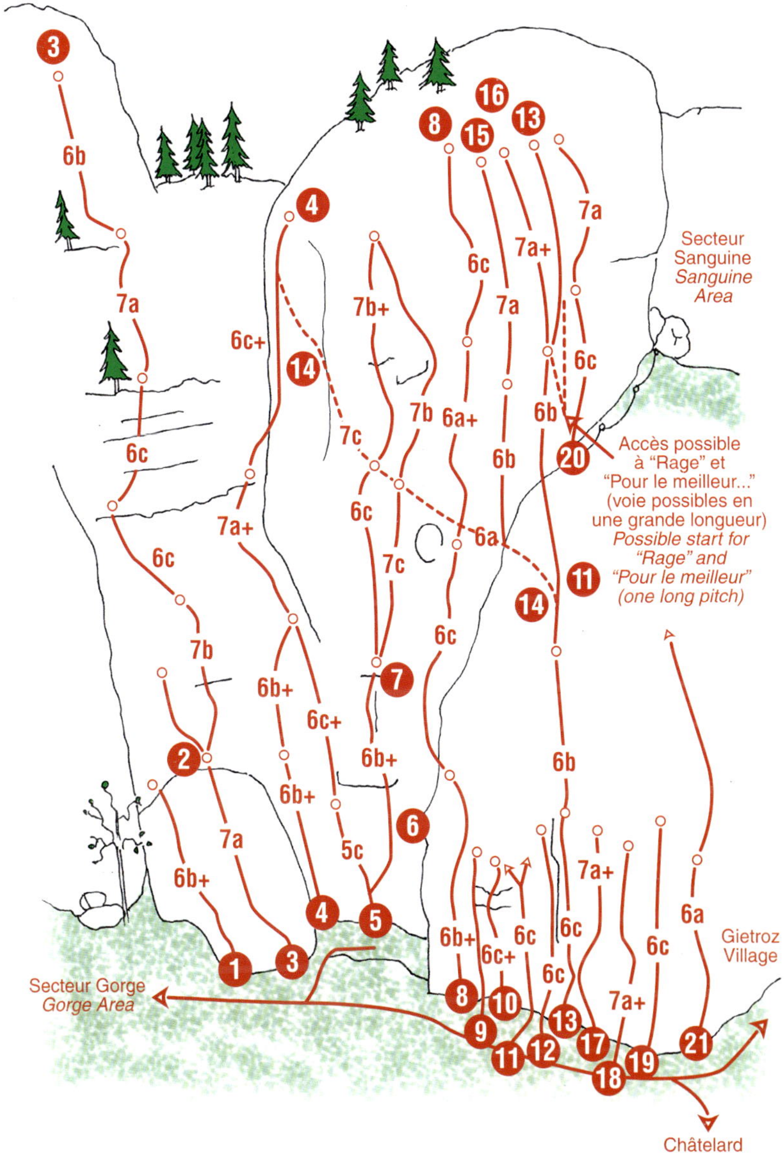

La Gorge

1350 m S

40'

3

0 0 3 18 30-50 m

17 routes, from 1 to 3 pitches long. This area offers the most difficult routes at Giétroz: "Rêve de singe", 8a; "Objectif terre", 7c+. It is in the shade in the afternoon.

Access : from the base of the "Grande Face" continue along the path and up the gorge. From the Zone (right section) follow the footpath to the right 5 mins to reach the upper part of the gorge.

The routes

1a - **In absentia**: 7b

1b - **Mystique**: 7c, very often damp, 15m.

2 - **Happy Birthday**: 6b, 6b.

3 - **The full Monty**: 7a (32m).

4 - **Orage**: 7a+, boulder move. 32m.

5 - **Le sorcier**: 7c+.

6 - **Sortilège**: **P1**: 6b+, 25m; **P2**: 6c, 15m **P3**: 6b.

7 - **Senanga**: 7b.

8 - **Au fil du temps**: 7c.

9 - **Rêve de singe**: 8a, 25m, superb route.

10 - **Objectif terre**: 7c+. 35m! Not to be missed.

11 - **Samedi soir sur la terre**: 7c, superb.

12 - **Dimanche noir**: 7c (use the last 2 bolts of route 13).

13 - **La colombe est la vie**: 7a, 35m! Good route for an on sight attempt.

14 - **Le piège**: **P1**: 6c; **P2**: 6c, 60m. Can be climbed in one pitch (16 quickdraws).

15 - **Question d'Egout**: 7a+ (Crosses "Le piège"), 32m.

16 - **Mardi gras**: continuation of "La colombe". 100m rope necessary for top roping. 19 quickdraws.

17 - **Dreamer**: 7b, 25m. A good route, several hidden two fingers holds.

COMBINED ROUTES

10+11 - **La liaison**: 8a.

17+10 - **La petite ligne**: 7c+/8a.

9+10+11 - **Cauchemar**: 8b.

Rêve de singe, 8a

La Gorge

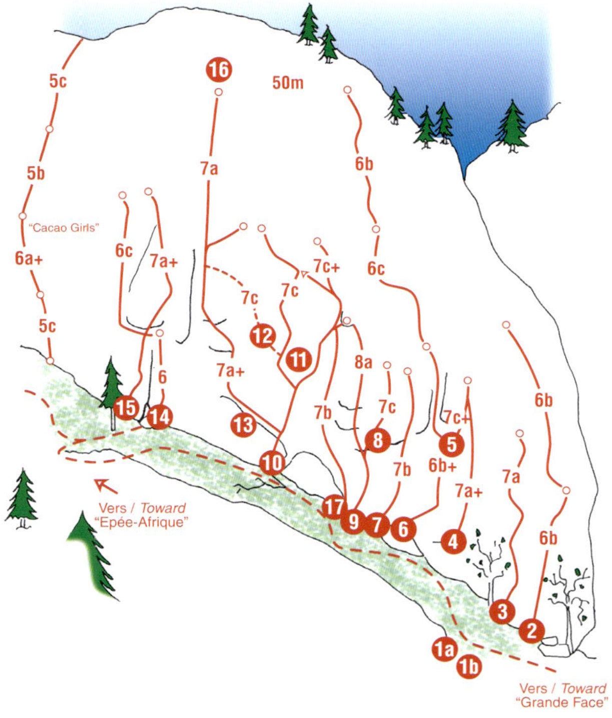

Afrique

1400 m	S
45'	
	3
0 0 11 13	12-35 m

23 routes, 1 to 2 pitches. Slab and steep wall climbing, from 6a to 7b+. A 70 m rope is necessary for most of the routes.

Access : go past "La Gorge" area and follow a rising footpath which leads to a large scree slope. From here the upper wall is clearly visible. From the Zone (right section) follow the path to the right 5 mins to reach the upper part of the gorge. Then go to the left.

The routes

1 - **Dure de dalle**: 7a+, 30m, delicate slab.

2 - **Dalle qui m'aille**: 7b, 30m, same but harder.

3 - **Le toit, la dalle et le surplomb**: 6c.

4 - **L'anormale**: 6b.

5 - **N'importe quoi**: 6b.

6 - **L'escalator**: 6c.

7 - **Charmant dévers**: 6c+, 35m. Committing start. Beautiful route.

8 - **The go between**: 7a.

9 - **Découverte directe**: 6c, 35m. Su perbe line.

10 - **Black Mamba**: 7b, 12m, short bu hard.

11 - **Djibouti**: 6c+, 35m. An othe beautiful trip.

12 - **Découverte classique**: 6a. Quit committing. Square hangers.

13 - **Guillotine**: 7a; not to be missed.

14 - **L'épée de Damoclès**: 6b+ to the first belay point. 6c in one pitch tc the "Guillotine" belay point.

15 - **Marée Noire**: 6c+; 30m.

16 - **Prestige**: 7b.

17 - **Colimaçon**: 7a+, on the white slab Crux move on slab.

18 - **Physiothérapie**: 6c+, sustained.

19 - **Psychothérapie**: 8a, 30m.

20 - **Traitement de choc**: 7b+, 25m, varied climb.

21 - **L'Epicondylite**: 7a+, 25m. Two boulder sections.

22 - **Luce-Ifer**: 6a, 25m.

23 - **Quel festin**: 7a, 25m.

24 - **Dynomight**: 7b, 20m.

25 - **Belles et Buts**: 7a+. On the far left, in the gorge.

26 - **?**: 6b+, 45m. A sustained difficulty long route.

27 - **?**: 6b+, 35m. An athletic wall and a uncomfortable corner.

28 - **?**: 6c, 25m.

29 - **?**: 6b, 32m. Start in a short overhang wall.

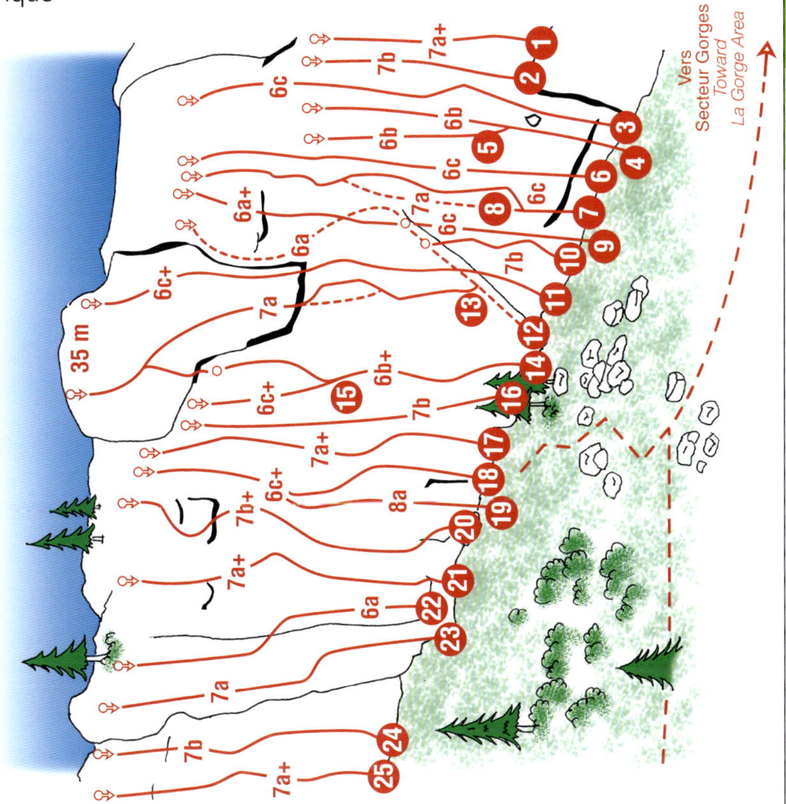

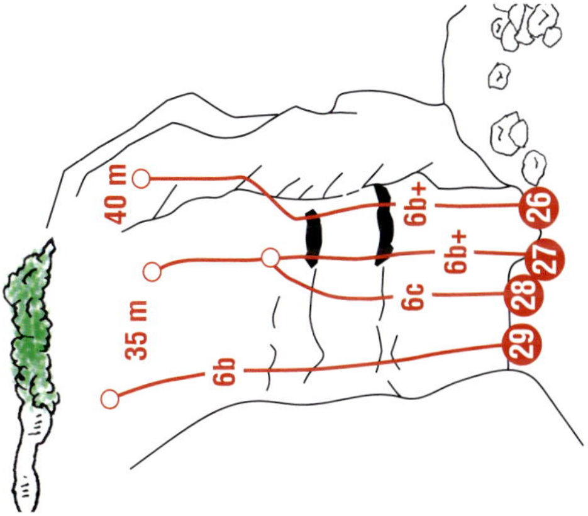

Acces to routes 26 to 29: go down bellow route 22 to reach the lower crag hidden in the forest. A promising new area. We present the 4 most right routes.

Châtelard sector

1150 m SE

15'

3

0 1 5 1 250 m

Four magnificent 250-300m high routes. By combining one of these with a Grande Face route, you can climb non-stop on more than 400m vertical height. Fifteen or so of middle difficulty routes on a magnificent rock are in the process of being equipped (Michel Piola) above the "Cacao girl" ledge (see access below). We indicate some of those new routes around "Autoroute Blanche" 4th's pitch.

Rock : excellent granite with good holds.

Climbing : varied climbing: slab, pillar, overhang.

Gear : 15 quickdraws, 50m abseil ropes for the multi-pitch routes; 80m single rope for the single-pitch routes.

Access :
- **by train**: Châtelard station (Switzerland);
- **by car**: from Chamonix follow the RD 1506 (24km). Cross the border and park in the first carpark after the custom post.

Approach : (10 to 20 minutes depending of the routes from the car park). Walk toward the custom and follow the narrow road indicated Giétroz. After the bridge over the railway take a trail to th right (signpost Giétroz).

- **Routes 1, 2 and 3**: follow the trail fc 5 mins until you reach a junction (cairn Turn left to go to the crag. "Autorout Blanche" start on a big boulder. The other routes are 50m to the left.

- **"Cacao Girl" route**: continue on th main path for an other 5 mins, turn lef (cairn and red dots) to reach the star of the route.

- **"Cacao Girl" ledge**: stay on the tra toward Giétroz, once you have passed zigzag, take to the left a path (cairn) tha leads to the start of the via ferrata tha goes up to the ledge.

Return : 15-20 mins. Once you are or the path above the finish, you have twc options:
- either you walk up on 50m and you take to the right, on the track following the Giétroz Gorge.
- or you take the path on the left and you continue until you get to Barberine, on a track equipped with ladders (underneath the climbing area known as "La Zone", whose equipment remains unknown, according to the wish of its discoverers...).

1 - **Custom m'aide**

ED. 6 pitches. Jon de Montjoye, Hilary Sharp, completed in 2005. Start 3m to the left of "Si le Lichen...". "Fixe" hangers (lizard logo). Unavoidable 6b. Excellent equipment. 250m.
P1: 6a, 20m, slab. **P2**: 5c, 20m. **P3**: 6b+, 40m, very good pitch on steep slab. Same belay as P3 of "Si le lichen...". **P4**: 7a. Tricky pillar. You need a determined stance. **P5**: 5c, 20m, slab. Belay

Châtelard sector
Descente
Descent
6a
6a
7a+
6c
5c
6c
2
1
6c
3
5c
5c
6c+
7a
6c+
6b+
6b+
5c
6a+
6a
5a
1
2
6b+
6a+
6a
3
4
Cacao
Girls

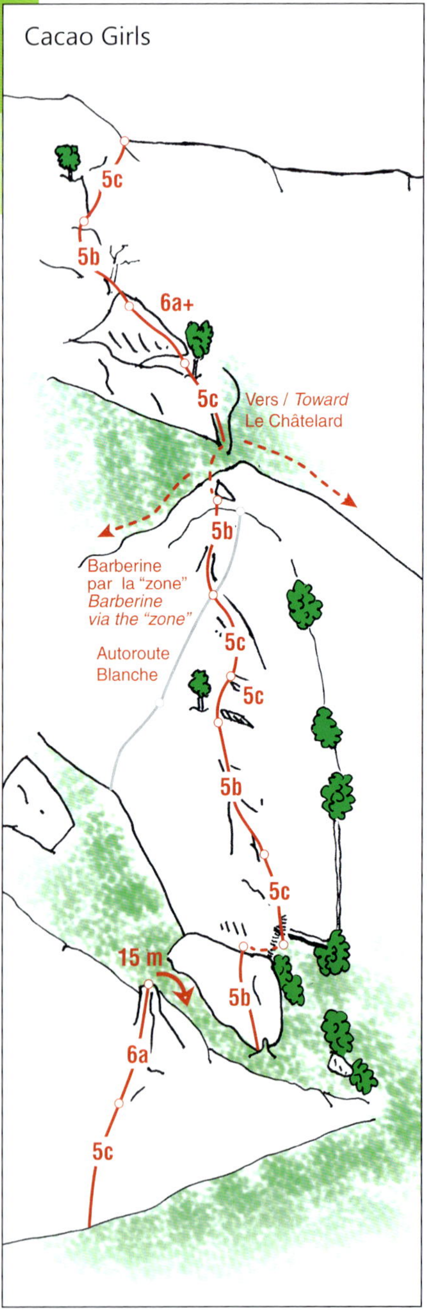

on a wide ledge. Traverse to the right. Follow the arrow and go down a couloir (handrail). Cross the finishing part of "Autoroute" and walk up to the last part. **P6**: 6c ,40m, an overhang and steep wall. **P7**: 40 m, 6b with two points of aid, or 7?. Start in a muscly overhang (A0), followed by a delicate slab. From the belay, a link with "Si le lichen..." is equipped.

2. **Si le lichen ne revenait pas...**
ED. Marc Valorio, 1985. 6b (unavoidable). 250m. Black hangers. Very well equipped.
P1: 5a, slab. **P2**: 6a+, 30m, succession of steps. **P3**: 6b+, 40m, tricky traverse on slab. **P4**: 6c+/7a, 35m, crack and boulder move in diedre. **P5**: 6c+, 30m. **P6**: 5a, 20m, slab. Follow the black arrow. Go down (handrail) and back up a steep couloir for 50m. **P7**: 6c, 45m, steep wall. **P8**: 6a, 45m.

3 - Autoroute Blanche
TD+. Jon de Montjoye, Hilary Sharp, 2001. Not to be missed - perfect rock. Abseil descent is not recommended from the summit (OK from the ledge). Traverse the ledge at mid-height above the angled slab (lichen).
P1: 6a; **P2**: 6a+; **LP3**: 6b+; **P4**: 6c; **P5**: 5c; **P6**: 6a.

4 - Cacao Girls
Cacao girl TD-. Raoul Crettenand, 2012. 10 quickdraws plus belays. An excellent consistent grade 5 route which climbs the whole face in 3 sections. One obligatory strenuous move of 5c on P10. Escape possible from belay 2 and belay 8. Fixe inox hangers. 360m. 12 pitches.

Approach : 80m to right of Autoroute Blanche start.

P1: 5c, 40m. Slab. **P2**: 6a, 35m. Superb slab and steep wall. From belay 2 decend 15 m to the base of the second ector - escape possible here on foot. **3**: 5b, 35m. Slab followed by small overhang at the top. **P4**: 5c, 20m. Start below the belay. Short overhang on awkward undercuts (not very nice to second). **5**: 30m, 5b. A great pitch up a red wall. **6**: 20m, 5c. The roof goes left of the bolt. **7**: 35m, 5c. Fine featured wall. Belay 7 n common with Autoroute Blanche. **P8**: 40m, 5b. Crack and slab. Go up 50m to reach the final sector. Name of the route at the foot of the starting crack. **P9**: 5c, 30m. Wide strenuous crack. **P10**: 6a+, 15m. The crux. Steep strenuous wall on cracks. **P11**: 5b, 20m. P10+P11 can be combined (so long as the second is at ease on the crux moves) **P12**: 5c, 30m.

Descent : on foot : go up to the cairn at the top of the route. Follow a path which descends towards 2 chalets. From here return to Giètroz or Châtelard. Abseil: 2 abseils (2x50m ropes) lead to belay 9, then continue on foot either via the Gorge or taking the via ferrata which goes down from La Zone.

"Autoroute Blanche" ledge

1 - **Custom m'aide**. **P7**: 6c.

2 - **Si le lichen ne revenait pas. P7**: 6c, 35m.

3 - **Autoroute Blanche**. **P4**: 6c, 30m.

5 - **?**. 6b+, 30m. Big ring. Start on the pillar. After climbing the crag (commun to route 6), go to the right on the pillar. A beautiful line.

6 - **?**. 6c, 30m. Inox ring. Next to the right of «Autoroute blanche». A steep wall to start.

7 - **?**. 6b+, 30m. Big rings. A beautiful route.

8 - **?**. 6c, 30m. Inox ring with red cement. An athletic finish.

8'- **?**. 7a, 30m. Same start as 8. A crescendo difficulty. Top route!

9 - **?**. 6a+, 35m. Quality of the rock improve during the climb.

10 - **?**. 6a+, 35m. Idem.

Pylône

1150 m S

10'

3

0 1 9 2 25 m

Strangely, for a long time this cliff was largely ignored by local climbers despite its easy access. Jon de Montjoye put paid to that, inspired (and exhausted!) by his efforts on the higher and more difficult to access cliffs of Barberine / Giétroz / Perrons. With Hilary Sharp he equipped and climbed 12 fine and varied routes on this cliff, providing a popular sunny sector.

Access : **by car**: from Chamonix follow the D 506 (24 km). Go over the border and park at the first parking after the customs post. **By train**: get off at the Châtelard frontière station.

Approach : look for a crag under the hydro pylone. From the parking, walk towards the border and walk up a small road, going over the train tracks. Take left at the road split. Leave road and go right and up a series of sheepback rock formations and follow the trail to the base of the crag.

The routes

1 - **Fine Line**: 6c, delicate thin slab climbing.

2 - **Les goulots du douanier**: 7a, 2 crux sections. The golots were placed by a customs officer years ago as an aid route.

3 - **Banane directe**: 6a+, technical wall at the top.

4 - **Banane**: 6a, traverse right before clipping the third bolt .

5 - **Les sudiste**: 6b+. Sustained start.

6 - **On va ramollir...** : 6b+. Slab

7 - **La belle Zig**: 5c. Crack with big jugs. Magnificent.

8 - **Ca va pas plus vite...** : 6a+. Crack with great moves.

9 - **Honey Badger**: 6b+. Start as for route 10. Delicate traverse; the top wall can be tricky if you don't find the right holds.

10 - **Le vent des câbles**: 6c. Awkward crack followed by a hard to read wall.

11 - **The ego has landed**: 7a+

12 - **Le contrebandier**: 6b+

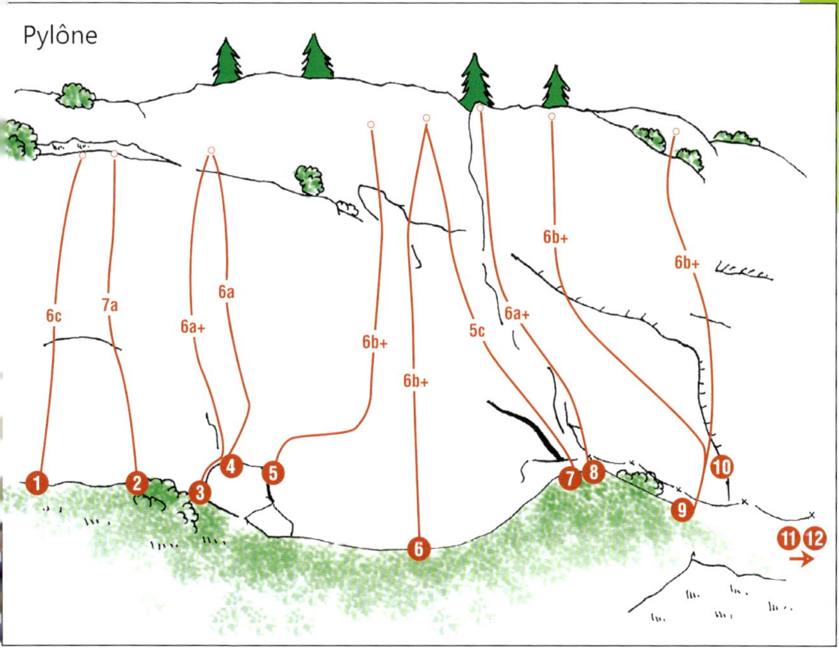

"Fine line", 6c

Fawlty Towers
Gorge de la tête du loup

Two superb towers in the surrounding area of Giétroz. Access is from the top, by abseil. Leave a rope in place.

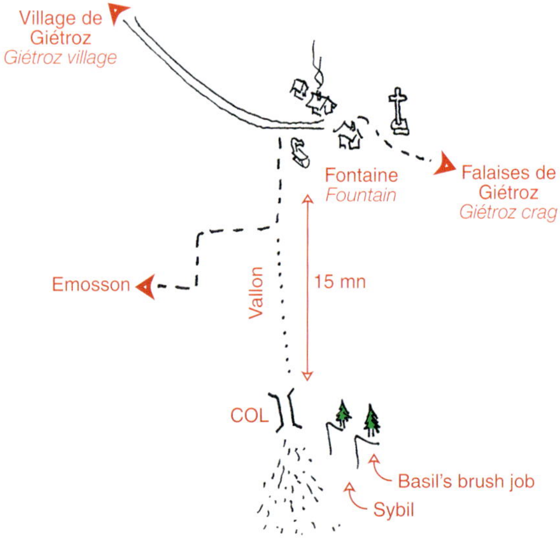

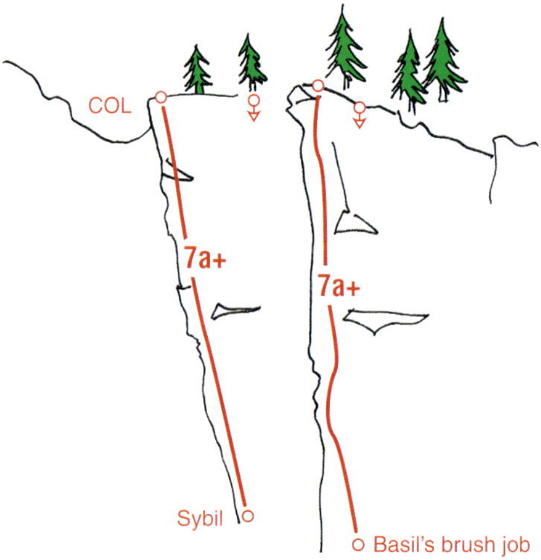

Scan me
French IGN SCAN25 map
Offline mode
40 maps

The locations